INTEGRATING THE HANDICAPPED INTO ORDINARY SCHOOLS

A STUDY OF HEARING-IMPAIRED PUPILS

WENDY LYNAS

CROOM HELM
London ● Sydney ● Dover, New Hampshire

© 1986 Wendy Lynas
Croom Helm Ltd, Provident House, Burrell Row,
Beckenham, Kent BR3 1AT

Croom Helm Australia Pty Ltd, Suite 4, 6th Floor,
64-76 Kippax Street, Surry Hills, NSW 2010, Australia

Croom Helm, 51 Washington Street, Dover, New Hampshire 03820, USA

British Library Cataloguing in Publication Data

Lynas, Wendy
    Integrating the handicapped into ordinary schools:
    a study of hearing-impaired pupils.
    1. Deaf—Education—England 2. Hearing-
    impaired children—Education—England
    3. Mainstreaming in education—England
    I. Title
    371.91′2′0942   HV2716

    ISBN 0-7099-1686-8
    ISBN 0-7099-1687-6 Pbk

Library of Congress Cataloging in Publication Data
Lynas, Wendy.
    Integrating the handicapped into ordinary schools.
    Bibliography: p.
    Includes Index
    1. Hearing-impaired children — Education — Great
Britain. 2. Mainstreaming in Education — Great Britain.
I. Title.
HV2716.L96   1986   371.91′2′0941   85-14995
ISBN 0-7099-1686-8
ISBN 0-7099-1687-6 (Pbk)

To B.B.

Filmset by Mayhew Typesetting, Bristol, England
Printed and bound in Great Britain by
Biddles Ltd, Guildford and King's Lynn

CONTENTS

FIGURES AND TABLES

Figures

Tables

ACKNOWLEDGEMENTS

I would like to thank all those who provided facilities for my research study or who participated in it: Directors of Education; Headteachers of schools; Heads of Services for the Hearing Impaired; and teachers of the deaf who co-operated so generously in giving me information and encouragement. My particular thanks go to those class teachers who allowed me into their classrooms to make observations and who kindly gave me a great deal of their time for interviews.

Likewise my thanks go to the normally hearing pupils who talked to me so freely yet so thoughtfully for long periods of time and to the hearing-impaired pupils and young deaf people who participated in the study for so generously giving up their time and for their patience in being interviewed.

I would also like to thank Professor Ian Taylor of the Department of Audiology and Education of the Deaf, Manchester University, for the support, encouragement and help he has given me throughout the period of my research, and my colleagues, Jean Huntington, Les Owrid and Geoff Redgate for their encouragement and advice concerning the content of the research.

Most of all, I must with great appreciation thank Dr B.M. Wild for the academic and emotional support he has given me throughout the years of study which have brought this book to fruition.

Last, but not least, I would like to thank my mother, Joan Lynas, not only for her constant support and encouragement but for typing, and retyping without complaint, the numerous drafts of this book.

PREFACE

The 1981 Education Act, following the recommendations of the Warnock Report (1978), is intended to encourage the integration of handicapped pupils into ordinary schools. This change in provision marks a policy shift which reflects changes in public attitudes towards the handicapped in recent years. It is expected that in the near future an increasing proportion of children, traditionally categorised as 'handicapped', will receive their education in an ordinary rather than a special school.

When recent trends in the education of the deaf are examined it is both intriguing and significant to note that the process of integration of hearing-impaired pupils into ordinary schools is already well under way. Indeed, for several years before the implementation of the 1981 Education Act it had been the case that the overwhelming majority of hearing-impaired pupils, including those with substantial hearing losses, were being educated in ordinary schools. Educators of the deaf have thus already had to confront problems arising from educating in ordinary schools and classes children with severe social handicaps and learning difficulties. In deaf education more than in any other area of special education, considerable experience and wisdom has been acquired concerning the education of handicapped pupils in an ordinary school environment.

It is the purpose of this book, therefore, to examine what appear to be the important issues connected with the integrated education of hearing-impaired pupils in ordinary schools and to explore some of the associated problems. In so doing I shall draw on material from my research investigation into aspects of the integration of hearing-impaired pupils into the ordinary school. The aim will be to increase knowledge and understanding of the situations that arise when hearing-impaired pupils are placed alongside normally hearing pupils in ordinary schools. The findings will, I believe, benefit not only those responsible for the education of deaf pupils in ordinary schools but also provide useful insights for educators in other areas of special education where integration has perhaps progressed more slowly and where knowledge and experience is at present more limited.

The work is divided into eight chapters. Chapters 1 to 3 are introductory and provide a necessary background to my own or indeed any recent investigation into the integrated education of hearing-impaired pupils.

In Chapter 1 historical developments in deaf education are traced and the many factors underlying the trends that have taken place over time are examined. Here the reasons are explored why in Britain educators of the deaf have 'pioneered' the integration of handicapped pupils into ordinary schools. Chapter 2 consists of a review of published research on the topic of integrated educational provision for deaf pupils and, where appropriate, other categories of handicapped children. In addition to revealing the knowledge and understanding which previous research provides attention is drawn to the many gaps in knowledge which remain.

One reason why the research literature does not supply all the answers to questions relating to the integrated education of deaf pupils in ordinary schools is that people are by no means clear about the meaning of 'integration'. In Chapter 3, therefore, at both a theoretical and practical level, the several meanings of integration are explored and related to the aims and objectives of educating deaf pupils.

Having provided a background orientation, in the first three chapters of the book, Chapters 4 to 7 refer directly to my own research investigation. The material for this book was acquired mainly through the method of participant observation in schools and through informal interviews with teachers, normally hearing pupils, and hearing-impaired pupils and former pupils. Chapter 4 sets out details of the study and of the research techniques used.

Chapters 5, 6 and 7, which form the greater part of the book, are concerned with the research evidence and findings. The aim here is to elucidate crucial aspects of the integrated education of hearing-impaired pupils. In Chapter 5 the integration of the hearing-impaired pupil is discussed from the perspectives and perceptions of ordinary class teachers, whilst Chapter 6 focuses on the responses and reactions of normally hearing pupils towards classmates with a hearing handicap. Chapter 7 looks at integration from the viewpoint of the hearing-impaired pupil himself. Here deaf pupils' attitudes and feelings on being placed in school classes alongside others with normal hearing are examined and some typical strategies adopted by hearing-impaired pupils for coping in the ordinary class are revealed. In addition, using evidence from interviews with hearing-impaired young people who had attended ordinary schools, the views of former pupils are explored concerning their experiences of an integrated education. More generally, the discussion includes a consideration of the feelings of deaf young people about themselves in relation to others in the adult world of hearing-speaking people, and their ideas about the value or otherwise of an education in an ordinary school as a preparation for life in the normally hearing world. Consideration is also given to the beliefs of these young people about themselves in relation to others who are deaf, and to what might be termed 'the deaf community', in order to throw light on the suitability or otherwise of an integrated education.

Finally, Chapter 8 consists of a summary of the main findings of my investigation and a discussion of the major conclusions to be drawn from it. This discussion includes a consideration of some policy implications for those responsible for the education of hearing-impaired pupils in ordinary schools.

1 BACKGROUND TO CURRENT EDUCATIONAL PROVISION FOR THE HEARING IMPAIRED

There is no denying the growing popularity in Britain of the idea of integrating handicapped children into ordinary schools. The trend towards integration practices in education has been particularly marked in deaf education and has gained momentum in recent years. As a consequence children with even severe hearing handicaps are now being educated in the context of the ordinary school. A similar trend towards placement of the majority of deaf and partially-hearing pupils in ordinary rather than special schools has been noted in many advanced industrial countries over the past decade (Dale 1984).

In this chapter the historical background to this shift towards the educational integration of the hearing impaired is examined and the major factors behind the current trend are identified. Major developments in the education of hearing-impaired children up to the Second World War are traced so as to show the significant events and circumstances leading up to the 'modern' period. Post-Second World War developments in deaf education are considered in more detail along with the social and ideological factors which have helped shape the current situation in which the overwhelming majority of hearing-impaired children in Britain are being educated in ordinary schools alongside pupils with normal hearing.

Major Developments in Education of the Deaf up to 1945

The history of the education of deaf children the world over is closely related to two broad social trends: the changing and improving status over time of handicapped people in general and the development and differentiation of universal popular education. The broad historical antecedents of both of these social trends will be considered first and then, with reference to Britain, developments in deaf education will be examined, from the time in 1870 when the State began to intervene in education, up to 1945 when the effects of the 1944 Education Act began to be seen.

1

The Changing Status of Handicapped People and the Implications for the Education of the Deaf

From Ancient Times right up to the Victorian Age, handicapped people had characteristically been accorded extremely low social status and this adversely affected their integration into the wider society. The Greeks and Romans displayed considerable intolerance of physical defect and were reputed to put to death at an early age those whom they believed would be a liability to the community (Hodgson 1953). The Middle Ages in Europe saw little change in the social position of anyone suffering serious physical or mental affliction and they were often outcast. In times that were indisputably harsh the medieval peasantry frequently sought scapegoats on whom to vent their anger and distress: scapegoats were often found in the handicapped. The deaf were particularly vulnerable to persecution and ostracism because of the 'mysterious' nature of their affliction. It was not, for example, difficult to believe that the deaf, with their 'curious' affliction and 'strange' ways were 'possessed of the devil' (Hodgson 1953).

More enlightened thinking emerged during the sixteenth and seventeenth centuries and a new interest developed in the 'scientific' approach to the solution of problems of all kinds, including those of handicapped people. There existed in some sixteenth-century intellectual circles a concern to understand deafness and its causes and to discover ways of curing the defect or at least of alleviating its worst consequences (Hodgson 1953). For the first time ever, there were recorded instances of successful attempts to teach the deaf to talk. Cardano, b. 1501 and Ponce de Leon, b. 1570 were probably the first European teachers of the deaf. Their tuition was, however, confined to a small number of deaf children fortunate enough to be born into aristocratic families. The lot of the deaf generally changed little during this period. Most deaf people continued to live as social outcasts, relying primarily on begging, stealing or individual charity for survival (Bender 1960). That deaf children generally were not at this time benefiting from the knowledge and techniques developed by Cardano or Ponce de Leon is perhaps not surprising. It was a time when none of the mass of the people received any kind of formal education. None the less, it was an important landmark in deaf education that someone had established that deafness was not necessarily equated with dumbness or mental deficiency and that, in principle, the deaf were *educable*.

The development of more widespread specific social and educational provisions for deaf children did not occur until the late eighteenth and early nineteenth centuries. The Industrial Revolution in Britain, and later elsewhere in Europe, brought with it far-reaching economic, social and political change. The rural, feudal, social and economic system ended and the era of industrialisation and urbanisation began. For the first time large populations of industrial wage-earners and their families were massed together in towns and cities. They often lived in conditions that were appalling and plain for everyone to see. Whether out of fear of mass rebellion or of epidemic disease, or of genuine concern for the plight of the less fortunate, some privileged and wealthy members of society in European countries felt obliged to make some provision for the health, welfare, housing and educational needs of the poorer sections of society. In Britain, a range of social services was developed during the nineteenth century, mainly as a result of private voluntary effort.

As the work of charitable institutions for the poor and afflicted developed so the scope of this work broadened to include the blind and the deaf (Pritchard 1963). These two groups, because their defects were so obvious and the effects of those defects so personally damaging, were the first categories of handicappped people to receive attention from voluntary institutions. It is during the late eighteenth and early nineteenth centuries that we see for the first time public acknowledgement of the specific misfortunes of the deaf, and the development of special provision for them.

Undoubtedly, people with severe handicaps were still regarded as burdens on society rather than potentially useful members of it, but they were grouped among the 'deserving poor' and thus seen to require and merit protection. Hence the first institutions which were developed for deaf children were termed, appropriately, 'asylums'. The asylums were designed not to restore the deaf to society but to protect them from its worst cruelties.

Asylums catering primarily for deaf children became established in all parts of Britain during the late eighteenth and nineteenth centuries. They were 'total' institutions in that they catered for the physical health and welfare needs of the residents. Mixing with members of 'ordinary' society was neither expected nor encouraged of asylum inhabitants. The isolation and segregation of the deaf from the wider society was reinforced by the fact that 'signing' rather than speech was the predominant form of communication used in the asylums. Not surprisingly, many who entered an asylum as children were forced to spend the rest of their lives there. There was simply nowhere else where they could gain social acceptance.

The prime purpose of the asylum then was to protect the deaf rather than to educate them, but there is considerable evidence to suggest that many of the asylums did attempt to offer some form of education and training to inmates (Bender 1960). Indeed the educative function of asylums became increasingly important as the nineteenth century progressed, influenced no doubt by the large-scale development of popular education for the 'normal' population, the second of the two broad social factors influencing the education of the deaf.

The Development and Differentiation of Universal Popular Education and its Implications for the Education of the Deaf

During the nineteenth century more and more British children came to receive an elementary education by courtesy of one or other of the two great religious organisations: the National Society (Church of England); and the British and Foreign School Society (Nonconformist). The impetus to provide popular education was both humanitarian and political. Over and above the idea of education as a humane and religious duty was a feeling that education would provide a safeguard against irreligion, vice and subversive tendencies among the poor. The stress on 'religious' education in the early voluntary schools stemmed from a belief that the poor must live upright and industrious lives, but as the century progressed the range of subjects offered broadened beyond the three 'Rs' to include, for example, history, geography, nature study and PE. None the less the education provided remained 'elementary': teaching was largely through instruction and drill; classes were large and provision patchy.

Cheapness was a key feature of elementary education throughout most of the nineteenth century and children with obvious and severe handicaps were quite firmly excluded from this system. It would seem that when education was basic, voluntary and optional and the number of 'ordinary' children far exceeded the number of school places, the time was not right for differentiating 'normal' education provision to take into account handicapped children. However, as ordinary schools became more widespread throughout Britain, so the ever increasing numbers of asylums for blind and deaf children came more closely to resemble ordinary schools in terms of their aims and activities.

The spirit of the late Victorian Age differed from that which predominated during the early nineteenth century and marked a new phase in both industrialisation and education. *Laissez-faire* economic and social philosophies and policies were challenged and more and more people came to believe that Britain's future progress and prosperity depended on a greater degree of State intervention in many spheres of economic and social life. The development of popular education was profoundly affected by this new thinking. It was agreed by industrialists, social reformers and government alike that the country needed an educated populace, and it was clear that voluntary effort alone would not achieve this. The two religious societies had made considerable progress with the education of Britain's children, but none the less, by 1870 only two-fifths of the school age population were actually receiving full-time education (Curtis 1968). State intervention, therefore, was increasingly seen to be necessary if universal popular education was to be achieved and this was most relevant to the development of special education for the deaf.

The Development of State Intervention in the Education of the Deaf 1870–1945

Parliament introduced legislation in 1870 to establish a statutory system of education in England and Wales. The 1870 Education Act created School Boards whose function was to support and enlarge existing voluntary schools, and establish new schools where necessary. The main purpose of the 1870 Education Act was, therefore, to fill the gaps in the voluntary system. Thus, by the end of the century, all 'normal' children were receiving full-time elementary education.

The 1870 Education Act also had important implications for the development of educational provision for handicapped children. Once education was made compulsory, the plight of children who appeared not to be educable by normal means become all the more apparent. And just as deaf and blind children were the first categories of handicapped children to be specifically catered for through voluntary effort, so they were the first to receive official attention of the State. In 1889 a Royal Commission was established to investigate the educational needs of these children. The main recommendations of the Commissioners were embodied in the 1893 Education (Deaf and Blind Pupils) Act. This legislation mandated the newly created School Boards to ensure specialist educational provision for all the deaf and blind children living in their local areas.

It is interesting to note that State intervention in the education of the deaf and blind in the latter part of the nineteenth century was not primarily the result of an ideology of benevolent humanitarianism or even charitable paternalism. The Government was motivated in this matter, as in most other policies, by economic self-interest: it wanted the deaf and the blind to become capable of gainful employment and thus self-sufficient, so that they would not be a drain on the nation's resources. That this is so is made clear in a statement made by Lord Egerton, Chairman of the 1889 Commission:

The blind, deaf, dumb and educable class of imbecile . . . if left uneducated become not only a burden to themselves, but a weighty burden to the State. It is in the interests of the State to educate them, so as to dry up, as far as possible the minor streams which must ultimately swell to a great torrent of pauperism. (Egerton Commission 1889)

Once School Boards had been given responsibility to provide education for deaf children facilities in deaf education advanced rapidly during the 1890s; conditions in existing asylums were improved and many new special schools were established. Thus by the beginning of the twentieth century the vast majority of deaf children were receiving full-time education in a special school for the deaf, whereas in 1800 it is estimated that only one deaf child in 20 received any form of special provision (Pritchard 1963).

The development of special schools for the deaf marks a major step forward along the route towards educational integration for deaf children: increasingly the deaf were being given the right not only to be looked after by society, but the right, as any other child, to be educated. Whilst there was little opposition to the policy of segregating deaf children from others, their education had become the responsibility of those same authorities responsible for the education of 'normal' children. This in itself was an important step towards the notion that the deaf were not 'a race apart' who should be kept apart. The notion of normality was reinforced by the fact that during the latter part of the nineteenth century oral means of communication had replaced manual means in most of the asylums. Teachers of deaf children came to perceive 'rehabilitation' as a proper goal in deaf education and the notion that schools for the deaf should prepare their pupils for life in the wider society rather than provide a means of escaping it gained greater acceptance at this time.

As more schools for the deaf were established, and they evolved during the first part of the twentieth century, there developed a greater concern for the nature of the education offered and the methods of teaching used within the schools. Just as standards of education in ordinary elementary schools were improving (Barnard 1961), so too new ideas and new philosophies were being put into practice in schools for the deaf. There was an increased professionalisation of teachers and as a result standards of teaching in schools for the deaf advanced during the first half of the twentieth century. Specialist knowledge, skills and expertise developed so that, for example, much more came to be known about the causes of deafness and the mechanisms of hearing. A new 'science' of audiology developed and with it the capability of accurately measuring hearing loss. For the first time it was realised that very few children were totally deaf:

most had some 'residual hearing' and some apparently 'deaf' children were found to have a considerable amount of useful hearing. Thus, professionals working with hearing-handicapped children came to perceive a new category of deaf child, the 'partially deaf'.

The discovery of residual hearing was accompanied by the development of more powerful electrical hearing aids. This in itself greatly boosted aural/oral methods in deaf education. By 1930 all but one school for the deaf were using predominantly oral methods (Pritchard 1963). Professionalism among teachers of the deaf was enhanced by the pioneering work of the Ewings at Manchester University. They not only provided examples of good practice in the education of deaf children, but also established a training department for teachers of the deaf. Increasingly, therefore, those who taught deaf children had received appropriate professional training.

The growth of knowledge, expertise and professionalism in deaf education in the first part of the twentieth century undoubtedly enhanced the status of special schools for the deaf within the education system as a whole. This was further helped by the fact that the State system itself was becoming more differentiated. More account was taken of the social and individual needs of children and a greater variety of schools developed, for example, trade schools, industrial schools, secondary schools and open-air schools. Thus schools catering for deaf children came increasingly to be seen as part of the normal differentiated system of education.

The principle of educating deaf children in separate special schools, however, remained on the whole unchallenged. This was so in spite of the fact that many schools for the deaf were residential, and set in remote country districts which meant that many deaf children were for a large part of their childhood cut off from their families and from the hearing world in general. It was believed by the majority of educators and parents that handicapped children needed to be in a segregated specialist environment in order to meet their special needs. (A limited experiment to bring hearing-handicapped children into closer contact with their hearing peers took place during the early part of the century but did not prove successful. Out of consideration for the particular educational needs of partially deaf children a special class in an ordinary school was opened in Bristol in 1908 (Pritchard 1963). However, as at that time there were no electrical aids to amplify sound, progress was regarded as not significant enough to justify the growth of the special class system of education. Thus the experiment was abandoned.) Moreover, during the 'lean years' of the 1920s and 1930s, any child permitted to live in a comfortable house in pleasant rural surroundings, and provided with clothes and three square meals a day was considered fortunate indeed.

Whilst in retrospect the policy of isolating hearing-handicapped children from the rest of the community may seem ill-advised, no one should underestimate the importance of this 'special school' phase. Valuable knowledge and understanding of the educational problems of deafness and the educational requirements of deaf pupils were developed and consolidated throughout this period of time.

It is clear from the foregoing that undoubtedly educational standards among the hearing handicapped had risen by the late 1930s. It was generally the case that most deaf young people during the inter-war years left school with some grasp of the English language and had some ability to communicate, albeit in a limited way, in a hearing-speaking world. Many had received sufficient education and training to enable them to get jobs on leaving school, often in skilled manual occupations. By the time of the Second World War, deaf adults may not have been equipped to become fully acceptable members of the hearing-speaking world, but they were certainly in a considerably better position to conform to the expectations of normally hearing society than their counterparts a century before. Deaf children had won the right to an education, and deaf adults had a place in society, which marks a considerable advance on the days when mere survival was a struggle for deaf people.

The Post-war Period

The advances made towards the educational integration of the deaf in the years during the post-Second World War period are perhaps even more remarkable than those preceding it. Many deaf pupils nowadays achieve standards of spoken language that would have been unthinkable earlier in the century. Furthermore severely and profoundly deaf children, who were believed in the pre-war years to need a highly specialised educational environment, are currently being educated alongside hearing pupils in ordinary schools. It is appropriate, therefore, to trace the significant developments in deaf education in the post-war period and to examine the major factors which have brought about this state of affairs.

Deaf Education 1945–84

The educational integration of deaf children in Britain was significantly advanced by the 1944 Education Act (for England and Wales — the corresponding Acts for Scotland and Ireland being enacted in 1945 and 1947).

As a result of the 1944 Education Act, local education authorities were required to identify all children needing special educational treatment and to ensure that each one received 'adequate educational provision'. Thus, as a result of the Act, the education of all handicapped children was placed firmly in the hands of local education authorities. Subsequent special education came officially within the general education framework. Moreover, the 1944 Act allowed a handicapped child to be identified as in need of special educational treatment without having to attend a special school.

The idea of offering specialist provision to handicappped children within the ordinary school was a new departure in educational thinking and very important as a basis for the further development of educational integration of the hearing impaired. The 1944 Education Act also laid down that the Minister would make:

> regulations defining the several categories of pupils requiring special educational treatment and make provisions as to the special methods appropriate for the education of pupils in each category.

The regulations published in 1945 were significant for the future development of deaf education because for the first time official recognition was given to the category 'partially deaf'. This meant that there were now two categories of hearing-handicapped children, 'deaf' and 'partially-deaf'. It was also established by the regulations that 'partially deaf' children did not need to be taught by 'the educational methods used for deaf pupils', and did not need to be educated in a special school. Children classified as 'deaf' were still required to attend special schools since it was felt that their educational needs were too specialised for them to be educated elsewhere.

In spite of the provisions of the 1944 Education Act, most LEAs in the immediate post-war period were more concerned with ensuring that the special schools were adequately funded, staffed and equipped than with experimenting with new forms of special provision for handicapped children in ordinary schools. Most LEAs during this period quite clearly interpreted 'adequate educational provision' for handicappped pupils as placement in a special school. Thus, even for the newly created category of 'partially deaf', the most common form of provision became separate classes within existing special schools. In some regions of Britain new schools catering specifically for the 'partially deaf' were established (Watson 1967).

A few LEAs, however, confronted with a new responsibility to make specific provision for partially-deaf children decided to establish special classes or units within ordinary schools. No doubt the motivation for creating partially-deaf units, in part, stemmed from the fact that such provision was relatively inexpensive. None the less it was also an acknowledgement of the benefits of ordinary school placement for children with considerable useful residual hearing. The first units, opened in London in 1947 and in Salford in 1948, provided a model of education for hearing-impaired children that was later to become very important.

With the growth in national prosperity, the 1950s and early 1960s witnessed considerable expansion in educational provision for hearing-impaired children as indeed for other categories of handicapped child. Facilities for detecting hearing loss greatly improved and during this period the proportion of pupils categorised as partially deaf rose considerably as can be seen quite clearly from the figures presented in Table 1.1.

Table 1.1: Growth in the Number of Partially-deaf Pupils 1947–64

Year	School population in England and Wales	No. of partially-deaf pupils in special schools or classes in England and Wales	Rate per 1,000 partially-deaf pupils to total school population in England and Wales
1947	5,174,674	895	0.173
1953	6,373,096	1,089	0.171
1958	7,027,156	1,357	0.193
1964	7,245,501	2,567	0.354

Source: DES 1968, Lewis Report.

The increase in numbers of partially-deaf pupils almost certainly reflects an improvement in *ascertainment* of hearing loss and not any change in the *incidence* of moderate hearing losses. More partially-deaf units attached to ordinary schools were established. The figures shown in Table 1.2 indicate this growth.

Table 1.2: Growth in the Number of Units for the Partially Deaf, 1947–62

	1947	1955	1960	1962
No. of partially-deaf units in England and Wales	3	5	25	43

Source: DES 1967.

The early established units suffered a number of problems and this may account for the fact that there was not more rapid expansion of this form of educational provision for partially-deaf pupils. One problem was a shortage of properly qualified teachers of the deaf to run them. Units which had just opened sometimes had to close for lack of suitable staffing (DES 1967). A further difficulty arose from the fact that at this stage units catered only for primary age pupils. Concentration on primary age pupils was a quickly established objective: the special class was to offer younger partially-deaf pupils the specialised remedial help they might need to develop normal spoken and written language skills. By the time the pupils were eleven years of age, it was assumed that they would be ready for transfer to full-time education in the ordinary secondary school. This objective was, however, rarely fulfilled. Many partially-deaf pupils were unable to make the educational progress necessary for coping with the demands of the normal secondary school and had then to be found places in special schools. Units were thus frequently criticised for 'failing' to fulfil their purpose.

A further characteristic of the early units was their relative separation from the ordinary school to which they were attached. The partially-deaf pupils, if integrated at all, attended ordinary classes for activities such as PE or craft rather than for academic subjects. They were not, therefore, offered many opportunities for mixing with their normally hearing peers. The emphasis was rather on providing specialist remedial tuition in the special class. Despite good intentions then, it is quite probable that many hearing-impaired pupils were over-protected in the special class and this in itself depressed their educational attainments (DES 1972).

In this period of the early development of units, then, a category of child who would formerly have been educated alongside other pupils at his local school was now being singled out by experts from a variety of professions and offered a specialised separate education. Many children with moderate hearing losses were removed from neighbourhood schools to another school some distance from their homes in order to receive most of their education in a special class, separated from the rest of the school. In an important sense, therefore, unit provision at this time represented exclusion and segregation rather than integration. Moreover, whilst 'integration' within the school was theoretically possible 'separation' was more typical.

Despite early problems with units matters improved. In the period from the mid-1960s to the present time, there have been definite signs of more optimistic views about the capabilities of hearing-impaired children. The Handicapped Pupils and Schools Amending Regulations,

1962 were of particular importance in promoting a more positive approach to the educational problems of deafness. First, the regulations changed the nomenclature referring to children with moderate hearing losses from 'partially deaf' to 'partially hearing'. This affirmed the growing realisation among deaf educators of the importance of residual hearing. Second, and very crucial to the development of the educational integration of children with a hearing handicap, was the elimination of the clause of the 1945/53 regulations which had excluded severely and profoundly deaf children from receiving special educational treatment in ordinary schools. In any case the distinction between 'deaf' and 'partially hearing' had become increasingly difficult to make. Many children who were deaf in the audiometric sense were achieving sufficiently good standards of spoken language to be regarded by professionals working with them as 'partials'.

The new legislation meant that children with more severe hearing losses could attend partially-hearing units if it was thought appropriate. Certainly the change in law coincided with a rapid growth in units from the early 1960s as can be seen from the figures presented in Table 1.3.

Table 1.3: Growth in the Number of Units for the Hearing Impaired, 1962–82

	1962	1965	1970	1976	1980	1982
No. of units	43	74	212	340	500	502

Source: DES 1967; NDCS *Yearbooks*, 1971–83.

It would be reasonable to assume that this growth was to an extent stimulated by the fact that LEAs, freed from the difficulty of having to decide whether or not a child was 'partially deaf', were more willing to establish unit provision in their areas. Moreover, in smaller LEAs where there were no special schools for the deaf or partially hearing, there were obvious financial advantages in keeping a hearing-impaired pupil in a special class within the local authority area rather than sending a child to a special school in another area. A further advantage of unit provision over special residential schools was that it enabled the deaf or partially-hearing child to live at home with his parents. Thus many LEAs were encouraged to establish units for both social and financial reasons.

Just as the number of units increased, so did the number of children attending them, as can be seen from Table 1.4.

Table 1.4: Growth in the Number of Hearing-impaired Pupils Attending Units, 1973–83

Year	No. of hearing-impaired pupils 5–16 years of age attending special classes attached to ordinary schools in England and Wales	Rate per 1,000 hearing-impaired pupils in special class to total school population, in England and Wales
1973[a]	2,008	0.24
1977	3,893	0.43
1983	4,049	0.48

Note: a. Hearing-impaired children attending 'designated special classes' were not counted by the DES until 1973.
Source: DES, *Statistics of Education, Schools*, 1975, 1979; BATOD 1984.

What is interesting, however, is that when the statistics of hearing-impaired children attending special schools over the last 15 years or so are examined, it can be seen that up until the mid-1970s there was growth here also. An examination of the figures presented in Table 1.5 below reveals that it was not until 1976/7 that the numbers of hearing-impaired children attending special schools started to decline.

Table 1.5: Growth and Decline in the Number of Hearing-impaired Pupils Attending Special Schools, 1968–83

Year	Nos. of deaf and partially-hearing pupils attending special schools in England and Wales	Rate per 1,000 deaf and partially-hearing pupils in special schools to total school population in England and Wales
1968	5,141	0.63
1972	5,781	0.64
1976	6,633	0.69
1977	5,938	0.65
1979	5,566	0.61
1980	4,847	0.55
1983	3,808	0.45

Source: DES, *Statistics of Education, Schools*, 1970–1982; BATOD 1984.

The 'buoyancy' of the special school population up until the mid-1970s may reflect the attendance of an increased proportion of multi-handicapped deaf children. These would be children who in previous years either would not have survived infancy or, prior to the 1970 Mental Health Act, would have attended training centres for the mentally handicapped. However, the major reason why special schools for the deaf not only survived but flourished over this period is that in the main they continued to attract the majority of severely and profoundly deaf children. In most parts of the country the special school was considered to be the most appropriate educational setting for pupils with substantial hearing losses. The growth in the number of units up to the mid-1970s does not, therefore, reflect a nationwide switch in placement policy from special school to unit. The major reason for the increase in unit provision for hearing-impaired pupils up to this time was almost certainly a result of the consistent improvement in the detection rate of pupils with moderate hearing losses combined with a greater willingness on the part of LEAs to offer these children special educational provision in their local area.

The popularity of units as a form of provision for these 'newly discovered' hearing-impaired children also owes something to the fact that they became much more flexible in function and purpose. The objectives broadened beyond those of simply preparing younger partially-hearing pupils for full-time secondary education. Many secondary school units were established and hence special classes began to cater for hearing-impaired pupils who were likely to need the special support of the unit for the whole of their school lives.

Thus up until the mid-1970s the predominant form of educational provision for children with severe and profound losses was the special school and for children with moderate or moderate to severe losses, the partially-hearing unit. Children with less severe or fluctuating losses were increasingly being catered for by peripatetic teachers of the deaf — a service provided within the child's local school.

The peripatetic service has grown considerably since the late 1950s and this has significantly helped to improve the educational support for children with less severe hearing losses in ordinary schools. The figures presented in Table 1.6 give evidence of this growth.

Table 1.6: Growth in the Number of Peripatetic Teachers of the Deaf

Nos. of peripatetic teachers of the deaf employed by LEAs, England and Wales	1959	1962	1965	1967	1974	1976	1981	1983
	24	42	95	138	200	363	420	440

Source: NDCS 1984.

The principal role of peripatetic or visiting teachers of the deaf is to offer whatever help is felt necessary to those hearing-impaired children who are placed full time in their local school. The support can vary from direct remedial tuition of the hearing-impaired child to advice and counselling for class teachers or parents.

The growth of the peripatetic service, as with the growth of units, reflects better detection of slight or moderate hearing losses coupled with an enhanced awareness of the special educational difficulties caused by such losses. That this is so is reflected in the dramatic rise in numbers of pupils in ordinary schools issued with hearing aids, as we can see from Table 1.7.

Table 1.7: Growth in the Number of Pupils with Hearing Aids Attending Ordinary Schools, 1957–83

No. of children attending ordinary schools issued with hearing aids	1957	1967	1972	1983[a]
	714	6,006	17,010	25,000 (approx.)

Note: a. Estimated figure, NDCS 1984.
Source: DHSS, *The Health of the School Child*, 1972.

With the growth of units and of the peripatetic service of teachers of the deaf, a considerable amount of educational provision has been developed for hearing-impaired pupils *outside* the special school system. As we have seen, neither units nor the peripatetic service were originally intended to cater for the educational needs of hearing-impaired pupils with severe and profound losses. But once these services were established there was a framework of provision which, over the last decade, has come to be extended to the more severely hearing-handicapped pupil. From the mid-1970s onwards greater numbers of children with substantial hearing losses have been placed either in units or full time in their local schools under the supervision of the peripatetic service. Increasingly, therefore, some form of ordinary school placement has come to be seen as an appropriate educational context for even the most deaf of children. This has led to the closure of several special schools for the deaf and it is likely that more will close in the near future (Peatey 1984). The progressive phasing out of many special schools has been reinforced by a fall in the total number of pupils with severe and profound deafness as a consequence of a general drop in the birth-rate in Britain. Moreover, because of medical advances, it has been predicted that there will be a reduction in the proportion of children born with substantial hearing losses (Taylor 1981).

Where deaf children are individually integrated, that is placed full time in their local school, they clearly have considerably more contact with the everyday hearing-speaking world than if placed in a special school. These children are in an important sense more 'integrated' than they formerly would have been. The same can also be said of many hearing-impaired children attending units. A significant recent development is that units have become far less segregated from the school to which they are attached. More deaf children are spending more time in ordinary classes alongside normally hearing pupils. This is demonstrated, for example, by an examination of the educational experiences of those deaf children attending units who featured in the film produced at Oxford Polytechnic, *1980 — One Hundred Years after Milan*. This group of 22 children, with a mean hearing loss of 96.2 dB in the better ear, spent, on average, 68 per cent of their school time in ordinary classes (Braybrook 1980). This is very different from the picture presented by the DES of pupils attending units in the late 1960s. The large majority of the children surveyed by the DES — 600 of the 721 for whom audiograms were available — had average hearing losses of less than 90 dB. Yet, only a minority of the total number of hearing-impaired children spent time in ordinary classes other than for non-academic subjects (DES 1967).

Thus, clearly, recent trends are towards the greater participation of hearing-impaired children, including those with substantial hearing losses, in both the social and academic life of the ordinary school. It would be incorrect, however, to conclude that all deaf children in Britain are progressing in a uniform way towards increased integration in their education. An examination of different types of provision for hearing-impaired pupils in different LEAs indicates wide variations in educational placement policies.

Differences between LEAs in the structure of educational provision for hearing-impaired pupils have been noted in the past. Hemmings (1972), for example, demonstrated several years ago in her investigation of units in a number of LEAs in South-east England, the West Country and the South Midlands that authorities varied a great deal in their attitudes towards the placement of deaf children. She cited two extreme examples to illustrate this point. In one LEA $2\frac{1}{2}$ per cent of deaf children attended a special school, 16 per cent were in units, and 81 per cent attended ordinary schools full time. In another LEA, 45 per cent of the hearing-impaired children attended residential schools for the deaf, 25 per cent were placed in units, and 30 per cent remained in their local schools.

It is extremely doubtful if discrepancies in provision such as these reflect differences in attributes of the hearing-impaired children. That this is so was confirmed by the work of Gregory and Bishop (1981) in their study of younger deaf children. They noted that the educational placement of the children studied did not relate to factors such as hearing loss and linguistic attainment.

A more recent unpublished investigation, conducted by the author in 1984, confirms that LEAs continue to differ in their placement policies for hearing-impaired pupils. Broad categories of educational provision were recorded in four different LEAs in England for hearing-impaired pupils, five to 16 years of age, with average hearing losses in the better ear of more than 70 dB. The data is presented in Table 1.8.

Table 1.8: The Educational Placement of Hearing-impaired Pupils, 5–16 Years of Age with Average Hearing Losses in the Better Ear Greater than 70 dB in four LEAs in England

LEA	Type of Educational Placement			
	Special School for the hearing impaired	Unit	Full-time individual placement in ordinary school	Total
LEA A	28 (82%)	—	6 (18%)	34
LEA B	7 (28%)	18 (72%)	— —	25
LEA C	10 (26%)	23 (61%)	5 (13%)	38
LEA D	13 (33%)	14 (34%)	13 (33%)	40

Source: Lynas 1984.

As can be seen there are marked variations between the LEAs in their provision for deaf children who, in terms of their hearing loss, are similarly handicapped. Possible reasons for these differences in provision will be discussed in Chapter 3.

It is significant, however, despite the differences in provision, that out of the total number of 137 severely and profoundly deaf pupils referred to in Table 1.8, 79 (58 per cent) attended an ordinary school. (That such a high proportion of deaf pupils continue to attend a special school in LEA 'A' undoubtedly reflects an absence of unit provision in that area.) Overall, these data confirm the general picture presented, namely, that a considerable proportion of children with substantial hearing losses are currently receiving their education in an ordinary school setting.

That ordinary schools should have become the preferred educational placement for deaf children reflects a belief among many educators that the best way to 'normalise' even the severely handicapped hearing-impaired child is to place him in a normal rather than a special, separate educational environment. The ultimate aim of integration and rehabilitation into 'normal' society has not changed from the earliest days of special educational provision for the deaf; it is rather that the perceived means of achieving this end have altered. As a means of attaining ultimate integration into society educators have moved positively in favour of educational integration itself.

Social and Ideological Factors Underlying Current Trends in Deaf Education

The shift in policy towards integration of the hearing impaired into the normal classroom deserves explanation, all the more so because developments towards integration for other categories of handicapped pupils have been considerably less marked (Tomlinson 1982). It is certainly true that society generally, and educational institutions in particular, have become more capable of accommodating the needs of handicapped categories of people such as the hearing impaired. There are, however, factors peculiar to the education of the hearing impaired which have combined powerfully to facilitate the integration of deaf pupils into ordinary schools. There are, therefore, special as well as general reasons why deaf children are the most educationally 'integrated' of all categories of handicapped children in this country.

If the more general reasons for the current educational integration of deaf children are considered, clearly relevant is the modern policy advocated by welfare and community workers of keeping all handicapped children and adults within the community rather than segregated from it. Health and welfare policies have increasingly been directed towards enabling the handicapped person to live as independent a life as possible in everyday society. The segregated institution has been severely criticised as a form of provision for the handicapped. Writers such as Townsend (1962) and Goffman (1968) have given much publicity to the harmful 'institutionalising' effects on individuals of 'total' institutions, such as residential schools and homes. The policy of segregating young children into special residential schools was particularly criticised by psychologists, for example by Bowlby (1965) who drew attention to the detrimental effect of separation from home on a child's emotional and social development.

Attempts towards enabling the handicapped to take their rightful place within the community come not just from those who frame social policy but from the handicapped themselves. During the 1960s and 1970s handicapped people, along with other minority groups, formed pressure groups (for example, Disablement Income Group; Association of Disabled Professionals; National Federation of the Blind; National Union of the Deaf) to further their rights in society. A common plea of the various groups was, and is, that handicapped people should have the right to lead useful, dignified lives and be given every opportunity to compete on equal terms with the non-handicapped. They argued, and still do, for the right to be different without being made to feel inferior (Hunt 1966).

'Normal' society has, on its part, shown a corresponding willingness over the past 20 years to accommodate and discriminate positively in favour of handicapped people. The wide range of community care and public services designed to help handicapped people participate as fully as possible is evidence of this positive discrimination. The position in the USA, which holds equally well in Britain, is nicely summed up by the words of President Carter addressing an audience of handicapped people at the time of the US Rehabilitation Act 1975. He suggested that to facilitate the integration of the handicapped in society: 'the buses should come up to you on the sidewalk and kneel to let you in' (*Guardian*, 1 June 1977).

There is thus a political and ideological climate opposed to the isolation and segregation of the handicapped and favouring their integration and self-determination. This in itself has contributed to educational principles and policies favouring the integration of handicapped pupils.

Furthermore, important changes in philosophy and practice in mainstream education in the post-war period have made it easier to integrate handicapped children into ordinary schools.

Over the past 30 or so years in Britain, and in many other countries, there has been a noticeable trend towards the individualisation and personalisation of education. Modern child-centred thinking, perhaps most coherently summed up in the Plowden Report (1967), stresses that teaching must take into account individual differences in pupils. Different children learn in different ways and therefore a good school, according to Plowden: 'sets out deliberately to devise the right environment for children to allow them to be themselves and to develop in the way and at the pace appropriate to them'.

The trend towards individualised education has, in recent years, been reinforced by the growth of mixed-ability classes in British schools at all stages of education and facilitated by an overall reduction in class size (DES 1978, 1979). The notion that 'all children are different' and that differing needs should be catered for in the one classroom is not far removed from the idea of educating all children together regardless of difference. The principle is further reinforced by the ideology of non-selective 'comprehensive' education at all stages of schooling. According to this view, schools should take the responsibility to educate 'all-comers', including the handicapped.

Whether in practice schools routinely accommodate the diverse needs and interests of all individual children in the community is, of course, questionable. Generally speaking, however, the modern school teacher is more attuned than her predecessors to coping with individual differences in the classroom and arguably in a better position to cope with a child whose special needs might derive from a specific handicap. Furthermore, the established principle of 'positive discrimination' encourages teachers to pay more attention within the class to 'those who need it'. (The extent to which class teachers adjust their teaching to suit the needs of hearing-impaired pupils is discussed in Chapter 5.)

Given the social and educational climate just described, it is perhaps not surprising that official policy has come to favour integration in education. Policy statements from the DES over the last ten years or so indicate a strengthening resolve to educate a greater proportion of handicapped children in an ordinary rather than a special school environment. For example, the DES Report *Special Education — A Fresh Look* (1973) states:

> Departmental policy has long been that no handicapped child should attend a special school if his needs can be met by an ordinary school.

In their document *Integrating Handicapped Children* (1974) the DES reaffirm:

> There is no doubt that the trend in this country, as in all those countries with highly developed educational systems must be (and already is) directed towards making it possible for increasing numbers of handicapped children to receive their education in ordinary primary and secondary schools.

More recently, in the Warnock Report (1978), a concept of handicap has been offered which in itself strengthens the notion of educational integration. Here a plea is made for the breakdown of the old medical model of disability and a demand for a more flexible consideration of the complex educational needs of the individual child. Instead of seeing handicap as an absolute characteristic of the individual, educators are asked to be aware of the relativity of handicap. A disability is a handicap in some situations but not in others. A so-called 'handicapped' child has, therefore, many 'normal' as well as 'different' qualities. With the emphasis on the learning problems rather than the handicap *per se*, we can discern a blurring of the distinction between handicapped and non-handicapped children. This sentiment is clearly expressed in the Education Bill (1980): 'In one sense every child's education needs are "special" because they are peculiar to him and nearly every child from time to time has difficulties which distinguish him from others.' The recognition that the gap between special and ordinary education is narrowing leads inevitably to the view that further integration is desirable. The 1980 Bill makes this quite clear with the statement: 'The Government takes as its starting point the principle that children and young people who have such (special) needs should be educated in association with those who do not.'

Many of the recommendations of the Warnock Report (1978) and the 1980 Education Bill are embodied in the 1981 Education Act. The 1981 Education Act, implemented on 1 April 1983, legislated that all children are to be included in ordinary schools unless this is not financially viable, interferes with the instruction of other children, or is incompatible with their receiving the education they require.

The 1981 Education Act, despite the 'let-out' clauses, is intended to provide a general framework of thinking encouraging more integration of handicapped children than is currently the case. How far-reaching the consequences of the 1981 Education Act will be for the future education of handicapped children only time will tell. Its significance must be seen, however, in the context of a general situation in which the majority of handicapped children are currently still receiving their education in segregated, special schools or classes (Booth 1983). The rhetoric of official statements from the DES (1973, 1974, 1978) has led to a belief that there has been steady progress towards the greater integration of handicapped pupils into ordinary schools over the years: yet figures from the DES (*Statistics of Education, Schools 1961–1984*) reveal that up to 1980 there was not a decline but a substantial increase in the proportion of children attending special schools. Since 1980 there has been a relative decline in the proportion of handicapped children attending special schools, but to date this has only been slight.

Whilst the changed social attitudes, shifts in ideology, educational philosophy and policy have created a facilitating background to developments towards the integrated education of handicapped pupils generally, the impact has been considerably more noticeable in deaf education than in other areas of special education.

That integration in deaf education has advanced far more than for other categories of handicapped children, and to the extent that it has is the result of special factors peculiar to deaf education and these merit further explanation.

Special Factors Facilitating Integration in Deaf Education

One special factor is that in a significant sense deaf children have become less handicapped than they used to be and it is important to understand the principal reasons leading to what might be seen as their 'normalisation'.

Of considerable importance has been the expansion in recent years of health and educational services for the pre-school hearing-impaired child. Hearing losses are more likely to be diagnosed early in a deaf child's life and appropriate hearing aids supplied. The deaf infant can now receive the benefits of amplified sound throughout the critical years of language acquisition. Furthermore, the general quality of hearing aids has improved in recent years so that hearing-impaired children can now benefit from greater amplification over a wider range of frequencies. Thus many deaf children are today quite literally hearing sounds that ten years ago they would not have been able to hear. The residual hearing of even very deaf children can now be used more effectively for the development of natural sounding spoken language.

The young deaf child benefits not only from better hearing aids, but also from improved parent guidance services and expanded facilities for the tuition of the pre-school child. In most areas of Britain, teachers of the deaf, who specialise in work with pre-school hearing-impaired children, are employed to help the child make best use of his residual hearing to develop his oral communication skills. Parents are advised as to how to offer experience in the home which will enable the deaf child to acquire more easily his mother tongue. Hence, by the time the 'average' deaf child reaches school age, he can hear, talk and understand the spoken language of others in a way that would have been thought exceptional several years ago.

The development of spoken language in the deaf child has, furthermore, been aided by more sophisticated and effective techniques of teaching used by teachers of the deaf. 'Natural' approaches to language acquisition, which owe much to the ideas of modern linguistics, emphasise a high 'input' of everyday, colloquial language to the deaf child in order that he may use his natural language acquisition capacity to learn the rules of his mother tongue. Advocates of 'natural' approaches stress the need for teachers and learners to use language that is appropriate and functional 'to the situation' regardless of syntactic complexity. Many claims have been made for the success of 'natural' approaches in developing normal language patterns in even the deafest of children (Van Uden 1977; Clark 1978). Where these approaches are used effectively with young hearing-impaired children, such children are more likely to be achieving relatively good standards of spoken language by the time they reach school age.

Equipped with improved oral communication skills, the deaf child is thus more easily able to assimilate into the ordinary school and more capable of benefiting from normal educational provision and facilities. Given that deaf children these days are talking more fluently and intelligibly and more readily comprehending the speech of others, then it is not difficult to understand why they are more acceptable in the ordinary school to both staff and pupils.[1]

Developments in hearing aid technology, as previously indicated, have greatly helped the pre-school deaf child acquire more normal language. These technological developments have also benefited the school-age deaf child and facilitated his integration into the ordinary school. Not only have individual aids improved in quality, they have also reduced in size. The miniaturisation of hearing aids, even very powerful ones, has meant that the majority of deaf school children can now wear behind-the-ear aids instead of the 'box' type bodyworn aids. Post-aural aids are less likely to get damaged in the rough and tumble of everyday school life and have the additional advantage for the integrated deaf child of easy concealment. This is particularly important in facilitating the integration of the older deaf children, some of whom may feel embarrassed and uncomfortable when wearing a highly visible and potentially stigmatising hearing aid.

A further 'breakthrough' in the development of hearing aids which has been of special significance for the integrated deaf child has been the invention of radio hearing aids. The wireless aid offers the hearing-handicapped child extremely good quality amplification of a teacher's voice without subjecting him to the interfering noises of the ordinary classroom and this enables him to follow lessons more easily. Many teachers believe also that the use of the radio aid by deaf children, both in the home and at school, has made a large contribution to the improvement of their spoken language and hence to their normalisation.

---

1. Just how acceptable deaf children are to class teachers and normally hearing pupils was a topic of my research and one which will be discussed in Chapters 5 and 6.

So far in this section concerned with special factors facilitating integration in deaf education only the positive factors behind the development towards the educational integration of hearing-impaired children have been outlined and discussed. However, an undoubtedly important factor underlying the development of various forms of integrated educational provision for hearing-impaired pupils has been the disillusion and dissatisfaction with the achievements attained by deaf children in special schools.

Evidence from Britain, the USA and Canada, that presented, for example, by the DES (1968), Montgomery (1968), Moores (1971) and Mac-Dougall (1971) revealed not only distressingly low academic standards, but also poor standards of oral communication in many of the special schools. Whilst it was probably unrealistic of educationalists to expect of severely hearing-impaired children educational standards that were the same as those achieved by normally hearing children, it was, and is, quite justifiable to be concerned that a large proportion of deaf children have been leaving special schools with poor spoken and written language competence. Special schools have been seen and are seen by many educators to fail in terms of their explicit objective of rehabilitation and eventual integration. This failure has led many teachers to the belief that for the majority of deaf children an ordinary school education is preferable. The experience of a normal hearing-speaking environment through integration into the ordinary school is perceived by educators to facilitate the attainment of more normal academic and linguistic standards. Integration, whilst perhaps not a sufficient condition for rehabilitation and normalisation, is increasingly coming to be perceived by many as a necessary one.

The practical realisation of ideas supporting the increased integration of deaf children has, of course, also been vastly aided by the pre-existence of reasonably large-scale services in ordinary schools for pupils with lesser hearing handicaps. As indicated earlier, provision originally intended for children with moderate or slight hearing impairments has come to be extended to those with more substantial hearing losses. Without the growth of the peripatetic service and the system of unit provision in the 1950s and 1960s, it is doubtful whether deaf children — that is those with the more severe hearing handicaps — would currently be the most 'integrated' category of handicapped pupil. Furthermore 'political' considerations in deaf education have not hampered the progress of integration as perhaps in other areas of special education. Tomlinson (1982) has pointed out that in special education generally, vested interests, particularly those of LEA administrators and Headteachers of special schools, have acted as a conservative force encouraging the maintenance of the special school system. In deaf education this has not to the same extent been the case because in many LEAs, Heads of special schools are also Heads of educational services for hearing-impaired children. Where this dual role is the case Headteachers retain their 'empires' as Heads of services whether or not integration takes place: power and status position remain unchanged regardless of whether deaf children are educated in ordinary or special schools.

In this chapter the most crucial factors which have led to the integration of the hearing impaired into the ordinary school have been identified but they probably do not offer a 'total explanation' of modern developments in the education of the hearing impaired. Idiosyncratic factors such as the ideas of powerful individuals may have played a large part in bringing about the present state of affairs: developments in deaf education in the past have always been significantly affected by influential individuals. Also, once the process of integration has begun, particularly in the relatively small, close-knit world of deaf education, there is inevitably some 'bandwagoning' effect.

The fact remains that in spite of the variations in provision described in this chapter, many, if not most, LEAs have become increasingly reluctant to place all but the most severely handicapped deaf children in a special school. In the future, therefore, the concerns of educators are likely to be not so much in deciding *whether* to place a hearing-impaired pupil in the ordinary school, but *how* to do so, in order that his intellectual, linguistic and social potential is most fully realised. Those who have responsibility for the education of deaf children in ordinary schools and are concerned about the quality of the education deaf pupils receive would benefit from informing themselves of the experiences of others and of the research findings on all aspects of integrated education. In Chapter 2 the accumulated experience of the research literature on the topic of integration will be examined.

2 THE ACADEMIC AND SOCIAL INTEGRATION OF HEARING-IMPAIRED PUPILS IN ORDINARY SCHOOLS: A REVIEW OF RESEARCH

A review of the literature on the integrated education of deaf children should be regarded with some caution. Any survey of research in special education, as Cave and Madison (1978) have pointed out tends 'to become a review of research undertaken in the United States so greatly does its volume exceed that of any other country'. Thus, whilst British material has been used where available, it is indeed the case that much of the work reviewed in this chapter comes from the USA. Care is needed before attempting to apply the results of research from one country to another where circumstances may be different. The United States system of education differs considerably from British education in terms of curriculum, organisation, and the bureaucratic, legal and cultural setting. Definitions and classifications of pupils with special needs inevitably vary between countries. Terms such as 'regular grades' and 'mainstreaming', for example, have no exact equivalent in Britain. Thus, whilst the research from the USA and indeed other countries undoubtedly offers interesting insights it would be unwise to assume that all the findings are precisely applicable to special education in Britain.

The research on the integrated education of deaf children falls into two broad categories. First, there is material which attempts to correlate integrated education with various aspects of the hearing-impaired child's academic, intellectual, linguistic, social and emotional development: such studies are generally termed 'efficacy studies' (Cave and Madison 1978). Some of these efficacy studies are comparative in that they attempt to compare the academic or social attainments of hearing-impaired children in ordinary schools with, say, hearing-impaired children in special schools, or alternatively with non-handicapped children in ordinary schools. This type of research can be further differentiated according to whether it results from what might be called 'controlled investigation' or from what can be regarded as 'case study' material. The controlled investigations involve the use of conventional research techniques, such as tests of attainment, surveys, questionnaires, behaviour rating scales, etc., in order to quantify relationships between selected variables such as the reading ages, or self-concepts of hearing-impaired pupils and, say, the type of school attended or the amount of time spent in ordinary classes. The case-study material is qualitative in nature and is based, for the most part, on reports of individual educators about their experience of integration at a particular school or within a local education authority area. In addition, there are a number of personal case studies: accounts of individual hearing-impaired children, written usually by parents, though sometimes by the pupils themselves, of their experiences in ordinary schools and classes.

Generally speaking the research in deaf education which one might term efficacy studies has been done in an attempt to clarify such questions as: how well do hearing-impaired children achieve academically in ordinary schools, or how well do they do in terms of social and personal development in ordinary schools, or is the educational experience in ordinary schools acceptable and appropriate?

The second broad category of research focuses attention on people within the ordinary school and attempts to describe attitudes towards pupils with a handicap and to uncover the factors underlying those attitudes. It examines the ways in which 'normals' in the ordinary school, that is, teachers and non-handicapped pupils, react to the presence of a hearing-impaired child in the class and the nature of the social relationships between them. This type of research attempts to answer questions such as: what happens when we place a hearing-impaired child in an ordinary class, or how do people feel about him and how does he interact with others, or can we identify factors which facilitate social integration? It assumes that if these questions can be answered then educators will be in a better position to understand the process of integration, and to take whatever action might be necessary to improve the education of the hearing-impaired child in the ordinary school. Most, though not all of the investigatory work into what might be termed 'social acceptance' makes use of formal research methods such as questionnaires and sociometric techniques rather than qualitative methods.

Efficacy Studies on Academic Attainments

Much of the research which might be termed efficacy studies attempts to relate school placement to the academic and intellectual progress of the hearing-impaired child. It must be stated at the outset, however, that large-scale published statistics on the academic performance of deaf children in ordinary schools are not available (Ross, Brackett and Maxon 1982). Whilst current research does not provide us with a complete picture of children's academic attainment and progress, there have been formal studies on this subject and they undoubtedly offer us some useful information concerning attainments.

A broad generalisation that can be made about these formal investigations is that they indicate significant educational retardation among hearing-impaired pupils regardless of educational setting (Quigley and Kretschmer 1982). Nearly all the studies demonstrate that degree of hearing loss is the greatest single factor affecting educational performance. Interestingly, whilst the evidence is not entirely overwhelming and unequivocal, the studies suggest that the educational environment is a significant independent factor and, furthermore, that the more 'normal' the school setting the greater the academic achievements of the hearing-impaired child. These points can be illustrated by considering some examples of efficacy studies undertaken in Britain and in other countries which attempt to relate placement in an ordinary school setting to the intellectual and academic progress of hearing-impaired pupils.

Earlier research, undertaken in the 1960s, though indicating some superiority of the ordinary over the special school for the hearing-impaired pupil on certain measures of educational achievement, does not paint as favourable a picture of integrated education for the deaf pupil as more recent research. An example of the earlier research is the study undertaken in Britain by M. Johnson (1963) on behalf of the Ministry of Education. In her investigation M. Johnson examined and evaluated the educational progress of 33 severely deaf pupils, 7–17 years of age, who had been transferred from special school to the ordinary school. The pupils were selected for transfer in the belief that they had the necessary competence to cope in the ordinary school. Yet after a specified period of time, only ten of the 33 hearing-impaired pupils were considered to be 'clearly successful' in terms of their educational progress and social adjustment. Insufficient specialist support and a lack of awareness on the part of class teachers were believed by M. Johnson to be important factors underlying the difficulties of hearing-impaired pupils in ordinary schools.

An investigation by J.C. Johnson (1962) undertaken in Britain at about the same time as that of M. Johnson, whilst not as pessimistic about the prospects of integrated deaf pupils, nevertheless revealed serious educational retardation in reading and arithmetic attainments among his sample of 68 hearing-impaired pupils attending ordinary schools. J.C. Johnson found his results 'extremely worrying'. However, when he compared the attainments of the ordinary school hearing-impaired pupils with those of a sample of hearing-impaired pupils of similar hearing loss attending a special school, he found that the special school pupils were even further behind on measures of attainment of reading, arithmetic and speech. Thus, J.C. Johnson's evidence confirmed disquietingly poor academic standards of hearing-impaired pupils wherever placed but indicated that attendance at the ordinary school might be relatively advantageous to the hearing-impaired pupil compared to attendance at a special school.

A later investigation again in Britain undertaken in the early-to-mid-1970s by Conrad (1979) produced some findings which were similar to those of J.C. Johnson. Conrad's study comprised an extensive survey of the attainments of 468 hearing-impaired pupils of school-leaving age attending special schools (359 pupils) and partially-hearing units in ordinary schools (109 pupils). On measures of reading, lip-reading and speech intelligibility Conrad found his hearing-impaired school-leavers to be considerably below average in attainments when compared to the normal school population. His findings on speech intelligibility confirmed those of J.C. Johnson that the unit pupils, educated in an ordinary school environment had better speech than the special school pupils, but on other educational measures there was no significant difference between the two groups. Generally Conrad interpreted his data to support the belief that it was hearing loss and not school placement which was critical for educational attainment, particularly for pupils with severe and profound hearing losses.

The evidence so far considered, based on research in Britain in the 1960s and early 1970s, suggests that hearing-impaired pupils achieve better academic and speech attainments in ordinary rather than in special schools, but that the standards are nevertheless low when compared to national norms of educational attainments. The academic and linguistic benefits of a normal school education for a deaf pupil do not, therefore, appear to have been substantial. However, it is almost certainly the case that in the early days of integration in deaf education relative lack of experience and resources, as suggested by M. Johnson (1963), limited the effectiveness of an integrated education for deaf pupils. Specialist support services and technical aids for the hearing-impaired pupil in the ordinary school were much less well developed than they have more recently become. Indeed an examination of more recent evidence offers stronger support for the superiority of the ordinary over the special school for the academic attainments of hearing-impaired pupils including those with greater hearing losses.

A study by Dale (1978) undertaken in London, for example, provides evidence that deaf children achieved better academic attainments the less segregated their educational environment. Dale reports that during 1972, six children, mean age 10.3 years, mean hearing loss 76.7 dB, were transferred from a junior unit to their local ordinary school: seven children in the control group, mean age 10.7 years, mean hearing loss 78.6 dB remained in the unit. Later, a further 'experimental' group of five children 6–13 years, drawn from both units and from a special school for the deaf, mean hearing loss 81.0 dB, were transferred full time to their local school. A control group of seven children, mean hearing loss 72.2 dB, remained in their special school or unit. The experimental groups and the 'controls' were assessed in 1977 for reading attainments and speech. The findings indicated that children in both hearing-impaired groups who transferred to full-time placement in the ordinary school made greater educational progress than those who remained in a more specialised environment either in the unit or in the special school for the deaf. The individually integrated children were significantly superior in reading attainments and speech intelligibility. The author concluded that 'carefully thought out individual integration schemes' should be extended as a form of educational provision for hearing-impaired children. He emphasised, however, that, when the individually integrated children are placed full time in their local school, they should receive a considerable amount of special support. Each hearing-impaired child featuring in Dale's study was withdrawn from the classroom for 45 minutes each day for specialist tuition in speech and language. In addition, each of these pupils had a support teacher working with them in the classroom for half of the school day. It would be wrong to conclude from this research, therefore, that the mere placement of a hearing-impaired pupil full time in his local school will produce superior academic achievements.

The study by Dale (1978) was small in scale but none the less his finding that hearing-impaired pupils make better academic progress the less specialised their educational setting appears to be confirmed by evidence from North America. An example is a study reported by Rister (1975) in the USA referring to the education of both moderately and profoundly deaf pupils. The study was conducted by the Speech and Hearing Institute, Houston, Texas, USA: the subjects were 88 deaf children aged 6–16 years; 62 per cent of these pupils attended ordinary school classes and 38 per cent were in special schools or segregated special classes. Out of the pupils enrolled in regular classes 81.1 per cent achieved 'adequate academic performance', compared to only 6 per cent of pupils enrolled in special schools or classes ('adequate academic performance' being defined in terms of being on a grade level appropriate to chronological age). However, the special school pupils did have greater average hearing losses; 87.8 per cent of special school and special class children had hearing losses greater than 85 dB compared with 56.4 per cent of children in regular classes. Rister argued, however, that as the majority of the profoundly deaf children in ordinary classes were achieving adequate academic attainments, and as the overwhelming majority of children in special schools and special classes were not achieving anywhere near 'on grade levels', then this was clear evidence of the superiority of ordinary classes over special classes for most deaf children. The Speech and Hearing Institute research findings, therefore, lend support to the idea that ordinary class placement is educationally beneficial to hearing-impaired children, even those with substantial hearing losses. However, we are not told in this study precisely *how* the 'regular class' children were integrated, nor what supplementary assistance, if any, they received.

A study in Canada by Reich, Hambleton and Houldin (1977), on the other hand, compared not just segregated with integrated schooling for hearing-impaired pupils, but investigated the effect of different degrees of segregation/integration. Four educational programmes were compared ranging from full integration with no specialist support to partial integration where hearing-impaired pupils were integrated for non-academic subjects only. The data collected on the children included measures of their hearing, oral and aural functioning, speech and intelligence, tests of academic attainment and measures of social adjustment and self-concept. The results of this study indicated that overall the fully integrated children were doing better academically at both primary and secondary level than those who were partially integrated. It was this fully integrated group, however, that had the least severe hearing losses and significantly better oral functioning. In an attempt to eliminate the 'hearing loss' factor and isolate the 'degree of integration' factor, a regression analysis was done on each of the groups according to the length of time they had been in the programme. If the fully integrated pupils' superiority had been the cause rather than the consequence of their integration then children who had just been integrated should have performed as well as those who had been in ordinary classes for some time. The results did, however, indicate that integration *per se* had some *independent* role in the pupils' superior achievement; the hearing-impaired children continued to improve the longer they were in the integration programmes, whilst those in the partially segregated classes fell further behind. The authors noted also that although most of the 'fully integrated' children were only moderately deaf, there were a few with severe and profound hearing losses who were considered to be more successful in terms of their academic achievements.

The picture that is beginning to emerge from the evidence so far considered is that, first, even those children with severe and profound hearing losses achieve better academic attainments in ordinary rather than in special schools. Second, hearing-impaired pupils, regardless of degree of hearing loss achieve better academic attainments the more fully they are integrated. This latter finding is corroborated by a thorough and extensive study undertaken by Jensema (1975), Jensema, Karchmer and Trybus (1978) and Jensema and Trybus (1979) in the USA.

These researchers, on behalf of the Office of Demographic Studies, studied a sample of 945 hearing-impaired children with different degrees of hearing loss and in different educational settings from all over the country. In addition to analysing academic achievement as a function of hearing loss, the authors also analysed the effect of school placement on academic achievement. As expected, children performed differently because of differences in their personal and social attributes, particularly their degree of hearing loss. However, after correcting for some of the major personal and social factors, differences in academic attainment as a function of type of educational setting were evident. (The influence of degree of hearing loss, aetiology, age of onset of loss, number of additional handicapping conditions, presence of mental retardation and reported ethnic background were corrected for in the data.) A range of categories of educational environment was considered: residential school for the deaf, day school for the deaf, full-time special class and full-time placement in an ordinary class. Jensema and Trybus (1979) found that as the educational settings became less specialised so the children's academic performance improved. A small but marked trend was evident that the less segregated the educational environment the higher the scores of the hearing-impaired pupils on all of the following measures: vocabulary, reading comprehension, speech intelligibility, maths concepts and maths computation. The authors remark that other variables not accounted for may have been responsible for the differences noted, as indeed they may. For example, there is no information on precisely what is meant by 'part-time special class' or 'full-time regular class' nor whether these categories of educational setting meant the same thing educationally for the children within each type of programme. These categories of educational setting are all the more difficult to interpret for British educators given the differences in the social and institutional context of education in the USA. Nevertheless, it is not difficult to agree with Ross *et al.* (1982) who, referring to this study, say: 'considering the important variables eliminated, the large population included, and the clear trend in the data it is more likely that the results can be interpreted as given'.

That the more recent research work on integration gives consistent evidence for the superiority of the ordinary school over the special school in respect of academic attainments should be taken seriously, if cautiously. It can always be argued that it is never possible with absolute precision to evaluate and control for all the individual, social and institutional variables. It is this kind of evidence, however, which leads Ross *et al.* to conclude: 'In our mind there is little doubt that hearing loss and other variables aside the more fully "mainstreamed" the average hard of hearing child is the greater his academic achievements.' ('Hard of hearing' according to Ross *et al.* (1982) refers to pupils with hearing losses not exceeding 95 dB.)

Explanations of why hearing-impaired pupils do better in ordinary schools can only be speculative and, as Ross *et al.* (1982) suggest, they are bound to be based on common-sense reasoning. What might be happening in ordinary classes is that teacher expectations are higher and also that deaf children have more exposure to normally hearing norms of spoken language and educational standards. As a consequence deaf children may be better motivated to 'achieve well' and 'speak intelligibly'. It is also likely, given that recent evidence is more positive than earlier findings about the academic advantages of placement in ordinary classes for hearing-impaired pupils that wisdom acquired by educators through years of experience has helped make integration more successful. Furthermore, the amount and quality of supportive services offered to hearing-impaired pupils in ordinary schools has almost certainly improved in most countries, as was seen to be the case in Britain in Chapter 1.

The research examined up to this point suggests that better educational standards are a consequence as well as a reason for ordinary school placement. However, this does not mean that a deaf child, just because he is placed in an ordinary class, is getting close to fulfilling his intellectual and academic potential. Whilst the research indicates that educators should acknowledge the benefits of the ordinary class for the hearing-impaired child, it would be unsafe on the basis of it to conclude that the ordinary class will, of itself, eliminate the educational problems associated with deafness. As we have seen, Dale (1978), for example, suggests on the evidence from his study that the individually integrated deaf child in an ordinary class needs both specialist support and supplementary assistance if he is to make adequate educational progress. That this is likely to be the case is supported by a study conducted in New Zealand in 1976, cited by the same author (1984). He reports that whilst hearing-impaired pupils enrolled in regular classes achieve 'reasonable' academic standards, they by no means comprehend all that is going on. In this investigation 44 hearing-impaired pupils, most of whom were severely deaf, were asked how much they understood of what the teacher said when she addressed the class as a whole. The results were as follows:

23 said they could understand the teacher — 'sometimes'
12 said they could understand the teacher — 'often'
 9 said they could understand the teacher — 'usually'

If one can generalise from the New Zealand study, it would appear that deaf children are missing a great deal in ordinary class lessons.

McCay Vernon (1981) paints an even gloomier picture about the deaf child's experience of the ordinary class. He suggests that, left to themselves, deaf children in ordinary classes 'cannot hear or understand what the teachers say'. He claims that at best a hearing-impaired pupil 'may get 5 to 20 per cent of what the teacher says'. McCay Vernon does not, however, support his claim with any evidence, therefore caution must be exercised in respect of this rather extreme 'finding'. Common sense tells us, however, that deaf children in ordinary classes will almost certainly experience some kind of difficulty and unless special measures are taken many will not be able to follow all the lessons all of the time.

In sum, then, the research evidence offers encouragement to those wishing to promote policies of integration for the hearing-impaired child, but it does not suggest that all the problems of educating deaf children will be solved simply by offering them more integrated education. The major educational problem remains: hearing-impaired pupils, for the most part, greatly underachieve academically when compared with normally hearing peers. This is true at all levels of hearing loss. Even a mild hearing loss is associated with academic retardation (Peckham, Sheridan and Butler 1972; Hamilton and Owrid 1974; Needleman 1977; Zinkus and Gottlieb 1980). Children with more severe hearing loss are at a much greater educational disadvantage than those with mild losses, as we have seen from much of the evidence cited. Deafness is a fundamental educational handicap because it interferes with normal linguistic and intellectual development and this is the case for the vast majority of deaf pupils no matter what the form of school setting.

Efficacy Studies: Social and Emotional Adjustment

Educators in favour of some form of ordinary school placement for the hearing-impaired child often argue that normal schools help promote normal social and emotional behaviour and that this is at least as important as academic achievement. The research material on the relationship between school placement and social and emotional adjustment is, however, considerably more equivocal than that on school placement and the relationship to the hearing-impaired child's academic achievements.

The only generalisation one can make about most efficacy studies from Europe and America on the social and emotional adjustment of hearing-impaired pupils in ordinary schools is that they indicate that such pupils show 'greater than average' maladjustment (Madebrink 1972). Whether the long-term social and emotional adjustment of the deaf individual is impeded or promoted by attendance at an ordinary rather than, say, a special school has yet to be demonstrated.

The evidence arising out of much formal research does not support the idea that normal schools necessarily produce 'normal' adjustment in the hearing-handicappped child. The findings of many studies confirm the view of writers such as Katz, Mathis and Merrill (1974), who have noted that:

> Hearing-impaired children do not necessarily feel more 'normal' in a normal setting. They may suffer experiences in a public school which emphasise their disability and constantly remind them of it.

J.C. Johnson's (1962) study, cited earlier with respect to academic achievements, indicated that many deaf children do suffer emotionally in a 'normal' school setting. In his investigation of 68 hearing-impaired children attending ordinary schools he found, using a Stott's Bristol Social Adjustment Guide (BSAG), that 53 per cent of the sample were 'normally adjusted', 38 per cent 'unsettled' and 9 per cent 'maladjusted'. These findings compare with those of Stott himself (1958) that 70 to 72 per cent of children in a typical junior class in an ordinary school can be expected to register as well-adjusted. J.C. Johnson suggests that the considerably greater amount of maladjustment found in his survey of hearing-impaired children is related to factors within the ordinary school environment itself. J.C. Johnson points to a lack of understanding on the part of class teachers in ordinary schools of the special educational problems caused by partial deafness as a major cause of the relatively poor adjustment of hearing-impaired pupils.

Fisher (1965) came to a very similar conclusion to that of J.C. Johnson as a result of his investigation into the social and emotional adjustment of hearing-impaired children attending ordinary classes. He compared 83 hearing-impaired pupils with 82 normally hearing 'controls' aged 5–16 years. Using Stott's BSAG and Cattell's Personality Questionnaire he found that 47 per cent of the hearing-impaired group, compared to 28 per cent of the control group, were found to show unsatisfactory adjustment. He explained the discrepancy in adjustment between hearing-impaired and normally hearing pupils in terms of:

> a serious lack of understanding among parents, teachers, school doctors and family doctors of the significance of moderate hearing impairment in pupils in ordinary classes.

Thus both Fisher (1965) and J.C. Johnson (1962) point to a lack of understanding on the part of other people in schools and outside them as significant factors in the relatively poor adjustment of hearing-impaired children in ordinary classes.

Reich *et al*. (1977), cited earlier in relation to academic attainments, suggest on the basis of their evidence concerning the emotional adjustment of hearing-impaired children in ordinary schools, that the way a child perceives himself in relation to others is a key factor in social and emotional adjustment. They believe that placement in ordinary schools can foster a poor self-concept in the hearing-impaired child. The hearing-impaired child in the ordinary school, they argue, can only adjust adequately if he sees himself as being able to cope effectively with his normally hearing peers. Where this is not possible, then integrated education can have a detrimental effect on the hearing-impaired child's social and emotional maturity. Hearing-impaired children who do not see themselves as competing on anything like equal terms with other pupils in the ordinary school are likely, the authors suggest, to be better adjusted socially and emotionally if placed in a special school.

The argument of Reich *et al*. that some hearing-impaired children might be better adjusted in a special school is supported by the work of Van den Horst (1971) with a sample of Dutch hearing-impaired children. Van den Horst compared the emotional adaptation and social stability of 50 hearing-impaired children attending ordinary school with 50 hearing-impaired children at a special school. His research, he acknowledges, suffers methodological weaknesses because the assessments of the children are based largely on school records and a number of different teachers' subjective reports. None the less, the findings bear considerable similarity to those of the other researchers previously cited. Van den Horst found that of the hearing-impaired group attending ordinary school, 54 per cent showed normal adjustment, whereas 86 per cent of the special school hearing-impaired pupils showed normal adjustment. The author, like J.C. Johnson (1962) and Fisher (1965), suggests that the poorer adjustment of the ordinary school group was caused by 'lack of understanding on the part of the environment'.

It is interesting that whilst the study of Van den Horst (1971), like those of Reich *et al*. (1977) and J.C. Johnson (1962), demonstrated that ordinary school placement produced higher academic and linguistic attainments in hearing-impaired pupils such placement resulted in less satisfactory social and emotional adjustment. It would seem from this research work that less than satisfactory social and emotional adjustment is a price that often has to be paid for greater academic achievements. But the question arises as to whether or not maladjustment in hearing-impaired pupils is a necessary feature of ordinary school placement: several writers seem to think that it is. Madebrink (1972), for example, discussing the integration of hearing-impaired children in Sweden observes that the very fact of deafness involves an unavoidable isolation which is all the more apparent when the deaf individual is surrounded by the normally hearing. Markham (1972) in his study of three deaf children integrated into ordinary schools comes to a similar conclusion. The deaf children featuring in Markham's investigation were each of high intelligence and had 'attained a very high degree of linguistic competence'. None the less they experienced considerable isolation in the ordinary school and suffered from a variety of emotional problems. Markham believes his study demonstrates that it is unrealistic to expect the complete integration of the deaf into a hearing society.

A more recent study in the USA by Farrugia and Austin (1980) does nothing to change the view just described. They found that deaf children integrated into normally hearing classrooms had poorer self-concepts and self-images than residentially placed pupils in spite of the fact that the non-residential pupils had higher academic attainments. They infer from their study that deaf children in the 'normal' community are continually measuring themselves against others and are perpetually troubled by their failure to be equal to the normally hearing.

Generally, then, the results of formal investigations into the social and emotional adjustment of hearing-impaired children placed in ordinary schools tend to show two main findings. First, that hearing-impaired children in ordinary schools are less well adjusted than normally hearing pupils in ordinary schools. Second, that hearing-impaired children in ordinary schools are less well adjusted than those in the protective environment of the special school. These results may be dispiriting to those educators keen to promote the educational integration of hearing-impaired children. However, the findings of the researchers cited above must be evaluated with caution and circumspection for a number of reasons.

First, all research which attempts to make precise measurements of social and emotional maladjustment inevitably suffers methodological weaknesses. 'Maladjustment' is difficult to define, let alone measure. Hence the amount of maladjustment found in any particular population tends to reflect the measuring devices used as much as the actual or real degree of maladjustment (Chazan 1970). Several writers, for example, Sussman (1973), Garrison and Tesch (1978) and Macdonald (1980), acknowledge an awareness of the problems of using conventional research tools for evaluating the personal adjustment of hearing-impaired pupils. They suggest that findings such as those which purport to demonstrate that deaf children in ordinary schools have poorer self-concepts, are socially and emotionally immature, etc. may be faulted because the effects may be as much a function of factors such as limited vocabulary, restricted experiences and insufficient exposure to 'worldly' ideas, as they are of individual psychological disturbance.

Second, even if we take into account the methodological difficulties of assessing the maladjustment of hearing-impaired children in ordinary schools, it must be pointed out that *every* investigation on the personality and adjustment of hearing-impaired children so far undertaken has indicated that deaf and partially-hearing children show an above-average degree of maladjustment, for example, Levine (1960), Mykelbust (1960), Craig (1965), Meadow (1969), Hine (1970) and Ives (1973). This is the case whatever the school placement of the hearing-impaired child. It cannot be said, therefore, that 'maladjusted' behaviour is a special feature peculiar to hearing-impaired children placed in ordinary schools.

Third, where research techniques other than personality inventories and behaviour rating scales are used, hearing-impaired pupils in ordinary schools appear less maladjusted than where these formal methods are employed. Evidence derived, for example, by seeking the feelings and views of the handicapped child himself suggests better adjustment to ordinary schools than we have been led to believe from the results of other types of research methods. Dale (1984) citing some of the findings of the New Zealand survey (1976) of hearing-impaired pupils in ordinary schools reports that of the 44 pupils interviewed, three-quarters liked being in an ordinary school, only three did not. The remaining pupils thought that school was 'all right'. Only one child said she would like to go back to a school for deaf children.

There have not been many studies in which the feelings and ideas of hearing-impaired pupils have been sought directly so it is difficult on the small amount of evidence available to formulate generalisations. Nevertheless, it is probably significant that the findings of the New Zealand Study (1976) are paralleled by some research in England into the integration of physically handicapped children in ordinary schools.

Anderson and Clarke (1982) interviewed 119 severely disabled teenagers, 31 per cent of whom attended special schools, 69 per cent ordinary schools. They found that all of those pupils placed in ordinary schools said they liked being there and all but one preferred ordinary to special school placement. But nearly 25 per cent of the pupils in special schools said they would have preferred to be in an ordinary school and a further 25 per cent were undecided. The chief advantage of ordinary schools, according to these pupils, was that it was more 'normal' to be in a 'normal' educational environment.

Of course, that handicapped pupils like ordinary schools does not necessarily mean that they are well adjusted, socially mature or emotionally stable. However, given serious methodological problems with 'objective' techniques for assessing adjustment in a hearing-impaired or any handicapped pupil, the method of asking the pupils directly how they feel about school seems as useful a way as any for deriving some 'measure' of their adjustment to the ordinary school. This method receives recent support from Ross *et al.* (1982). These researchers argue that:

> There does not yet seem to be an acceptable substitute for judging the psycho-social status of the hard-of-hearing child than talking to him and his parents, asking about his friends and after-school activities and observing him in classrooms, cafeteria and recess.

Even if it is accepted that hearing-impaired pupils in ordinary schools are not as well adjusted, socially competent or as self-confident as their non-handicapped peers, it must be acknowledged that a hearing impairment is an undesirable handicap and one that makes many aspects of life, particularly social life, difficult. It is, therefore, not surprising that many hearing-impaired children have to suffer more than a fair share of frustration, tension, anxiety and general discomfort whilst growing up. Sustaining adequate social interaction and maintaining satisfactory relationships is a problem for all human beings, but the problems are exacerbated for those whose handicap leads to communication difficulties. It may well be the case that adjustment to a hearing-speaking world at an early age, painful though it may be, is likely to lead the hearing-impaired child to more successful integration later on.

A more segregated educational environment, on the other hand, might offer a hearing-impaired child protection from the harsh, outside world and this may give him a greater sense of emotional security as a child, but that security may be short-lived. The high incidence of psychiatric disorder that has been reported in the past among the adult deaf (Denmark

1981) is testimony to the fact that a protective special school environment does not necessarily lead to emotional stability later in life. Thus it can be argued that the earlier in life a hearing-impaired child learns to bear the 'slings and arrows' of hearing-speaking society through placement in the ordinary school the better he will be able to withstand and overcome the special difficulties associated with his communication handicap that will confront him throughout his life. This argument has yet to be verified, but it undoubtedly has a large measure of common-sense appeal, and is worthy of serious consideration by educators responsible for the school placement of hearing-impaired children. This issue will be taken up in Chapter 7.

There are, then, a number of reasons for being sceptical concerning existing research material which indicates relatively 'poor' social and emotional adjustment of hearing-impaired children in ordinary schools. The research does not by any means prove that integration does not work, nor that ordinary school placement leads necessarily to permanent and irreparable emotional damage to a deaf person. The fact that a great many educators are anxious to promote integrated, as opposed to segregated, education suggests that educators likewise do not accept at face value the findings of formal research on this topic. This non-acceptance may be for any one of several reasons. First, the methodological weaknesses of the research material may be such that those concerned with decision-making in deaf education feel they can safely ignore the rather negative findings. Second, a significant factor may be the influence of modern ideological and political ideas, referred to in Chapter 1, which support trends towards 'integration' and oppose 'segregation'. These ideas may lead to firm beliefs in the philosophy of integration in deaf education which override any 'scientific' consideration of its effectiveness. Third, and perhaps most important of all, the day-to-day experience of teachers and parents of integrated education for hearing-impaired children have been considerably more powerful in influencing educational policy than have research papers in relatively inaccessible journals. Many teachers at the 'chalk-face' feel convinced, because of the evidence before their eyes, that the ordinary school offers considerable advantages to the majority of hearing-impaired children. Teachers and parents witness what they believe to be attainments in spoken language, academic work and social behaviour that could not have been achieved in a segregated special school.

Efficacy Case Studies of Experiences of Integration

That personal experience rather than the evidence of 'hard' research has been a powerful influence in promoting the educational integration of hearing-impaired children is supported by the written material from Britain and abroad which is in the form of individual case studies. Most, though not all of these accounts, are of success stories and they generally offer a warm view of the value and benefits of integrated education for the deaf. There is not the space here nor the necessity to review all such reports. Some citations from a few typical accounts are offered to indicate their nature and the contribution that they make to the understanding of integration of the hearing impaired into the ordinary school.

Professor Löwe (1977), for example, expresses obvious enthusiasm for integration when referring to the hearing-impaired children who attend an ordinary primary school in Switzerland. He states:

> For me it is always an exciting experience to observe the integrated deaf children at Meggan. Instead of the former inferiority complex and shyness around ordinary school children, they know the joy of studying and playing together and their consciousness of equality is growing.

There are many equally optimistic accounts of specific integration programmes from the USA. For example, Charles H. Cosper (1976), reporting on the Andrew Gautenbein programme, Michigan, and the Jane Brooks integration scheme in Chickasha, Oklahoma, appears to have no doubts about the high level of all-round educational standards achieved by the hearing-impaired pupils in these schemes, as his statement illustrates:

> Emotional adjustment can be just as natural for a hearing-impaired child as it is for the child who can hear. Most of the hearing-impaired students at the Jane Brooks School and at Berrien Springs have healthy self concepts. They have academic ability, sports prowess and rapport with other people in the community just like any hearing child.

Also from the USA is a report of a programme adopted by the Lexington School for the Deaf, NYC, which admits both deaf and normally hearing pupils. Blumberg (1973) describing the work of the school justifies integration on the grounds that:

It is the only way to provide the hearing-impaired child with what he cannot gain from his ordinary 'deaf' environmental experiences . . . Integration is one of the logical steps in the chain of events which will prepare a child with a hearing loss to take his place in society as a contributing individual.

Parents as well as teachers frequently offer glowing reports of the post-integration success of their hearing-handicapped children. For example, the parents of a ten-year-old severely deaf girl made the following comment about the educational success of their daughter since enrolling at an ordinary American primary school (Yater 1977):

Bonnie has blossomed! She is making many friends and is learning to enjoy the give and take of friendship. This same attribute has transferred to her participation in groups outside of school life. Although she integrated a grade below her chronological age level, we are satisfied with her progress . . . She is gaining self-confidence.

From the same source (Yater 1977) Bena, a profoundly deaf teenager, comments on her own experiences of integration at American elementary and junior high schools:

Being deaf is not so hard once you adjust to it. Going into third grade in a public school was a hard move for me to make . . . Being surrounded by twenty-five or more children was quite a change after having had five in my class . . . Each year in elementary school had helped me to gain confidence and now I was in an entirely new situation again. However, this time I adjusted much more easily and it seemed easier to fit in.

Not all personal accounts of an integrated education support the views of Bena, cited above, that an education in an ordinary school increases self-confidence. Paddy Ladd (1981), now a deaf adult, referring to his own experiences in an ordinary school in Britain suggests that these experiences undermined rather than boosted his confidence. His account expresses a feeling of being:

Stuck out on my own, bumbling along, trying to catch on to the coat-tails of the hearing world, pretending to be a hearing person instead of accepting myself for what I am.

It is, of course, impossible to weigh the account of Bena against that of Paddy Ladd and come to any sensible or valid conclusions. That deaf pupils might perceive their education in a different way from their teachers, however, demonstrates a need for more 'consumer' research into the integrated education of deaf children.

In addition to written accounts of integration, many educators in Britain have had the experience of seeing video recordings prepared by members of staff at Oxford Polytechnic of conversations with a large number of severely and profoundly deaf children, all of whom have been educated in an ordinary school environment (Oxford Polytechnic 1980). Probably no one who has viewed these tapes would deny the impressive levels of spoken language achieved by these hearing-impaired children. Though educational placement in the ordinary school may not be the sole factor behind the success of the hearing-impaired pupils, it is none the less hard to doubt that being surrounded by the everyday talk of normally hearing school children and teachers had made a significant contribution to their high levels of spoken language competence.

A question that needs to be considered most carefully by educators is the extent to which they must balance 'hard', 'objective' research findings which offer positive but not unequivocal support for integrated education of deaf children with the case-study material and findings derived from the views of the pupils themselves, which tend in the main to provide a more enthusiastic view of ordinary school placement for the hearing impaired. Clearly, it would be imprudent to overlook the fact that there are many problems highlighted by the research material associated with integration practices in deaf education. These problems have to be overcome if the hearing-impaired child is to receive an optimum education in the ordinary school and be helped to achieve acceptable academic standards and social and emotional adjustment. Many of the writers of the case-study material referred to emphasise strongly the need for certain conditions to be met if integration is to be succcessful. Few are so naïve as to believe that a hearing-impaired child will automatically prosper educationally simply by being placed in an ordinary class. As Dale (1966) so rightly says:

> Integrating deaf children into ordinary schools will not make them hear. Many of them will probably remain deaf throughout their lives and will have very serious communication difficulties.

Placing a handicapped child in a normal school environment does not through some mysterious process remove his disability and make him normal. The research literature on the attainments of hearing-impaired pupils educated in ordinary schools suggests that there has probably been some improvement in educational standards with the new form of provision. It also demonstrates that integrated deaf pupils continue to 'underachieve'.

The efficacy studies into the academic and socio-emotional achievements of handicapped children reviewed above do not on the whole set out to offer reasons other than speculative ones for what the research reveals. As examples of what might be termed input/output analysis they attempt to correlate broad variables, such as educational environment, to a handicapped child's academic attainments and emotional adjustment. They do not, however, tell *why* matters are as they are. For 'why' explanations, a closer look at the day-to-day occurrences in classrooms and the attitudes of the people in them is necessary. It is this second broad type of research which gives some knowledge and insight into the process of integration and it is this kind of understanding which will help to ensure that the hearing-impaired pupil gets as much benefit as possible from ordinary school placement.

Most of the research which has in any way attempted to investigate 'within-school factors' which might affect the process of educational integration has been concerned with the attitudes of class teachers and 'normal' pupils to the handicapped child and the way in which the two groups interact. (By 'class teachers' is meant teachers of 'ordinary' or 'regular' classes in ordinary schools who generally do not hold specialist qualifications to teach handicapped pupils.) The literature referring to the process of the integration of hearing-impaired children is not, to date, extensive. References will be made, therefore, to research material concerned with the integration of categories of handicapped pupils other than the deaf in order to offer fuller insights into the process of the educational integration of the hearing impaired.

Studies of Teacher Attitudes Towards Handicapped Pupils

In the consideration of this category of research the literature relating to teacher attitudes towards handicapped children will be examined first because favourable teacher attitudes are thought by many educators to be crucial if integration is to succeed. The majority of reported investigations are from the USA and indicate a widespread use of formal attitude scales to determine teachers' views of handicapped pupils.

Many investigators have sought to establish the nature of class teachers' attitudes. Most of these studies report relatively unfavourable teacher attitudes towards working with a handicapped pupil and a certain amount of unwillingness on the part of teachers to receive a handicapped child into their classes, for example, Alexander and Strain (1978), Horne (1979), Baum and Frazita (1979), Byford (1979), Baker and Gottlieb (1980) and Schultz (1982). However, some other investigators, for example, Cope and Anderson (1977), Hegarty, Pocklington and Lucas (1981) and Loxham (1982) have found more positive attitudes among teachers towards their handicapped pupils. The findings beg the question of *why* some class teachers willingly accept handicapped pupils into their classes and others do not, and what are the specific factors underlying such teacher attitudes? Many researchers attempt to correlate attitudes with other 'teacher' or 'institutional' variables in order to gain insight into the reasons why teachers' attitudes might be 'favourable' or 'unfavourable'.

Cave and Madison (1978), in their review of the research literature on special education, suggest that unfavourable teacher attitudes towards accepting handicapped children stem from insecurity, and sometimes resentment, arising from ignorance and inexperience of handicapped children. According to these writers what seems to be important in influencing teachers' attitudes is their *knowledge* of the implications of handicap and their *experience* of children with a particular handicap. There are many examples from the research literature concerning all categories of handicapped pupils which illustrate that this is so, and some typical studies will be cited to demonstrate the point.

That 'knowledge' is a critical factor in determining a teacher's attitude towards handicap is confirmed by the study undertaken some years ago in the USA by Murphy, Dickstein and Dripps (1960). These researchers investigated teachers' feelings about different types of handicapped children and related this to teachers' knowledge of the different handicaps. The study revealed that a handicapped child's position on the teachers' 'desirability' scale had a direct relationship to the teacher's knowledge of that handicap. It is significant to specialist educators of the deaf that hearing-handicapped children, along with the visually handicapped and delinquent children, were the lowest ranked groups on the 'desirability' scale. It was concerning these groups that teachers, overall, were least knowledgeable. The authors concluded from their data, that:

The more informed a teacher feels about a handicapping condition, the more inclined she is to feel comfortable with the child having the

condition and the more accepting will be her attitude towards the child
. . . There is no fear like the fear of the unknown.

More recently a survey conducted by the DES on behalf of the Warnock
Committee (1978) in schools in England, Scotland and Wales confirms
that knowledge and information are very important in favourably dispos-
ing a teacher to receive a handicapped child into her class. The Committee report states that:

> The evidence we have received strongly supports the view that ordinary
> schools need better and more comprehensive advice and support if
> they are to make efficient provision for children with special educa-
> tional needs.

Many more examples could be cited of research from a variety of countries which indicates that class teachers' attitudes towards their handicapped pupils improve as they become more knowledgeable about their
pupils' special features and special needs and how to serve them — for
example, from Britain: Anderson (1973), Hegarty and Pocklington (1982);
from the USA: Alexander and Strain (1978), Stephens and Braun (1980),
Allsop (1980), Larrivee (1981), Ringlaben and Price (1981); and from
Israel: Naor and Milgram (1980). Most of these writers stress the
desirability of both pre-service and in-service training for all teachers
to appraise them of handicapped children and their special educational
needs. Several suggestions are offered as to what might constitute
appropriate training; these include lectures, films, group discussions,
simulation exercises and regular workshops.

Research on teacher attitudes towards hearing-impaired pupils reveals,
perhaps not surprisingly, conclusions very similar to those concerning
other categories of handicapped children. For example, that knowledge
of hearing-impaired children is an important factor in the promotion of
positive attitudes in teachers is confirmed by the Project NEED (Bitter
and Johnston 1973). Project NEED was concerned with many aspects
of the integration of hearing-handicapped children. It consisted largely
of a series of seminars in which teachers and administrators from all over
the USA came to share their experiences of integrating hearing-impaired
children into ordinary schools. Significantly, the most frequently stated
problem of integration was 'lack of knowledge of hearing impairment
on the part of receiving class teachers'. Likewise Porter (1975), describing her experiences as an administrator of an integration programme for
hearing-impaired pupils into ordinary schools in the USA, confirms the

need for teachers to be knowledgeable about handicap and stresses the need for the teacher to receive on-going advice and information. She states: 'not only must teachers be prepared in advance but advised continuously'. Kindred (1976) in her account of integrating hearing-impaired pupils into regular classes at a secondary school in Virginia, USA, similarly refers to the critical importance of continuous education of the ordinary class teacher concerning the special problems of hearing impairment. She suggests that: 'A continuing program of teacher orientation is one of the most important factors for successful integration of hearing-impaired students at the secondary school level.'

That most teachers do not understand the implications of deafness for the educational development of a pupil as part of their general knowledge is indicated by an investigation by Paul and Young (1975) on deaf children educated in ordinary classes in the USA. The majority of pupils featuring in the investigation were found to be achieving academically 'well below average', yet 50 per cent of their class teachers did not think that the pupils' hearing loss was a factor underlying their low achievements.

The research cited above thus leaves no doubt as to the importance of 'knowledge of handicap' to the class teacher in facilitating the process of integration. In the case of the education of deaf children it may be particularly important that class teachers are given advice and information about the implications of a hearing handicap as there is evidence to indicate that the 'invisible' handicap of deafness is not generally well understood by teachers.

That teachers need knowledge and understanding of handicap if they are to feel competent to teach a handicapped pupil and to receive him willingly into their classes accords very much with common-sense reasoning. So also does the idea that 'experience' with a pupil helps teachers feel more confident in having such a child in their class and this is confirmed by research evidence. The investigation of Haring, Stern and Cruickshank (1958), for example, on teacher attitudes towards handicapped pupils in the USA, suggests that experience may be even more important than abstract knowledge. This research attempted to separate the two variables, experience and knowledge, and concluded that whilst knowledge of handicap was important, previous direct experience of working with handicapped pupils was more critical to the positive acceptance of these children by class teachers.

A more recent piece of research by Johnson and Cartwright (1979) in the USA, was likewise aimed at investigating the differential effect of knowledge of handicap, and experience of handicapped children, on the attitudes of ordinary class teachers towards mainstreaming. In this study one group of 29 teachers had attended an Information Course on children with special needs *and* had some classroom experience of handicapped children. Another group of 27 teachers were enrolled on an Information Course but had no experience of teaching handicapped children. A third group of 28 teachers had classroom experience of children with special needs but were not enrolled on an Information Course. The research indicated that teachers' attitudes towards mainstreaming significantly improved as a result of a combination of information about, and experience with, handicapped children. Johnson and Cartwright's conclusion differed from that of Haring *et al.* (1958) in that they believed both variables to be of equal importance and complementary to each other.

Anderson (1973) in her investigation into the integration of physically handicapped children into primary schools in England confirms the findings of Johnson and Cartwright (1979) in the USA, that the two crucial factors in producing favourable attitudes among class teachers towards handicapped children are the amount and quality of information that teachers have about the children *and* the degree of contact and experience teachers have of handicapped children in the classroom.

It would seem, therefore, that teachers need to be given the opportunity to apply their knowledge of handicap in the classroom itself in order to feel more generally confident in their ability to cater for the special needs of a handicapped child. None of the research discussed relating to 'experience' concerns children with a hearing handicap, but there is no reason to suppose that the conclusions would be any different for class teachers of hearing-impaired pupils.

In addition to 'knowledge' and 'experience' there are two other major factors which have been demonstrated to be important in fostering positive attitudes among class teachers towards handicapped pupils: these are an ideological commitment to the principle of integrating handicapped children into normal society and the provision of adequate resources and support services to help the teacher cope with the additional responsibility of a handicapped pupil. With regard to the issue of ideological commitment the research findings from the USA of Stephens and Braun (1980), along with those of Ringlaben and Price (1981), suggest that a belief that handicapped children *should* be educated in ordinary schools is a significant independent factor in promoting attitudes in teachers towards handicapped pupils. One might speculate that teachers with such a view would be more highly motivated to seek information about the special needs of handicapped children and ways of catering for those needs in the ordinary classroom.

Likewise, the provision of special facilities and extra resources for class teachers receiving handicapped children into their classes has been shown to be important by several investigators, for example, Cope and Anderson (1977); Schultz (1982). These writers emphasise that class teachers, as well as being given information and advice, should receive additional help such as the services of a classroom or welfare assistant or specialist support teacher. Again, it seems to accord with common-sense reasoning that teachers given extra assistance will feel more favourable to the presence of a handicapped child in the class and more confident in their ability to serve his often very time-consuming special needs.

According to the research evidence then, it would appear that the factors which foster positive attitudes in teachers towards handicapped pupils all have something in common, and that is, they contribute to a feeling of confidence on the part of the teacher. Feeling confident in their ability to cope with the teaching of handicapped children might be presumed to be a crucial overarching factor influencing the way teachers feel about handicapped children. That this may indeed be the case is confirmed by the work of Larrivee and Cook (1979), who conducted a large-scale survey of the attitudes towards handicapped children of 1,000 New England schoolteachers. Larrivee and Cook found that the most important variable for creating a favourable and accepting attitude in a teacher towards handicapped children was 'the perception of degree of success with special needs students'.

A conclusion that can thus perhaps be safely reached from the currently available research material is that ordinary class teachers are more likely to have positive attitudes towards a handicapped pupil if they believe they can make a contribution towards his educational development. In order that this can occur, it would seem that both knowledge of the handicap and familiarity with the handicapped child are critical factors. Also of importance are the quality of the supportive services offered to a teacher receiving a child with special educational needs and a commitment on the part of the teacher to the idea of integrated education for the handicapped.

That teachers have favourable attitudes towards handicapped pupils is not, however, exactly equivalent to saying that they are positively willing to have them in their classes, nor that they teach them effectively. There is evidence that such a willingness is considerably influenced by institutional variables such as class size, the organisation of teaching and the mode of administration in the school. For example, Bitter *et al.* (1973) found that one of the most frequently stated problems by class teachers receiving handicapped children was that they had to cope with them in already overcrowded classes. That class load is an important factor is strongly emphasised in the Warnock Report (1978) also, and is illustrated in the following statement:

> The importance of favourable staff-pupil ratios if individual pupils with disabilities are to be successfully assimilated into ordinary classes was confirmed by the responses from headteachers and teachers in ordinary schools to a survey which was administered on our behalf by the Department of Education and Science of the views of teachers in England, Scotland and Wales about provision for children with special educational needs. Staffing ratios, which facilitate smaller classes in general and smaller teaching groups in particular, were considered to be the most important factor contributing to successful integration.

The importance of improving conditions for class teachers receiving handicapped children into their classes is emphasised even more strongly by Rauth (1981). She suggests in relation to the integrated education of handicapped children in the USA that:

> many handicapped children are not getting the education they should in the 'least restrictive environment' simply because teachers have not the time to spare. Requests for extra resources are frequently met with 'Sorry, you'll have to make do . . .' Given appropriate training and conditions teachers can indeed be expected to help all children in their classes learn and grow. Until such a commitment is made, until it is recognised that additional resources must be channelled into public services, we will be forced to pretend that rhetorical good intentions are reality.

In comparison, it is interesting and significant that in Britain the National Association of Schoolmasters and Union of Women Teachers have advised members 'not to accept handicapped children into their schools unless the resources are available to provide proper care for them' (*Guardian*, 12 April 1985).

Class load is, however, but one factor affecting a teacher's working conditions. An investigation by Payne and Murray (1974) in the USA suggests that the nature of a class may also be important. If, for example, a class already contains a significant proportion of 'problem children', then the teacher cannot be expected to take on another 'special needs' child. Payne and Murray (1974) found that Principals of suburban schools were more willing and prepared to accepted handicapped pupils into their schools than the Heads of urban schools, which is, of course, to accept the widely-held, and probably correct, assumption that urban schools contain more 'problem' children than suburban ones.

That class teachers need favourable working conditions in order to offer adequate service to special needs pupils seems a reasonable assumption but it has been further suggested that if a handicapped child is to receive an 'optimum education' in an ordinary class, a teacher must also adopt a particular teaching style. A number of writers, for example, Bitter *et al*. (1973), Porter (1975) and Kindred (1976) have stressed the need for a teacher receiving a handicapped child to individualise and personalise her teaching strategies in order to cater for the individual special needs of the handicapped child.

That teachers should be sensitive to the different educational needs of their pupils seems to be axiomatic if they are to cope adequately with a child with a disability. There has, however, as yet been little investigation into the precise relationship between the way a teacher organises her class and her preferred mode of teaching, for example, whole class methods, individual approaches, etc., and her actual response to a handicapped child. One cannot assume that a teacher who, say, relies more on 'whole class' techniques will be any less accommodating to a child with special needs than a teacher who prefers what might be called 'individual' approaches. Clearly the way teachers teach is not amenable to easy and simple classification into rigid categories. None the less, how a teacher normally behaves in the classroom — her everyday style of teaching — is likely to affect the ease with which a handicapped child can cope in the ordinary class. Indeed, this topic merits further investigation and is a matter which is considered in Chapter 5.

Throughout the discussion of the research into variables affecting teacher attitudes towards handicapped children information has been drawn from the literature relating to all types of handicapped children. A factor which relates specifically to the special problems of pupils with hearing handicaps, namely, their difficulties of communication merits some special consideration. Generally speaking, the greater the hearing loss the greater the communication problems. One might hypothesise that a major difficulty for class teachers receiving hearing-impaired pupils into their classes would be associated with communication problems. It would also seem to be likely that the deafer the child the greater the problem for the teacher. Surprisingly, however, the research evidence available does not confirm either hypothesis. Bitter *et al*. (1973) for example, found that neither communication difficulties nor degree of deafness were mentioned by class teachers as 'problems' when teaching hearing-impaired pupils. The authors found this puzzling but suggested that perhaps it was the case that the problem was too obvious to state. Another point of view stated by several writers, for example, Rodda (1970), is that children with more substantial hearing losses evoke sufficient sympathy and compassion in teachers to offset their perception of deaf children as problems. Generally though, it is the case that the problematic nature of the communication between class teacher and hearing-impaired pupil is not one that has received a great deal of attention from researchers and this is a deficiency. Indeed, the matter of communication between ordinary class teachers and hearing-impaired pupils is one which is reported and discussed in Chapter 5.

The evidence reviewed and considered so far on the attitudes of class teachers towards handicapped children gives helpful information and insights to educators wishing to pursue a policy of integrating handicapped children into ordinary classes. Clearly, the research suggests that there is a need to provide teachers with in-service training, short courses, opportunities for familiarisation with children who have specific handicaps and appropriate and continuing advice from specialists. There is also evidence which indicates a need to create favourable working conditions for teachers if they are to receive handicapped children willingly into their classes.

A criticism that can be made of currently available research material is that it tells us nothing of the dynamics of the processes operating in the classroom itself when a handicapped child is placed in an ordinary class. Educators responsible for the placement of hearing-impaired children need to know, for example, not just whether or not a teacher is likely to have favourable attitudes towards a deaf pupil but how she actually *behaves* towards him. It is apparent, therefore, that there is a need for more awareness of, and research into, the day-to-day practices of ordinary class teachers and the way they respond to the presence of a hearing-impaired pupil in the class.

A further criticism that can be made of the research material on the attitudes of teachers towards handicapped children relates to the methodologies used. Most of the studies referred to attempt to assess teacher attitudes by means of an attitude scale or a questionnaire designed by the investigators to measure teachers' attitudes, beliefs and feelings about teaching handicapped children. As suggested earlier in this chapter there are methodological problems in attempting to determine *precise* measurements of complex features of human beings such as their attitudes and beliefs (Wild 1976). Likewise similar methodological

criticisms can be levelled at much of the work investigating the relationships between handicapped and normal children in ordinary schools. Most
such studies make use of formal techniques such as sociometry, classroom
interaction analysis and peer status scales and can thus be accused of
aiming at a degree of objectivity which is, arguably, unattainable. None
the less, it is useful to examine any work which attempts to provide us
with information and understanding about the way the handicapped and
non-handicapped react and respond to each other in ordinary schools,
and available studies do indeed provide us with some useful insights which
have relevance to the integration of the hearing impaired.

Studies of Interaction Between Handicapped Pupils and Non-handicapped Pupils and Teachers in Ordinary Schools

Investigations which focus on relationships between handicapped and non-
handicapped pupils indicate fairly consistently that hearing-impaired
children, and indeed all categories of handicapped children, are less well
accepted in the ordinary school by non-handicapped pupils and also by
teachers than those who are physically normal. The findings are not,
however, straightforward and unequivocal as will become apparent from
the following examination and discussion of this research evidence. Those
studies relating to hearing-impaired children specifically will be discussed
first because these are clearly of most relevance.

In an early study of interaction between handicapped and non-
handicapped pupils in ordinary schools Force (1956) investigated 63 partially hearing children aged 6–13 years in ordinary classes in the USA.
Sociometric instruments were used to assess the choice behaviour of
school children on three criteria — friends, playmates and workmates.
On all three dimensions the partially hearing children scored lower than
the non-handicapped pupils. Force attributed this finding to the relative
visibility of the hearing handicap; the hearing-impaired children in this
study all wore prominent, body-worn hearing aids and this, argued the
author, led to negative stereotyping on the part of the normal pupils.

Elsner (1959) on the other hand offers a different point of view by
suggesting that the more 'visible' a child's hearing loss, the greater the
degree of social acceptance of that child. Elsner used the Moreno Peer
Nomination Scale to evaluate the social position of 45 hearing-impaired
children aged 9–12 years in ordinary classes in the USA. The hearing
losses of the children in the sample ranged from 36–79 dB with a mean
hearing loss of 49 dB. Elsner divided the sample into two groups: one

group had a mean hearing loss of less than 50 dB and did not wear hearing aids; the other group had a mean hearing loss of more than 50 dB and wore aids. Elsner found, as Force had done, that hearing-impaired children were not, overall, as well accepted as normally hearing classmates. However, he found also that it was the children with the least visible abnormality, that is, the children with the less severe hearing losses, who were less accepted than the deafer children who wore hearing aids. Elsner explains his findings in terms of the fact that a visible handicap may actually reduce awkwardness between disabled and non-disabled peers; the need to explain the handicap is minimised and the non-handicapped respondent knows what is required of him in order to accommodate to the other person's condition.

An investigation conducted by Kennedy and Bruininks (1974) on the other hand produced findings which differed in some respects from those of both Force and Elsner. This study examined peer status and self-perceived peer status of fifteen 5–7 year old hearing-impaired children. Four children had hearing losses of between 45–74 dB; eleven children had losses of 75–110 dB. Three sociometric tests were used: the Moreno Peer Nomination Scale; the Ohio Social Acceptance Scale and the Perceived Social Choice Socioempathy Scale. The results indicated that among these young children, the pupils with severe or profound losses achieved greater social acceptability than those with moderate or slight hearing losses, and perhaps surprisingly, greater than those with normal hearing. All the hearing-impaired children were found to be as perceptive of their social status as children with normal hearing. Thus Kennedy and Bruininks seem to confuse still further the picture presented to us by Force and Elsner. The authors were aware of this and suggested that the sociometric techniques may not be enough to achieve a full understanding of the situation when hearing-impaired and normally hearing children are placed in a school class together. There was, Kennedy and Bruininks emphasised, the need for:

> a clear understanding of the social dynamics of regular classrooms which include handicapped children and that such knowledge will contribute to the development of effective strategies to achieve their successful integration in normalised school settings.

McCauley, Bruininks and Kennedy (1976) studied the interactive behaviour (positive/negative) and the verbal/non-verbal interactions of these same children after one year employing observational techniques in the classroom itself. The investigators compared the behaviour of the hearing-impaired children with a group of non-handicapped 'controls'. They found that as a group the hearing-impaired children did not behave differently from their non-handicapped classmates in respect of positive/negative interactions. There were, however, some differences between the two groups, although the differences were not large: the hearing-impaired children directed significantly more behaviour towards the teacher than did the non-handicapped 'controls'. The non-handicapped children directed significantly more behaviour towards their peers than did the hearing-impaired children. There were more verbal interactions between non-handicapped children than between hearing-impaired children. These findings were confirmed more recently by Antia (1982). This study, which compared the social behaviour of 32 partially mainstreamed hearing-impaired children with 84 normally hearing children in five urban schools, revealed that the hearing-impaired children interacted more with other hearing-impaired than with normally hearing peers and more frequently with teachers than did normally hearing children. None of the findings is particularly surprising given the nature of a hearing handicap. The important thing that emerges from the studies is that there was, overall, not much difference between the classroom behaviour of the hearing-impaired children and the non-handicapped children. The deaf children behaved very normally.

Hemmings (1972) also found a considerable degree of normal behaviour in her comprehensive study of hearing-impaired children attending units in ordinary schools in Britain. Her information was derived mainly from teachers' reports rather than from her own direct observation. None the less, in spite of the fact that her data was largely 'second-hand', she gained many useful insights from her investigation into the nature of the social relationships between deaf and normally hearing children in ordinary schools. Overall, she reported 'good relations' between deaf and normally hearing pupils. Most hearing children were reported to be friendly to hearing-impaired pupils. A few non-handicapped children were particularly concerned to be helpful and kind to a deaf classmate. Sometimes this 'helpfulness' would result in what teachers regarded as 'over-protective' behaviour. A minority of normally hearing children, on the other hand, avoided deaf children as a matter of policy because of what teachers believed to be fear or shyness or embarrassment.

Whilst most non-handicapped children were found by Hemmings to be friendly to hearing-impaired peers a common feature of the social relationships between hearing-impaired and normally hearing children was that friendships between the two groups were often short-lived. It was the hearing-impaired children who did the 'dropping', demonstrating, according to Hemmings, 'their immaturity'. It was also noted that it was sometimes a special kind of child who befriended a deaf pupil, one who had problems of his/her own. This was especially the case with shy and withdrawn children who, according to Hemmings, found another child with 'problems' relatively non-threatening.

Overall, Hemmings' findings suggest that hearing-impaired children often did have more problems than non-handicapped children in ordinary schools in sustaining relationships with others. On the whole, however, the majority of deaf children were believed to have achieved adequate levels of peer acceptance.

A similar conclusion to that of Hemmings was reached by Cameron (1979) in a study which aimed 'to compare the degree of social acceptance enjoyed by hearing-impaired children and non-handicapped children in the same class, and the perceptiveness of both groups in estimating their own relative social status within those classes' and furthermore 'to compare the interactive behaviour of hearing-impaired children with non-handicapped children in the same classes'. Cameron's investigation relied on similar sociometric and observational techniques used in the studies from the USA quoted above.

The hearing-impaired children were divided into two groups: one group comprised 20 hearing-impaired children of primary age who were fully integrated into ordinary classes; the other group comprised 20 hearing-impaired children who had been placed in partially-hearing units and attended ordinary classes on a part-time basis. Cameron employed the Moreno Peer Nomination Scale on the 40 hearing-impaired children and 1,037 non-handicapped children who were in the classes attended by the hearing-impaired children. In addition, she used a Classroom Observation Schedule to collect data on the behavioural interactions of both the hearing-impaired children and an equal-size sample of non-handicapped children randomly selected from the same class.

The major findings of Cameron's investigation confirm, overall, that hearing-impaired children are 'happy at school' and have reasonably good relations with others, but also that they are not as socially accepted as non-handicapped children. On the whole the hearing-impaired group occupied a position of 'neutrality' rather than 'rejection' in the ordinary class. Significantly, but perhaps not surprisingly, the hearing-impaired children who were integrated on a part-time basis were found to be less socially accepted than those who were integrated on a full-time basis. Children attending units 'identified' with other unit children rather than those from ordinary classes.

Cameron's findings on behavioural interactions confirm also those of

McCauley *et al.* (1976) and Antia (1982). The behavioural interactions of hearing-impaired children in the classroom did not differ a great deal from those of the non-handicapped pupils. There were small differences, however. First, teachers initiated and sustained contact more often with the hearing-impaired children. Second, hearing-impaired children had more non-verbal interactions with other pupils than the 'controls'. Overall, Cameron believed her research findings indicated that socially the integration of hearing-impaired children in ordinary schools was successful.

Whilst the research findings cited above tend to indicate that the quality of interaction between hearing-impaired and normally hearing children in ordinary schools is not quite as good as that between pupils generally, the evidence, particularly the more recent evidence, suggests that usually the relationships between the two groups are satisfactory. The extensive study by Hegarty *et al.* (1981) of the integration of several different categories of handicapped children into ordinary schools produced similar findings and led the authors to conclude: 'We encountered many examples of natural relationships and good friendships between pupils with special needs and their peers.'

Hegarty *et al* (1981) also looked specifically at a feature of handicapped/non-handicapped pupil interaction which is of great concern to many people, namely, the problem of teasing and victimisation. A common anxiety of teachers and parents of handicapped children is that the abnormal child will be the object of ridicule in school and subject to teasing or, even worse, bullying. Hegarty *et al.* (1981) found evidence of non-handicapped pupils teasing handicapped ones but did not believe it be a common or serious problem. This finding is corroborated by Hemmings (1972) in her study of hearing-impaired children in ordinary schools. Hemmings found that deaf pupils did not on the whole suffer any serious amount of teasing.

The study by Anderson and Clarke (1982) into the education of secondary age physically handicapped children in both special and ordinary schools provides the further insight that whilst physically handicapped children were indeed teased in ordinary schools, they were no more teased than any other pupils in the school. That is to say, non-handicapped pupils in ordinary schools are as likely to be teased as handicapped pupils. Moreover, the authors found that physically handicapped pupils are as likely to be teased in a special school as in an ordinary school. Anderson and Clarke's investigation indicates, therefore, that teasing is not peculiar to handicapped pupils in ordinary schools. What is perhaps significant, however, is that interviews with the handicapped pupils featuring in Anderson and Clarke's investigation revealed that they believed they were victimised more than other children and that they thought that this was because of their handicap. Thus, the authors concluded, handicapped children are more sensitive about themselves than their non-handicapped peers.

The subject of teasing in schools is a difficult one to investigate because, although a common feature of school life, it is generally an 'undercover' activity. Furthermore, informants, that is school pupils, do not always tell the truth about the subject. It was one of the purposes of my own investigation to attempt to explore the issue of teasing and victimisation of hearing-impaired pupils in ordinary schools as fully as possible. The matter is particularly important because a child who believes he is perpetually being made fun of and discriminated against because he has a hearing handicap is clearly not 'integrated' into the ordinary school in the way most educators would wish him to be.

In general, there are grounds for optimism about the ability of the handicapped child to adapt socially to life in ordinary schools and be reasonably well accepted by his peers. Currently available research findings provide some encouragement to those who wish to promote and extend integration policies. However, given that most studies indicate that there is some room for improvement in social relationships between handicapped and non-handicapped children in ordinary schools, it is important to attempt to discover those factors which might further improve attitudes and relations between the two groups. Indeed, there has been more emphasis in recent research in uncovering the variables underlying good social relations between pupils. The work concerned with handicapped children in general, in addition to research relating specifically to hearing-impaired children will be considered.

Several studies suggest that administrative and spatial arrangements can be influential in achieving better social relations between pupils. For example, the research of Cope and Anderson (1977) revealed that handicapped children who were integrated individually into an ordinary class were twice as likely to be chosen as friends by other children in the class, as handicapped children who went into the ordinary class as a group. Dale and Hemmings (1971) in their investigation of hearing-impaired pupils in ordinary schools in England arrived at a similar conclusion. They noted that if two or more deaf children were placed together in an ordinary class 'interaction is greatly reduced' between them and non-handicapped children.

A further finding of Cope and Anderson (1977) was that physically handicapped children were more likely to have non-handicapped friends if their special class was situated within the school building rather than apart from it. Similarly the case studies of Hegarty *et al.* (1982), of examples of the integrated education of different categories of handicapped children, show that the segregation of handicapped pupils from others in a separate special class affects the social relationships between handicapped and non-handicapped pupils. The authors found that segregated handicapped pupils tended to be 'at best tolerated' by other pupils in the school. Eyre and Hall (1983) conclude from their study of the integrated education of deaf children in Leicestershire that where hearing-impaired children were placed in a special unit in an ordinary school they tended to congregate together and mix mainly with each other. Where they were individually placed, however, they were found to make friends with normally hearing children. Eyre and Hall recommend the individual placement of handicapped pupils in ordinary schools if social integration is to be a major goal.

The investigation of Johnson and Johnson (1980) in the USA, however, suggests that the physical proximity of handicapped and non-handicapped children in ordinary classes does not, of itself, promote good social relations between the two groups. The research indicates that it is necessary to contrive situations in which the handicapped and non-handicapped child can co-operate and the handicapped child can be seen to be making a genuine contribution to the task at hand. That teachers should aim to create opportunities in the classroom for contact and co-operation in a non-competitive atmosphere between handicapped and non-handicapped pupils is supported by the work of Antia (1982) and Esposito and Peach (1983), also in the USA.

Other writers have shown that the social integration of handicapped pupils can be made more successful simply by educating non-handicapped children about the nature of handicap. Teaching children directly about difference and similarity, dependence and interdependence and respect for one another as unique individuals, giving lectures, showing films, setting up workshops and group discussions about different handicaps and their implications, simulation exercises — all these reasonably simple measures have been found by several researchers, for example, Hoben (1980), Gottlieb (1980) and Handlers and Austin (1980) to improve the attitudes of pupils towards handicapped peers and increase their preparedness to offer positive support.

Further evidence, for example from Gresham (1982), suggests that counselling and training the handicapped child himself in order to improve his social competence and social skills can help make him more acceptable to non-handicapped classmates and thus improve social relationships between the two groups.

A technique, popular in the USA, which is in part designed to promote sociability between the handicapped and non-handicapped child is the 'buddy' or 'good companion' system. Here a 'responsible' pupil or pupils are selected to befriend a handicapped pupil and offer assistance where necessary. According to the experience of Cope and Anderson (1977), however, the 'good companion' scheme, as applied in some English schools, appears to have its dangers. They found that 'good companions' tended to patronise and 'baby' the handicapped child and thus hinder rather than promote his full acceptance into the ordinary class.

The research of Hodgson, Clunies-Ross and Hegarty (1984), similarly referring to integration in English schools, presents a more favourable picture of 'pupil helper', 'peer tutor', etc. schemes for handicapped pupils in ordinary classes. Their findings suggest that organised schemes of pupil assistance ensure more comprehensive and consistent support.

Whilst many of the studies cited on social integration do not refer especially to hearing-impaired children it does not seem unreasonable to infer that the factors described which encourage the mutual liking and respect of handicapped and non-handicapped children are likely to apply whatever the category of handicapped child. An important conclusion which appears to derive from the studies is that it is possible to modify features of the school environment to facilitate the social integration of handicapped children. Fairly small changes in school and classroom organisation, and 'consciousness raising' activities with 'normal' pupils it would seem, make a significant contribution to improving social interaction between handicapped and non-handicapped groups.

The studies quoted concerning the social relationships and behavioural interactions of handicapped and non-handicapped pupils all seem to suggest that social integration is reasonably 'successful' and, furthermore, that educators can take steps to facilitate good relationships. What the research studies lack is detailed information about the many different views handicapped and non-handicapped pupils may hold of each other, and the several ways pupils interact with others. Sociometry, for example, may tell us in a broad sense the peer status of a handicapped pupil but it does not tell us about the many different stances and postures that, say, hearing-impaired and normally hearing pupils adopt in respect of each other; it does not reveal the statements they make about each other, nor what several beliefs or attitudes the two groups have towards each other. Interaction-analysis has the advantage that it is based on observation in the classroom itself but the observation is controlled in the sense that it follows pre-constructed timed observation schedules and, as argued earlier in this chapter, such analysis is likely to be distorted. Delamont and Hamilton (1976) further suggest that since interaction analysis is usually confined to small, measurable bits of action and behaviour it is usually very incomplete. Qualitative data such as individual intentions is generally ignored because less easily accessible. Hence both sociometry and interaction analysis suffer from the methodological difficulties associated with quantitative techniques already mentioned in this chapter.

Whatever the limitations of the research material discussed in this chapter on the academic and social integration of handicapped children into ordinary schools, the research literature clearly offers many valuable insights. The findings are reasonably encouraging to those who wish to promote integration policies and they have obvious common-sense appeal. However, because of the methodological weaknesses of much of the research we are not given a complete picture of 'what goes on' when handicapped and non-handicapped come together in ordinary schools.

A further problem with currently available research material is that there is a lack of definition of the term 'integration'. Investigators generally use the word 'integration' in very broad terms to mean the ordinary school placement of a handicapped pupil. Yet, an 'integrated education' for a handicapped child can refer to a wide variety of forms of educational provision within the ordinary school. Moreover, the word 'integration' refers to a complex of notions relating to the several ways in which handicapped children adapt, cope with and are accommodated in the ordinary school and this adds to the ambiguity of the term. It would be helpful to the reader, therefore, to clarify the many meanings, overtones and interpretations of the term 'integration' in order for him to get a more refined perspective on my own and other research material. Thus, before reporting and discussing my own investigations into the practical processes of integration the concept of 'integration' will be explored in Chapter 3.

3 THE CONCEPT OF INTEGRATION: SOME BROAD THEORETICAL AND PRACTICAL CONSIDERATIONS

Integration has meaning at both a theoretical and a practical level and both levels are concerned with the relationship between the hearing impaired and the wider society. The broad theoretical concept of the integration of the hearing impaired is concerned with issues such as adaptation, acceptance, assimilation and mutual accommodation — matters which are closely related to aims in deaf education, for example, whether we expect the 'normalisation' or 'separate development' of handicapped children. If on the other hand integration is examined at a practical level the integration of hearing-impaired children in education might mean a consideration of some form of placement policy and practice with reference to the ordinary school. Here the concern would be with what is the most desirable type of association between the handicapped pupil and the ordinary school. Integration in this sense might imply a variety of educational practices from full-time placement of the handicapped pupil in the ordinary class to full-time placement in a special class or unit within the school.

The broad theoretical concept of integration together with placement ideology will be considered first and then attention will be focused upon what is claimed to be going on in placement-practice. The primary objective in discussing the thoeretical concepts and practice of integration will be to introduce and clarify ideas pertinent to the understanding and later discussion of my own research findings relating to the deaf. In so doing issues will be touched on which are relevant to the integration of other categories of handicapped pupils into ordinary schools.

Theoretical Aspects of Integration

Individuals can be integrated into society in different ways so it is necessary to identify these in order to facilitate discussion of the different concepts of integration in relation to the education of deaf children. In its widest usage 'integration' entails a process of making whole: of combining diverse elements into a unity.

Assimilation/Normalisation

One way of unifying diverse elements into a whole is through the process of 'assimilation' or 'normalisation'. These terms imply a process of 'making similar or the same', of rendering differences less apparent, of losing as far as possible a distinctive identity, of making 'abnormal' people more 'normal' according to current definitions of normality.

There is no doubt that in relation to the education of hearing-impaired children the term 'integration' is taken by many to mean assimilation or normalisation. For example, Nix (1977) suggests that integration should mean:

> helping the hearing-impaired child to live his life in as near normal a manner as possible and making available to him patterns and conditions of daily living that are as close as possible to the mainstream of society.

Making the hearing-impaired child as like or as similar as possible to his hearing peers means attempting to eliminate as far as possible those differences that distinguish him from 'normals', such as poor speech, lack of comprehension, limited language and consequent low academic attainments. If assimilation is the aim then educators should develop, as far as is feasible given the handicap, normal speech, normal language, lip-reading skills and the ability to make maximum use of hearing. Academically the aim would be to help the hearing-impaired pupil to compete on as near equal terms as possible with normally hearing pupils. Socially, educators would have to try to ensure that unconventional or anti-social behaviour did not develop. The key notion here would be 'adaptation'. It would be essential for the hearing-impaired person to adapt his ways to those of the majority.

A complementary notion to 'adaptation' would be that of 'acceptance'. Not only would the hearing-impaired person have to adapt to majority ways but the hearing majority would have to be willing to allow the deaf individual to become 'one of them'. Unless there was prejudice against the deaf, in which case little or no acceptance would be possible, it would be likely that the willingness of the majority group to accept would be dependent, to a significant extent, upon the willingness and the ability of the minority group to adapt. According to the 'normalisation' paradigm of integration a deaf child who could talk would be more acceptable than one who could communicate only by means of sign language. One might suggest that the more normal the speech and language, the more acceptable the hearing-impaired child would become.

However, whether a hearing-impaired pupil is accepted or not by the hearing group may depend on a number of other factors. For example, the opportunities normally hearing children have to associate with a deaf child will clearly influence their acceptance of him. Furthermore, it is possible to conceive of different levels of acceptance. A hearing-impaired pupil, for example, may not be openly rejected by hearing peers but may still not be 'accepted as an equal' among them. The notion of acceptance is plainly a complex one, not capable of simple definition, and dependent on many variables. The fact remains, though, that for hearing-impaired children to be fully assimilated they would need to be fully accepted as equal members of the normally hearing group. A fully assimilated hearing-impaired child or adult is one who enters into all spheres of activity, such as education, occupation, friendship, on the same terms as anyone else.

It is, of course, possible to support assimilation as a central objective in deaf education whilst at the same time acknowledging that it is unlikely to be wholly achieved. Many deaf educators see their aim as making the deaf child 'as near normal as possible'. 'Near normalisation' permits 'partial assimilation' into normally hearing society.

Mutual Accommodation

Making normal or similar is but one way diverse elements can be unified into a whole. Another process, that of mutual accommodation, likewise demands acceptance and adaptation but here there is less emphasis on 'making similar'. Mutual accommodation suggests that differences between groups are maintained and that members of the groups acknowledge respective differences but go some way to meeting each others needs and demands. Unlike in the case of assimilation the hearing impaired need not aspire to become 'normal' but should make some attempt to gain acceptance by the normally hearing. Similarly the normally hearing would be expected to make the necessary adjustments in attitudes and behaviour in order to accommodate to the needs of the handicapped person. A concrete example of mutual accommodation occurs when hearing-impaired children make attempts to communicate by talking to their hearing peers, albeit in a defective way, whilst normally hearing children, for their part, observe certain 'rules' which they think will aid communication with their hearing-impaired age-mates. For example: facing them when talking, speaking more slowly, exaggerating lip movements, making use of gesture and mime. Another instance occurs when the teacher who has a hearing-impaired pupil in her class makes sure the radio microphone is switched on, avoids talking to the blackboard and writes points up on the board for the pupil's benefit. The hearing-impaired pupil accommodates to the situation by concentrating hard on the teacher's face and making use of all other available clues as to what is being taught. Particularly important questions concerning ordinary class placement are: how far teachers or normally hearing pupils can or should accommodate to the special needs of hearing-impaired pupils and how far the hearing handicapped can reasonably be expected to accommodate to the demands of the ordinary classroom. These are matters which will be taken up in Chapters 5 and 7.

Mutual accommodation is, of course, a typical everyday social process. No two members of society are exactly alike and part of being a socially competent person is to be able to adjust to and accommodate differences in others. A normally hearing person adjusting to the style of communication of a person with deficient hearing is, in a sense, essentially no different than, say, a rural farm labourer from Scotland adapting to and accepting the norms, values and way of talking of a car worker from the Midlands. In other words, 'It's normal to be different.' A question that arises, however, is whether in the eyes of others a deaf person falls outside the range of the normally differentiated population. For example, how 'different' is a deaf individual permitted to be whilst still being able to be accommodated within the 'normal' group? Is it possible, say, for the deaf pupil with poor receptive language skills and virtually unintelligible speech to adjust to and be accommodated by normally hearing classmates in any socially significant way? These questions raise the issue of how realistic it is to expect an individual with a substantial hearing loss to be 'normal' and how far it is 'proper' for the deaf to accommodate all the demands and expectations of normally hearing society. It is this issue which will be considered next.

Normalisation: A Realistic Goal?

Assimilation and mutual accommodation can both be seen as social processes that actually occur 'in the real world' but they can also be regarded as aims in the education of handicapped children, that is, ideal states to be sought after. The extent to which it is thought such aims can be realised depends both on opinions about the ability of hearing-impaired children to adapt to the world of the hearing-speaking community and beliefs about the extent to which the normally hearing are willing to display favourable attitudes towards the hearing impaired and make whatever adjustments might be necessary to accommodate the needs of those who may have communication difficulties. So, for example, if it were believed that a particular hearing-impaired child, given sufficient early support, can adapt to the demands of a normal environment, and if there was an assurance that people with normal hearing would fully accept that child, then assimilation becomes a possible aim. It is probably true to say that most educators in Britain regard both assimilation and normalisation as proper goals in deaf education whilst at the same time acknowledging a need for the deaf and the normally hearing mutually to accommodate ineradicable differences. In this sense, normalisation and mutual accommodation are not incompatible goals.

However, there are those who believe that 'normalisation' is an inappropriate goal for severely and profoundly deaf children. That is, they do not agree with the idea that the best way to prepare a deaf child for life in a hearing-speaking world is to make maximum use of residual hearing for the development of oral language and the ability to understand speech. It is important to examine this viewpoint for two reasons. First, influential organisations such as the British Deaf Association and the National Union of the Deaf are increasingly putting their names to the 'anti-normalisation' position (BDA 1982) and, therefore, they may well shape the meaning of integration in deaf education in the future. Second, an analysis of this view will make a contribution to an understanding of the concept of integration.

What is being challenged by those who might be termed the 'anti-integrationists' (Lynas 1984) is not that integration is unimportant for the deaf but that 'normalisation' is an essential component of integration. A common belief found, for example, in the writings of Merrill (1979), Montgomery (1981) and Ladd (1981), and one from which a number of other significant notions derive, is that a deaf person is not essentially 'abnormal'. This belief stems from the view that although a deaf person cannot develop oral language in the way that hearing people can, he can, nevertheless, develop language. This language, which it is claimed he acquires through his own 'biologically preferred mode', is sign language: a visual/manual form of communication which should be judged as simply another language. The deaf signing person, according to this judgement, is no more abnormal than one who is, for example, Chinese. The argument that is advanced by the above listed writers is that since the deaf have the ability to develop a language there is no justification for regarding them as deficient or abnormal. Rather, they should be respected as different but equal members of society just as any other ethnic minority group with a special life-style and culture of their own should be respected. Thus, given that one accepts the supposition that deaf people are not 'deviant' or 'abnormal' then the objective of 'normalisation', by whatever means, is an inappropriate and illogical goal.

Normalisation as a goal is also insulting to the deaf in the eyes of some, as it indicates a lack of respect for the deaf community and their special language, norms and values. McGrath (1981) even goes so far as to suggest that in a hearing-dominated society the deaf group, because they are unhearing, are oppressed and stigmatised just as other groups are accorded inferior social status for being 'unrich' or 'unwhite'. There is a 'normalisation conspiracy' it is alleged, which forces the deaf person 'to deny his deafness, imitate a hearing person, and pretend that he enjoys it' (Merrill 1979). A better way of perceiving integration, according to Jordan (1981), is in terms of breaking down the barriers between deaf and hearing people. This writer believes that: 'This means a lot of hard work and *not* denying that these barriers exist.' Accommodation, Jordan implies, is about normally hearing people being exposed to and accepting the exceptional qualities of deaf people.

Many, though not all of those who are deeply critical of the 'integration = normalisation' idea, decry present trends towards the educational placement of severely and profoundly deaf children in ordinary schools. This is in part because mainstreaming policies, by their very nature, disperse deaf children into many different schools and are thus believed to undermine the development and continued existence of the deaf community with its special culture and language. Furthermore, it is believed that the deaf child in the ordinary school is at a disadvantage because he is only acceptable and successful as an individual to the degree to which, according to Merrill (1979): 'he can emulate a hearing person by reading speech on the lips and using his own speech in communication'. Since the deaf individual, it is alleged, can *never* receive or produce spoken language as well as a hearing person, and since his deafness cannot be cured no matter what educational strategies are selected, the deaf pupil will always have inferior status and be regarded as a second-class citizen within the ordinary school. As a 'pale version' of a hearing person he will never be properly integrated because he will never be accepted as an equal by the normally hearing. This, according to Turfus (1982), is not integration but 'pseudo-assimilation'. Much better, so the argument goes, for the deaf child to be 'a normally developing deaf person' and accepted for what he is rather than 'an abnormally developing hearing person'; much better for him to develop his own language, sign language, in a natural way than struggle to achieve the unachievable, namely, competence in oral language. It is not normal, according to Spredley (1980) for a deaf person 'to discover a world he cannot hear'.

Thus, in short, what some individuals and pressure groups such as the BDA argue is that normalisation, as usually defined, is not a suitable goal for most deaf individuals on the grounds that (a) it is unattainable and (b) what is normal for a hearing person is not normal for one who is deaf. Integration, for people with these views therefore, means allowing the deaf person to develop his special language — sign language — and to be socialised into deaf culture in order to acquire a sense of self-respect and self-worth. The integrated deaf individual is seen as one with personal integrity who is accepted in society for what he is — a normal deaf person. For people with these views integration is as much about normally hearing people learning to communicate with the deaf by using sign language as it is about deaf people learning to talk.

That normalisation represents for some people the key element in the integration of the hearing handicapped and for others that it means 'pseudo-assimilation' demonstrates clearly that integration is not a simple concept with a single straightforward meaning. Two major perspectives on integration have been identified: one, the 'normalisation' view which focuses on the notion that it is shared culture and values and common identities which bind different parts of society together and the other, the 'separate identity' view which emphasises the deaf as a separate distinct group in society linked together with other different groups to form a social whole. It is important to be aware of these different perspectives and their implications since, as ideas and ideologies, they have a profound influence on the way people think. They may affect attitudes and opinions about deaf education and indeed they may influence placement policy.

Placement Policy

Background Considerations to Placement Policy: Integration and Equality of Opportunity

The goal of integrating a person into a community, however the goal is defined, might be said to be meaningless without giving the person equal rights to those things that are generally desired in society. Any person, group or category of people, which does not have reasonably equal access to such socially desirable commodities as jobs, income, housing, prestige, could be said to be suffering injustice, that is, not possessing full democratic rights and hence not fully integrated. In advanced industrial societies educational qualifications are regarded as important and may be crucial to the achievement of many such socially desirable ends. It is for this reason that the notion of equality of opportunity in education has long been a major political issue and a force for change which has a bearing on the topic of integration.

The idea of compensatory education and positive discrimination, popular in both Britain and the United States in the 1960s in relation to the 'socially disadvantaged', has come to be applied increasingly in the 1970s and 1980s to other disadvantaged groups such as the physically and mentally handicapped. The idea that the disabled should be given something rather more than equal treatment in order to integrate them better is expressed forcefully in the Snowdon Report (1976):

> Integration does not mean treating everybody exactly as they would treat everyone else. It should go without saying that to compensate for their disadvantage in order that their lives may most closely approach 'normality' the disabled must have deliberately favoured treatment in every aspect. Discrimination in fact must be positive.

In the context of a policy of ordinary school education for the handicapped the important issue, with reference to integration in Snowdon's sense, seems to centre around how schools can be made sufficiently special so that special needs can be met. This is to ask how much and what kind of special support is required for a handicapped child to get maximum social and educational benefit from ordinary school placement: that is, to enjoy more genuine equality of opportunity? Many educators would argue that it is not enough to adopt what has been termed the 'limpet' approach to integration, that is, to attach a handicapped child to an ordinary school and hope that educational normality will wash over and adhere to him. A number of writers, for example, Hegarty *et al.* (1981) and Dale (1984) have argued that adequate resources and careful thought and planning are necessary if the ordinary school is to provide an appropriate environment for a handicapped child. Moreover, they have emphasised that educating handicapped children in ordinary schools should not be seen as a way of educating them in the 'least expensive environment'.

It would also seem to follow that integration should include paying attention to the general ethos of the school so that all pupils, handicapped or not, can be given the opportunity to participate in and contribute to the life of the school as a prerequisite to integration into the wider society. It thus becomes important for teachers to create environments in which every pupil can be recognised and valued as a unique individual whilst at the same time be recognised as a member of a community. The creation of a school climate in which each pupil is acknowledged as worthwhile and incorporated as part of the whole is not something that has been achieved in British schools to date. As Bookbinder (1983) pointed out, the education system as a whole is primarily designed to meet the needs of a small academic minority and, since it already fails to cater adequately for the needs of the majority of 'normal' pupils, conditions in schools are not generally conducive to the acceptance and integration of handicapped or any disadvantaged children. What Bookbinder appears to be saying is that the elitist traditions of British education, buttressed by the requirements of a type of economic system which does not require a universally highly educated workforce, creates far from ideal conditions for offering genuine equality of opportunity to all children. Furthermore, those likely to suffer most under such a system are those who are the least easy to educate. A child who has serious learning difficulties because of, say, some major emotional disturbance or a severe hearing loss might not, therefore, be expected to prosper in ordinary British schools unless special measures are taken. It is this kind of reasoning which leads Bookbinder to emphasise that we must attempt to create a situation of 'least disadvantage' for the handicapped pupil in the ordinary school rather than pretend to meet in full his special needs. Bookbinder believes this is the nearest one can get to the fulfilment of the ideal of equality of opportunity for the handicapped child in the ordinary school.

That deaf children ought to have equality of educational opportunity is, none the less, an ideal which most educators would almost certainly support and consider to be a prerequisite of genuine integration into society. But this still leaves the problem of defining what form of placement would achieve 'genuine' integration.

Some Practical Considerations of Placement Policy with Reference to Integration

Placing a handicapped child in the ordinary school might be seen as a means to the end of ultimate integration into normal adult society. Ross *et al.* (1982), for example, have recently emphasised that the prime reason for placing hearing-impaired pupils in ordinary schools is to prevent educators ever again producing 'a generation of under-employed, under-achieving' hearing-impaired people. It should be pointed out, however, that conceptually the integration of hearing-impaired pupils into normal society need not entail them being educated under the same roof as their normally hearing peers. There are some educators who believe, for example, that the integration of some deaf pupils may best be achieved by giving them special intensive educational attention apart from other pupils with normal hearing so that 'later on' they may be more readily assimilated and accommodated in the wider society.

Alternatively, if the major goal of deaf education is perceived to be the development of the deaf person as a separate and different individual with a special life-style, language and culture, those favouring this view might none the less seek an ordinary school environment for hearing-impaired children. Placement in an ordinary school would facilitate 'deaf society' and 'hearing society' being given the opportunity to come to terms with each other. Thus it can be seen that, conceptually, educational goals in themselves do not dictate educational placement, though in practice they are likely to influence the form of provision.

Those responsible for the education of deaf children, therefore, have to make decisions at two different levels. First, they have to decide on their educational goals: on what it is they are hoping to achieve in educating a deaf pupil. Second, they have to decide on the means that are most appropriate for achieving those goals. Thus, in the first place, educators have to decide, for example, whether they believe that 'normalisation' should be the major goal in deaf education or whether they think the major goal should be 'the development of the deaf person with a separate and special deaf identity'. Having decided on the level of 'ultimate aim', educators have then to determine the form of educational provision which will most effectively produce, say, the 'normalised' or the 'special' deaf individual. Hence, if it is believed that the ultimate integration of the hearing impaired demands that deaf people have the facility for the use and understanding of spoken language, then it has to be asked in which educational environment is this ability likely to be most effectively developed? Is it in the ordinary school, where hearing-impaired children are surrounded by normal speech and language, or is it in a special school where there is full-time specialist teaching, small classes and the possibility of optimum listening conditions, but where a child may be exposed to much defective spoken language and deviant modes of communication? If, on the other hand, the central goal for the deaf child is deemed to be the acquisition of sign language as a mother tongue then educators have to decide whether this objective can be achieved most easily in the ordinary or in the special school.

Integration can thus be seen as both an ultimate goal and a form of educational provision. What is important is that educators need to be clear about the ultimate goals before deciding what can and what cannot be achieved by any particular form of educational provision.

Types of Placement Available for the Hearing Impaired

Educators confronted with the problem of educating a handicapped child in an ordinary school want to ensure that the child is offered and receives an 'optimum education', that is, the most effective education possible in an ordinary school environment. At a practical level therefore, though they may differ in terms of their ultimate goals, teachers of handicapped children are preoccupied with the need to organise provision within the ordinary school so that a child benefits from appropriate 'normal' experiences, yet does not have his special needs overlooked. Several writers, for example, Deno (1970), Cope and Anderson (1977) and official reports, for example, the Warnock Report (1978) have offered models, structures and schemes of integration designed to assist educators of handicapped pupils in deciding on the most suitable form of placement for a handicapped child. These schemes might best be described in terms of the amount of association between the handicapped pupils and the ordinary school. At one extreme the handicapped child has minimum association with the ordinary school and maximum protection and special support; at the other he has maximum association with the ordinary school and minimal special support. The Warnock Report (1978), for example, distinguishes three main forms of school integration: locational, social and functional.

Locational integration exists where special units or classes are set up in the ordinary school or where a special school and an ordinary school share the same site. Social integration is:

> where children attending a special class or unit eat, play and consort with other children and possibly share organized out-of-classroom activities with them.

Functional integration is the fullest form of integration and is achieved when locational and social integration lead to:

> joint participation in educational activities . . . where children with special needs join, part-time or full-time, the regular classes of the school and make a full contribution to the activity of the school.

The chief problem with the Warnock model is that it is rather simple and does not take into account the many different types of provision for handicapped children which could be classed as 'functional' integration.

A more elaborate and popular scheme of placement is Deno's cascade model (see Figure 3.1).

Figure 3.1: Range of Special Education Provision

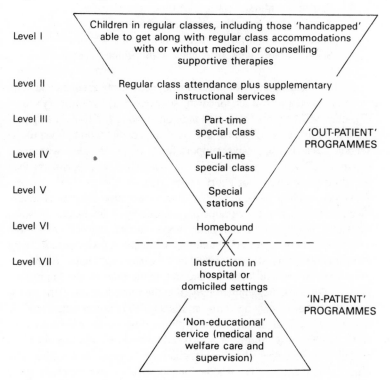

Level I	Children in regular classes, including those 'handicapped' able to get along with regular class accommodations with or without medical or counselling supportive therapies
Level II	Regular class attendance plus supplementary instructional services
Level III	Part-time special class
Level IV	Full-time special class
Level V	Special stations
Level VI	Homebound
Level VII	Instruction in hospital or domiciled settings

'OUT-PATIENT' PROGRAMMES

'IN-PATIENT' PROGRAMMES

'Non-educational' service (medical and welfare care and supervision)

Source: Deno 1970.

Deno's model seeks to describe organisational arrangements in terms of a continuum between placement of 'special needs' pupils in an ordinary class without support and 'in-patient' placement of 'special needs' pupils in non-educational medical/welfare care. English writers, for example, Anderson (1973), Snowdon (1976) and Cope and Anderson (1977) have devised similar continuums of school integration for handicapped pupils. The categorisations of school placement vary slightly but can be broadly summarised as follows:

1. Ordinary class without supportive services
2. Ordinary class with support in the classroom
3. Ordinary class with withdrawal for short periods
4. Ordinary class attendance with supplementary instructional

services
5. Part-time ordinary class, part-time special class
6. Special class in ordinary school, full-time
7. Special school with contact with ordinary school
8. Special school without contact with ordinary school.

Strictly speaking the above list does not necessarily entail a continuum since a pupil in a special school having some lessons in an ordinary school (7), may well be more integrated than one who is full time in a special class in an ordinary school (6) and has little contact with the rest of the school. Likewise, intensive support for a pupil provided within the classroom (2) could, under some circumstances, be more segregating than withdrawing the pupil for short periods (3).

Models such as those described above have been criticised because they provide no scope for evaluating the quality of interaction between the handicapped and the non-handicapped in ordinary schools (Booth 1983). Furthermore, no information or guidance is given as to the type and nature of special support offered to the handicapped pupil. Moreover, given the hierarchical format of presenting the models, the impression is given, albeit perhaps unwittingly, that the more 'ordinary' the provision, the better it must be. This, as Bishop (1977) points out, would be to confuse the goal of integration with the process. In other words for some handicapped children it may be educationally advantageous to be placed in a more specialised rather than a less specialised setting. Ordinary class placement is not something to be valued as necessarily 'good in itself'.

What all the models succeed in demonstrating, however, is that educational integration does not refer to a single pattern of educational provision. Thus, at a practical level, the notion of integration has several quite different meanings. Certainly a variety of forms of educational provision are plainly discernible in the integrated education of the hearing impaired and these will be examined in more detail so as to demonstrate the many different practical meanings of integration.

Forms of Integrated Educational Provision for Hearing-impaired Pupils

In terms of organisation four broad types of integration can readily be distinguished. There is individual integration when the hearing-impaired pupil is placed full time in his local school and is visited at varying intervals of time by a peripatetic teacher of the deaf, and three major patterns of provision available to hearing-impaired children attending units: the separate special class whereby deaf pupils are educated in an ordinary school but receive all, or nearly all, their education in a separate, special classroom; the part-time special class where the deaf pupil spends some time in the special class, some in the ordinary class; and the unit as resource centre, that is, a system whereby the hearing-impaired pupil is taught almost entirely in the ordinary class but returns occasionally to the unit for tutorial assistance. What all units have in common is that several hearing-impaired pupils are educated in one school which is, generally speaking, not the children's local school, and where there is at least one teacher of the deaf based at the school.

To suggest that there are four, and only four, types of integrated education for hearing-impaired pupils in ordinary schools in this country would understate the position. Indeed it is often said that there are as many kinds of integration in Britain as there are hearing-impaired children! To get a more thorough understanding of the integrated hearing-impaired pupil's education it is necessary to know the *amount* of specialist support, the *type* and *nature* of special help given and the *location* of that support.

The Amount, Type, Nature and Location of Special Support

The amount of specialist assistance offered to hearing-impaired pupils in ordinary schools by teachers of the deaf can vary from sporadic and infrequent to almost full-time support. Thus, a deaf pupil might receive all his education in the ordinary class with only occasional withdrawal for some kind of special attention. Alternatively, he might be placed in a special class within the ordinary school and receive all his education in that class from a specialist teacher of the deaf, thus participating minimally in the life of the main school.

The type and nature of special support offered to the hearing-impaired pupil in the ordinary school can include some form of language tuition; speech and auditory training; teaching of basic skills such as reading, writing and maths; teaching the deaf pupil manual communication; 'back-up' teaching designed to clarify or reinforce material taught in regular classes; 'preparation' teaching which aims to familiarise the deaf pupil in advance with the content of a future lesson for the class; a broadening of general knowledge; what might be termed 'moral support' where the specialist teacher offers friendly contact rather than direct tuition; counselling about all kinds of personal and social matters.

Just as the type and nature of support offered to hearing-impaired pupils in the ordinary school can vary a great deal, so too can the place where it is given. The location where suport might be given by the teacher of the deaf can vary from a specially equipped acoustically treated room to a corridor or empty hall. On the other hand it might be given in the ordinary classroom itself with the support teacher offering direct assistance to the deaf pupil whilst normal lessons are taking place. Another form of special support relating to location is that offered by the ordinary class teacher herself. She might, for example, spend extra time with the hearing-impaired pupil or perhaps modify her teaching style in order to help the deaf pupil follow the lesson.

It is often assumed that the reason why there is a great amount of variety in the types of education offered to deaf pupils in ordinary schools is that there is a corresponding variety in types of deaf children. Hearing-impaired children, it is claimed, have different personal characteristics and different problems and therefore different educational needs. In order to cater for individual needs educators thus have to decide between educational options: for example, to select the best provision for any one particular hearing-impaired child; judge which hearing-impaired children can cope with minimal support and which need considerable help; evaluate what sort of support to give and whether or not that support is best given in the ordinary classroom or elsewhere. (As a by-product of my research a summary of the major advantages and disadvantages of different types of support provision given to integrated hearing-impaired pupils in ordinary schools was produced — see Appendix 1.) Such decisions are not easy to make but it is assumed that they are guided by the belief that the less handicapped the child the less restrictive, less special need be the educational environment, and that the more handicapped the child the more specialised will be his education in the ordinary school. Given these assumptions it might be expected that educational decisions, made by educational professionals in the field on the basis of rational consideration of the hearing-impaired child's individual needs, would be similar and that children with similar problems would be educated in similar ways.

When integration practices in deaf education are examined, however, quite substantial variations can be observed between schools and LEAs in the way in which hearing-impaired pupils with apparently similar characteristics are educated (see Chapter 1). Thus whilst hearing-impaired children are, in theory, educated according to the principle of individual need it is clear that individual needs and ways of catering for them are perceived differently by professionals responsible for the educational management of hearing-impaired pupils. In order to illustrate this point further included in Appendix II are case studies of four hearing-impaired pupils featuring in my investigation who were integrated into ordinary schools together with a brief note offering some discussion of the discrepancies in provision.

Practical Dilemmas of Integration

Why educators value differently various integration practices in deaf education is probably related in the first place to the problem that in educating a hearing-impaired child in the ordinary school there are fundamental practical dilemmas which cannot easily be resolved. For example, given that there are only so many hours in a school day it is not easy to offer the deaf pupil the full range of 'normal' school experiences and at the same time give him an educational environment which is also sufficiently supportive of his special needs. A young deaf child may for instance derive considerable benefit from the point of view of language development by spending much of the day talking to a linguistically sensitive adult in a special, acoustically-treated room; yet in so doing he is not getting the social advantage of mixing with other children. Social development and language development are both important to the growing deaf child, yet to achieve both, fully, he may need to do the impossible, that is, be in two places at the same time. This kind of dilemma can only be resolved by a more or less satisfactory compromise.

Another dilemma arises from the difficulty of offering sufficient special treatment to a hearing-impaired pupil without drawing undue attention to his 'abnormality'. A fine line exists between providing an educational environment which is supportive and one which is segregating, isolating or even stigmatising.

A further conflict derives from the need to offer hearing-impaired pupils enough support so that they are not placed under intolerable strain, yet at the same time provide sufficient everyday experiences adequately to educate them. Whilst a deaf pupil educated in the ordinary school should not be put into situations which are too demanding he should clearly not be over-protected. Likewise a deaf child placed full time in his local school may come to feel much more at home in the normally hearing world than one who spends much of his school day in the protected environment of a special class. On the other hand, the individually integrated child may feel under more personal strain than the deaf child in a special class and furthermore be deprived of the opportunity of sharing his problems with other pupils who are similarly handicapped. It is because there are no easy solutions to these types of difficulties and dilemmas that educators must think very carefully about the pros and cons of the type of integration offered to a hearing-impaired pupil in the ordinary school.

Variations in placement, such as those cited and discussed, reflect different ideas about what constitutes the most appropriate educational environment for a hearing-impaired child. As Hegarty *et al.* (1981) point out, when referring to the education in this country of many different categories of handicapped children: 'What is common practice in some places does not seem even to have been entertained as a possibility elsewhere.' Even though educators may share common goals for the education of deaf children they often think differently about the best ways of achieving those goals; they quite often hold different notions about how the process of integration should be achieved.

It is clear, as seen earlier in the discussion, that differences of provision for hearing-impaired pupils in ordinary schools reflect the existence of a second set of variables, namely, educators' ideas about the goals of educating deaf children. Thus if a teacher of the deaf's prime objective in educating a profoundly deaf child is to enable him to acquire his so-called 'natural' language, that of sign language, then she needs to devote her specialist skills and time to teaching him manual communication. She might likewise, if she believes that there should be mutual accommodation between deaf and normally hearing pupils, need to ensure that normally hearing pupils are also given the opportunity to learn sign language.

If, however, the broad objective of deaf education is perceived to be the assimilation of the deaf pupil into hearing-speaking society then teachers of the deaf in ordinary schools need to use their specialist knowledge to facilitate the development of oral language. They would need also to ensure that there are opportunities for handicapped pupils to acquire the social skills necessary for acceptance into the normally hearing world.

What has therefore been demonstrated in this chapter is that there are many ways in which hearing-impaired children can be integrated into ordinary schools and that it is not an easy matter to decide on the 'best way' of integrating deaf pupils. Dilemmas arise out of both the practical aspects of school integration and out of more fundamental issues relating to philosophies and purposes of deaf education. The more awareness there is of the purposes, processes and dilemmas associated with integrating hearing-impaired children the more it should be possible to ensure that such children do in fact receive an optimum education in the ordinary school.

In attempting to clarify the concept of integration and in discussing certain practical issues connected with educating hearing-impaired pupils in ordinary schools, some insights into the education of hearing-impaired pupils have been offered and issues touched upon which are relevant to the integration of other categories of handicapped pupil. It is not enough, however, to consider these ideas in the abstract. Whether deaf children are judged to be, or judge themselves to be 'normal' or 'different' will also depend on the subjective experiences of those involved in the situation. Indeed it is a central purpose of this research-based book to explore notions of integration as they are manifest in the minds and expressed opinions of those most directly involved in the integration of hearing-impaired pupils in the ordinary schools, namely, class teachers, normally hearing pupils and the hearing-impaired pupils themselves. It is to my research material that I now turn.

4 THE RESEARCH INVESTIGATION: SCOPE AND NATURE OF THE ENQUIRY

Introduction

The broad aim of the research was to gain knowledge and insight into the education of hearing-impaired pupils in ordinary schools. Through my investigations I hoped to fill in some of the gaps in previous research on integration in deaf education and obtain for display data that was richer than that hitherto obtained. More especially I wanted to explore aspects of the situation that arise when we place a hearing-impaired pupil in an ordinary class from the point of view of three major categories of social participant, namely, the class teacher, the normally hearing pupil and the deaf pupil. In order to achieve this purpose a qualitative rather than a quantitative approach was selected. (The assumption here is made that the human social world is fundamentally different from the natural, physical world and, therefore, requires a different mode of investigation. These approaches, developed in fields such as psychology, psychiatry and sociology are variously labelled 'symbolic interactionist', 'phenomenological', 'illuminative', 'anthropological'. For a full discussion of the theoretical and methodological assumptions of qualitative approaches the reader is referred to Filstead (1971).) The data were acquired through participant observation and informal interviews.

The fieldwork took place at two different time periods. The first period began in May 1977 and was completed in December 1978: the second, a follow-up study begun in April 1983, was completed by March 1984. Details will be given first of the earlier investigation before looking at the reasons for, and features of, the later follow-up study.

Details of the Initial Study 1977/8

During the 1977/8 period of research one to two visits per term-time week were made to ten schools located within the Greater Manchester region. The schools were situated in three LEA areas which will be referred to as 'A', 'B' and 'C'.

In LEA 'A' three schools were visited: one infant, one junior and one secondary, each of which contained a special class for hearing-impaired pupils. The infant school had six hearing-impaired pupils, the junior school eight, and at the secondary school there were 22 deaf pupils. The hearing losses of the pupils ranged from moderate to profound. The patterns of integration varied between the schools but in all three the majority of the hearing-impaired pupils spent a considerable amount of time in ordinary classes.

In LEA 'B' six schools were visited: one infant, three junior and two secondary. In these schools the hearing-impaired pupils had been individually placed on a full-time basis. The six pupils had hearing losses ranging from moderate to severe.

In LEA 'C' one secondary school was visited which contained a partially-hearing unit attended by 22 hearing-impaired pupils. All the hearing-impaired pupils spent at least half their school day in ordinary classes. The hearing losses of these pupils ranged from moderate to severe.

The mode of investigation — participant observation and interviewing — remained the same throughout the investigation. Most of the time in school was spent in ordinary classrooms where at least one hearing-impaired pupil had been placed. The investigation involved observing pupils and teachers and occasionally participating in classroom activities where the situation was open and informal.

The amount of time spent in each classroom varied according to the wishes of teachers and Headteachers. Any one hearing-impaired pupil was observed for anything from between two to eight lessons or sessions. During breaks, free periods and occasionally after school, class teachers, hearing-impaired and normally hearing pupils were interviewed informally. It was sometimes convenient to talk to pupils and teachers during the lessons.

Most of the hearing-impaired pupils were interviewed individually. The normally hearing pupils, all of whom had some experience of attending classes alongside hearing-impaired pupils, were interviewed in small groups of two or three. They were selected either at random or because they were, in the minds of their teachers, 'co-operative', 'sensible' or simply 'talkative'. Most of the interviews were tape recorded, particularly those with both normally hearing and hearing-impaired pupils. The raw data thus consisted largely of notes recorded during periods of classroom observation, notes taken after informal talks with teachers and pupils and transcriptions from tape-recordings of informal interviews. Where notes were taken they were 'written up' immediately after the observation or interview sessions. It was this data which formed the basis for the ideas, concepts and themes discussed in Chapters 5, 6 and 7.

Special Considerations in the Selection of Pupils and Schools

There were two salient criteria underlying the choice of pupils and schools.

First, it was important to research in schools where the integrated deaf pupils had, on the whole, substantial hearing losses. As stated in Chapter 1 the trend towards educating severely and profoundly deaf pupils in an ordinary school environment has made rapid progress in Britain only during the past seven or eight years. It was important, therefore, that as far as possible the hearing-impaired pupils featuring in the study should come into this 'new' category of integrated pupil who, a decade previous, would in all probability have been educated in a special school, that is, those children who were perhaps likely to experience the greatest difficulties in a non-specialised school environment.

The mean hearing loss in the better ear of the pupils who featured in my investigations was 67 dB. Ten pupils had hearing losses of 90 dB or more. Thus in the main the principle of selecting 'deafer' pupils for the study was satisfied.

The second criterion underlying the choice of schools was that the schools should vary from each other in significant ways. It seemed to me to be important to investigate in schools which differed in ways that might be critical to the way in which hearing-impaired pupils might integrate into ordinary schools. Fortunately, no two British schools are alike and the schools in which the research was undertaken varied along several dimensions: stage of education, size, social environment, organisation, predominant teaching style, building, etc.

It also seemed particularly important to investigate the integration of hearing-impaired pupils at different stages of education because the social and learning environment, styles of teaching, etc. change so markedly as pupils progress through the educational system. Of the ten schools visited, therefore, there were two infant, four junior and four secondary schools. Within the schools different patterns of integration were operating. Some of the hearing-impaired pupils attended units contained in ordinary schools; others were individually placed full time in their local school. Of the unit pupils, some attended ordinary classes on an almost full-time basis; some on a part-time basis only; some attended ordinary classes individually; others in groups of two or three.

The reasons for my seeking to visit and observe in contrasting schools were twofold. Contrasting schools afforded a valuable opportunity to make interesting comparisons between the effects of factors such as different school features; ages of pupil and types of ordinary class placement on the practice of integration of hearing-impaired children. The significance of these differences is discussed in later chapters. Furthermore, the use of comparison groups helps focus attention on *essential* aspects of the integration of hearing-impaired children in ordinary classes. The point is well made by Glaser and Strauss (1971) who state:

> The constant comparison of many groups rather quickly, draws the observers' attention to many similarities and differences among groups that are important . . . category development is much slower in a single terrain and the result is a much less generalized category imbued with less meaning. In addition the differences and similarities among groups speedily generate generalized relations among the categories.

Investigating pupils and schools which contrasted in significant ways, therefore, was a strategy for facilitating the research process.

Some Data Collection Problems Associated with the Investigation

The objective of the initial study was to understand the integration of hearing-impaired pupils from the perspectives of class teachers, normally hearing and hearing-impaired pupils but there were difficulties in so doing in respect of some of the pupils. Tapping into the framework of meanings of some of the deafer pupils who had serious communication problems was at times difficult. Where a child's speech was almost unintelligible, and where his oral language competence and linguistic understanding were at a very low level, it was extremely difficult to gain an adequate understanding of his thoughts and feelings. Some of the deaf pupils I talked to, for example, were unable to understand the open-ended, non-directional type of question that had been generally used with interviewees throughout the investigation. The problem was particularly acute in the case of some young profoundly deaf children who were virtually impossible to interview at all.

Attempts to compensate for the many difficulties of communicating with young children were made by observing closely the actions and interactions of the pupils in classrooms and listening to the sorts of things they said. Furthermore, direct observations in classrooms were backed up by seeking teachers' accounts of the behaviour, responses and attitudes of the pupils. Attempts were made to overcome the problems associated with interviewing deaf pupils with serious communication difficulties by gathering the opinions of those nearest to them, such as their class teachers, teachers of the deaf and their more verbally fluent deaf friends. It did not seem that recourse to quantitative methods would have provided a solution to the difficulties. On the contrary, a researcher is far more likely to get closer to a child's mind and outlook through informal methods than with more 'remote' instruments such as behaviour rating scales and formal attitude schedules.

Despite the difficulties mentioned above much of the data derived from the initial study (which will be discussed in the next three chapters), provided the hoped-for information and insight into the integrated education of hearing-impaired pupils. It became clear, however, that the research would benefit by the addition of a longitudinal dimension so as to get additional information on the views and attitudes of hearing-impaired pupils and former pupils concerning their integrated education, and their ideas about themselves in relation to others in the wider society. Thus follow-up interviews were conducted with as many of the hearing-impaired pupils who had featured in the 1977/8 investigation as were reasonably accessible. This additional effort seemed to be worthwhile since generally so little is known about hearing-impaired pupils' feelings and ideas about being educated in an ordinary school.

The Follow-up Study, 1983/4

Between March 1983 and September 1984 interviews were conducted with 40 of the 50 hearing-impaired pupils and young people who had been observed/talked to and interviewed whilst at school during the earlier investigation of 1977/8. The remaining ten either could not be traced or had moved to a part of the country too distant to visit given the limitations of time and finance.

Most of those interviewed during this latter period, 30 in number, had left school. Of the remaining ten, eight were at the secondary stage of education. The interviews, which lasted for approximately 45 minutes to one hour, were held at the hearing-impaired young person's school, college or home. The interviews were informal and the questions were, for the most part, open-ended. However, as there were certain specific matters on which opinions were required, an informal interview schedule was used (see Appendix 3). The interviews, which were recorded on a sound tape recorder, were conducted in as relaxed a way as possible in order to encourage the hearing-impaired young person to talk as fully and freely as possible.

The interviews with the 40 hearing-impaired pupils and young people, which will be reported and discussed in Chapter 7, proved to be rich and rewarding. In the first place it was possible to overcome many of the data collection problems referred to earlier, namely, those of obtaining worthwhile information from 'interviews' with young deaf children who had severe communication difficulties. These older pupils and young people had not only developed linguistically and were, therefore, more proficient at talking but had also become more mature in their thoughts and ideas. They were thus in a better position to understand my statements and questions and it was easier to 'get on to their wavelength'. Hence, the follow-up interviews provided a useful means of checking earlier findings and of enlarging and deepening knowledge and insights already acquired. It was also possible to ascertain whether, on growing up, these deaf young people, with their greater capacity to reflect and introspect, had in any significant way changed their views about their experiences in the ordinary school. Furthermore, it was most valuable to have the opportunity to talk to a reasonably large number of young deaf people who had experienced an education in an ordinary school, but who were now members of adult society.

As will be seen in Chapter 7, talking to these young deaf people who had left school and entered the 'outside world' about how 'integrated' they felt in normally hearing society proved both informative and useful. I was able to acquire knowledge of whether or not these young deaf people felt their experiences in the ordinary school had helped them cope in the wider society; how they felt about themselves in relation to other people; whether they felt 'assimilated' into hearing-speaking society or 'isolated' from it and whether they perceived themselves to be similar to or different from those with normal hearing. This knowledge made an important contribution at a theoretical level to the research: it provided greater depth to an understanding of the concept of integration. Furthermore, this knowledge offers worthwhile 'feedback' information to educators responsible for educating deaf pupils in ordinary schools.

The follow-up study proved to be useful and important. Since many of those hearing-impaired pupils who had featured in the earlier investigation had reached, or were beyond, school-leaving age, it opened up the possibility of obtaining information about their academic attainments. It was beyond the scope of the research to make a detailed study of hearing-impaired pupils' educational and linguistic attainments using measures of, say, reading ability, speech intelligibility, English comprehension, etc. However, given that 38 of the original sample of 50 hearing-impaired pupils had completed five years of secondary schooling (this number includes eight hearing-impaired pupils who had left school but who were not, for the reasons stated, interviewed) it was a relatively easy matter to obtain information about their attainments in public examinations. This information was obtained either from the young people themselves or from school records.

The value of collecting data on deaf pupils' public examination results was that their attainments could be compared with national norms of pupil attainments. It was thus possible to make some assessment of the achievements of hearing-impaired pupils relative to those with normal hearing and this is reported and discussed in Chapter 7.

Since a central objective of the qualitative approach in educational research is to examine both individuals and educational practices in ways that preserve them intact much of the data presented is in the form of teachers' and pupils' own words and descriptions of events observed first-hand in classrooms. The basic validity of the qualitative approach lies in presenting a recognisable reality to those in the social world under study but a valuable and worthwhile qualitative study should go further than that; it should help increase sensitivity, understanding and interest in the topic. The data derived from my participant observation, therefore, is used to provide an interpretive commentary on the perceptions and views of those who featured in the investigation. The findings are discussed in relation to current issues in deaf education and, where appropriate, recommendations are made, to those responsible for the integrated education of deaf pupils. The aim is not just to produce a likeness of reality but to illuminate issues, problems and practices relating to the education of hearing-impaired children in ordinary schools.

5 THE CLASS TEACHER AND THE HEARING-IMPAIRED PUPIL

Published research into teachers' responses to the placement of handicapped pupils in their classes, as was seen in Chapter 2, reveals that investigators have tended to concentrate almost exclusively on establishing what are teachers' attitudes towards handicapped pupils, and on isolating the variables affecting those attitudes. They have revealed, for example, a relationship between knowledge and experience of handicap among class teachers and an accommodating attitude towards handicapped pupils. Attitudes tend to be expressed by researchers in rather simplistic terms, such as 'positive' or 'negative', 'favourable' or 'unfavourable' and research reports do not as a rule give detailed views or discussion on the variations of attitudes which might occur within a 'positive/negative', 'favourable/unfavourable' framework. Moreover, research which refers specifically to teacher attitudes towards hearing-impaired children is noticeably sparse.

There is no published research material revealing the ongoing day-to-day practical responses of teachers to the placement of a hearing-impaired pupil in their classrooms. That is to say, we know virtually nothing of how teachers act, or react, when a hearing-impaired pupil is placed in an ordinary class. Yet, if it is agreed that class teachers' actions, as well as their attitudes, may affect the ability of hearing-impaired pupils to adjust to normal classrooms, and benefit from normal educational provision, then it becomes important to know what those actions might be. Whether or not teachers treat a deaf child as 'just another pupil' or as an 'abnormal' member of the class; whether or not they modify their teaching practices to accommodate the special needs of a pupil with a hearing loss; whether or not they discriminate positively in favour of a deaf pupil and offer him special attention and extra help — all these variable reactions will affect the hearing-impaired pupil's view of himself and the way in which he integrates into the ordinary school.

Some attention will also be paid in this chapter to the way teachers ordinarily and routinely behave towards 'normal' pupils. In Britain, ordinary class teachers vary considerably in their style of teaching, but they generally work on the assumption that their pupils have normal hearing, so there is a need to examine some aspects of teachers' day-to-day teaching styles to see what effect these might have on the prospects of the hearing-impaired pupil adapting to life in the ordinary class.

Those responsible for placing hearing-impaired pupils in ordinary classes need to be aware of, and sensitive to, the many different types of educational treatment, and experiences deaf pupils receive there. It is on the basis of this awareness and knowledge that decisions can be made concerning the kind of special support that needs to be given to class teachers in their new role as 'teachers of the deaf', and the amount of intervention that might be necessary in order to ensure that hearing-impaired pupils receive the 'optimum education' in ordinary classes.

Class Teachers' Views of their Hearing-impaired Pupils

I want to begin by considering the ways in which class teachers perceive their hearing-impaired pupils and to discuss some of the implications of their views. The discussion here, as throughout this chapter, is based primarily on observations in schools and interviews with 45 teachers who were receiving one or more hearing-impaired pupils into their classes. The material was collected during the earlier period of the investigation — 1977/8. Much of the data is in the form of the teachers' own words.

As might be expected, class teachers do not share identical views about the presence of hearing-impaired pupils in their classes, but a general finding that emerged was that, with only one exception, the class teachers featuring in the investigation *were willing* to accept hearing-impaired pupils.

Typical teacher responses with reference to these pupils were:

Infant   'I don't mind at all.'
teacher
Infant   'She's most welcome.'
teacher
Junior   'I enjoy having him.'
teacher
Secondary 'No problem.'
teacher
Secondary 'I don't mind.'
teacher
Secondary 'I'm very pleased to have him.'
teacher

The one teacher who objected to having a deaf pupil in her class did so on the grounds that she could not spare the time to give a deaf pupil the attention she felt was needed. As a consequence of the pressure on her time she felt a considerable amount of anxiety about having a hearing-impaired pupil in her class. This matter of time demands will be considered in more detail later in this chapter.

Though hearing-impaired pupils were generally received willingly by class teachers this is not to say that all the teachers were equally 'favourable and enthusiastic' about having a deaf pupil in their class. There appeared to be a continuum of viewpoints, ranging from 'very favourable' to 'unenthusiastic', with another category of viewpoint which can be termed 'neutral' or 'indifferent'. Of the class teachers interviewed approximately 50 per cent were, on balance, 'positive' about receiving hearing-impaired pupils into their classes. It is both interesting, and important in its implications for integration, to understand why teachers, untrained to teach the deaf, should be favourably disposed and even pleased to have a deaf pupil in their class.

Reasons for Positive Attitudes Towards Hearing-impaired Pupils

A frequently stated reason for finding satisfaction in having a deaf pupil in the class was that teachers were pleased to be making some contribution towards conquering the handicapping effects of deafness, even if this did entail extra effort on their part. The following remarks by teachers at all stages of education concerning different hearing-impaired pupils they had taught or were teaching exemplify their views:

Infant teacher	'I don't mind a bit helping her and get so thrilled when she does something she's never done before.'
Infant teacher	'I think she's fascinating. I just marvel at how she manages given that she's so deaf. I enjoy thinking out how I'm going to explain something to Alison because it's so worth it if I get something across.'
Junior teacher	'Well you've got to do something for them, haven't you? They've got so much not going for them. I like to think I'm helping.'
Junior teacher	'She's very rewarding to teach. I get thrilled at every little breakthrough.'
Secondary teacher	'I'm always aware of them. I have a special sympathy for them. Some teachers don't bother, but I'm conscious of them. I know that they can't look at their text-book and follow what I'm saying. I know they can't hear when the gas comes on the bunsen burner so I have to help them. There's a lot of little

things. I think you've got to give them special attention otherwise they can't manage.'

The views cited above suggest that deaf pupils, because dependent and vulnerable in many ways, appeal to the sympathy of some class teachers and evoke a concern to help the handicapped pupil. This feeling of sympathy and concern can, in itself, be both satisfying for teachers and positively assist hearing-impaired pupils' integration into ordinary classes. Several teachers found hearing-impaired pupils interesting because 'out of the ordinary'. The following citations characterise their stance:

Junior teacher	'Oh I find him fascinating. I feel I've learnt a lot about deafness by having him here this year.'
Junior teacher	'He's just that bit different from the others and he makes me laugh — especially when he gets hold of the wrong end of the stick — which he does sometimes.'
Secondary teacher	'I like having deaf children in the class. It makes it more interesting really.'
Secondary teacher	'Well it makes a change, doesn't it? I think about them a bit and try out different things to see if it works or not.'

Any pupil, regardless of 'interest' or 'appeal' value, who behaves well and displays diligent attitudes towards work will almost certainly be popular with his teachers. The evidence suggests that many deaf pupils in ordinary classes often display 'good pupil' behaviour and this encourages class teachers to form favourable attitudes towards their integration. The following comments, from teachers referring to their hearing-impaired pupils, illustrate the point:

Infant teacher	'She tries so hard.'
Junior teacher	'He concentrates so hard.'
Junior teacher	'He's such a nice boy. So helpful. He often stays after lessons to put things away.'
Junior teacher	'Richard is very good. He works well, concentrates hard. He's good.'
Junior teacher	'Andrew's (hearing-impaired) fine. I could do with a class full of Andrews . . . it's the Stephens and the Deans and the Isaacs (normally hearing) of this world that I have to worry about.'

Secondary teacher	'I'm very pleased with the unit boys — they're quiet and they work hard. I've never had any trouble with them.'
Secondary teacher	'I like having the phu children because, on the whole, they're pleasant and polite and they work hard.'
Secondary teacher	'She's alert and attentive and gets on with her work by herself.'
Secondary teacher	'The unit pupils I've known have always had good attitudes to work.'

The good behaviour commented on by class teachers, and confirmed by observations in ordinary classes and discussions with deaf pupils, may stem from the fact that hearing-impaired pupils may feel rather overawed and possibly even slightly insecure in ordinary classes. This is more likely to be the case when hearing-impaired pupils attend ordinary classes on a part-time basis. Furthermore, deaf children, like all others, have individual personalities, and some of their 'helpfulness' and 'quiet behaviour' may be related to these individual features. Some aspects of 'good pupil' behaviour, however, seem to result directly from the hearing handicap itself.

Hearing-impaired people generally are often highly dependent for their understanding of speech on visual clues from the speaker's face. Hearing-impaired children, thus, generally need to look attentively at their teacher whilst she is speaking in order to obtain much needed clues to the meaning of her spoken words from such things as lip movements, facial expressions and other gestures. This behaviour, observed frequently in classrooms, whilst integrally related to the hearing handicap, nevertheless often earned the hearing-impaired pupils the compliment of 'attentive'.

A further characteristic of the deaf pupils observed, which helped give them the status of 'good pupil' in the eyes of the teacher, related to their problems in discriminating speech in a noisy situation. Noise in classrooms means that hearing-impaired pupils cannot easily participate with their neighbouring pupils in the 'chit-chat' and 'aside talk' that is so typical of normal classroom life. It was clear that deaf pupils in ordinary classes often found it easier to 'get on with their work' rather than attempt to participate in 'difficult' conversations with other pupils. This behaviour, quite naturally, encourages class teachers to perceive them as 'hard working' and 'diligent'.

As might be expected from any group of 50 pupils, there were a few deaf pupils featuring in the investigation, five in number, who, far from being regarded as 'well behaved' by their class teachers were thought to be 'naughty', 'aggressive' or 'disruptive'. Since emotional and behavioural disorders of one kind or another, according to many writers, for example, Levine (1960), Mykelbust (1960) and Meadow (1980) are commonly associated with deafness, it might seem surprising that there were only five who were regarded as a threat to peace and order in the ordinary classroom. However, observations and interviews indicated that whilst deaf pupils may have experienced feelings of emotional disturbance these feelings did not generally manifest themselves in unruly and disorderly behaviour in class.

In addition to displaying good behaviour many of the hearing-impaired pupils had special competencies, talents and personal features which were helpful in promoting favourable attitudes among class teachers towards integration. Certain hearing-impaired pupils were fortunate in having an above-average facility in subjects such as art, needlework, handwriting, cookery, PE, athletics, etc. Where this was so class teachers frequently remarked on the fact with some pride:

Junior teacher	'She's marvellous at needlework.'
Junior teacher	'He's meticulously neat. He takes tremendous pains in all practical activities. I wish some of the others would follow suit.'
Junior teacher	'He's the best swimmer in the class. I'm so pleased for him that he's really good at something, as this helps him win respect from other children.'
Secondary teacher	'She's outstanding at games. She's such a wonderful athletic build.'
Secondary teacher	'I would say that at this subject (metalwork) he's one of the best in the group.'

Teachers also seemed pleased to be able to point to what they perceived as endearing features of personality in their deaf pupils. The following statements illustrate this feeling:

Infant teacher	'She's got such a delightful sunny way. It's lovely to see.'
Junior teacher	'I love having him. He's got such a lovely personality.'
Junior teacher	'She's so gentle and smiling all the time.'

The research suggests, therefore, that if a deaf child has particularly pleasing qualities or special abilities his integration into the ordinary class will be facilitated. An implication of this finding is that those responsible for the education of deaf children should take every possible step to develop any talents or good personal qualities that a deaf child may possess.

That hearing-impaired pupils were welcomed by class teachers was, in some cases, however, not so much because of outstanding personal qualities but because in contrast to certain other pupils in the class they were relatively easy to teach and control. According to many teachers, particularly those who worked in what they believed to be 'difficult' schools, hearing-impaired pupils were often felt not only to be 'well-balanced' and 'well-motivated' towards work but also in some cases to have a greater ability 'to achieve' academically than their normally hearing classmates. (The hearing-impaired pupils attending units were drawn from a larger catchment area than that of the school they attended and therefore generally represented a broader social class spectrum.) A sample of opinions from these teachers characterises the feeling:

Junior teacher	'This is Hulme, Manchester 15. They've all got problems. Mark's (severely deaf) nothing of a problem compared to some of the other children.'
Secondary teacher	'I enjoy teaching Lorraine because she's intelligent and though she's quiet she catches on quickly. She's better than most of the others here — disturbed, dim and the like.'
Secondary teacher	'Often the deaf ones are better than the others. It's unusual to get the unit children in Band 3. There's a lot of low ability kids in the school. It's poor motivation really.'
Secondary teacher	'Some of them are so thick you just wouldn't believe. That's the reason why the deaf don't seem like problems.'
Secondary teacher	'The deaf ones are very good. They're *really* good and they're quiet. They're well up.'

Thus, some class teachers, especially those from schools in socially deprived areas, felt that deaf pupils were no more disadvantaged or difficult to cope with than other pupils in the school.

Up to this point in the discussion of class teachers' views of hearing-impaired pupils, reference has been made to features of the pupil which may encourage his acceptance in the ordinary class and evoke sympathetic attitudes in class teachers. Accepting attitudes were found also to be facilitated by certain characteristics of the teachers themselves. The two major facilitating factors appeared to be a commitment to the idea of integration, and some knowledge of deafness and its implications.

Some teachers felt strongly that the integration of handicapped children was a good thing, and this made them honour-bound willingly to accept deaf pupils into their classes. Citations of a few such opinions will exemplify their views:

Infant teacher	'I don't even like to think of a "unit". The deaf children are attached to different classes and they grow up together with the others. That's how it should be.'
Junior teacher	'Now I really think they must integrate. They need to be with other children, accepted as one of them — it helps them become more mature.'
Secondary teacher	'I think integration's a good thing — they've got to integrate when they leave school, haven't they?'
Secondary teacher	'I think it's very good they're in normal schools. This is where they should be. They've got to face normal people when they leave school.'

The views quoted above suggest a commitment to the idea of integration on the part of class teachers *prior* to receiving a hearing-impaired pupil into their classes, but a few teachers had clearly developed a positive attitude towards integration as a consequence of their experience of having a deaf pupil in the class. A powerful factor persuading these teachers of the benefits of integration was not only that it was 'good' for the handicapped pupil but that it was also good for the normally hearing pupils. They believed that the presence of a deaf pupil in the class made their non-handicapped pupils more aware of the problems of others, more sympathetic, and less selfish. The following comments on integration illustrate their beliefs:

Infant teacher	'I think integration is wonderful for the other children.'
Junior teacher	'It's so good for the others. It's good for them to be able to show kindness and sympathy.'
Junior teacher	Having Julie (deaf) in the class seems to be bring out the best in the others. The children are very kind to her. They help her a lot.'
Secondary teacher	'The unit's important in this school for the other pupils. They need to think beyond themselves. If they can get used to the deaf students now they'll be able to understand deaf people better when they leave school.'

Just as some teachers held prior ideological convictions about the value of integration as a principle, so a few, about six in all, held positive attitudes on the basis of previous knowledge and prior sympathy for the predicament of the deaf. Three teachers, for instance, found their own mother's deafness helped them to understand more fully the problems of their deaf pupils as their comments indicate:

Junior teacher	'My mother is deaf so I do know something of what it means and how it is for poor Julie.'
Secondary teacher	'I'm predisposed to be sympathetic to the deaf because my mother is deaf. I know what it's like for her. I've been to Randamwood Clinic to get hearing aids and batteries. I know what a fiddle all that is. And I know what it's like to hear through a hearing aid!'
Secondary teacher	'I'm very concerned for the deaf ones because of the noise here (open-plan science area). My mother's deaf and she just can't cope at all if it's noisy. That's why I'm very careful with them and help them all I can.'

Another teacher found that insights gained from her acquaintance with a deaf playmate of her own children could usefully be applied to a severely deaf pupil who joined her class:

Junior teacher	'I live near a deaf girl. She's extremely deaf, yet my own children take her completely for granted — in fact all the neighbours do. So when Mark came to this school I felt I understood him because of what I know about Karen.'

When teachers had previous acquaintance with deafness they felt their understanding of some of the problems associated with the handicap gave them more confidence and competence to cope with the special needs of a deaf pupil. Their knowledge thus facilitated the integration of hearing-impaired pupils into ordinary classes.

The knowledge of deafness and its implications possessed by the majority of teachers, however, was derived mainly from *ad hoc* contacts with teachers of the deaf and was somewhat limited and patchy. The major 'dark areas' in the minds of teachers included the uses and limitations of hearing-aids; the implications of different types and degrees of hearing loss on a child's perception of speech; the significance of prelingual deafness on language development; the limited value of lip-reading for understanding speech. Indeed, a survey carried out for the DHSS, *Public*

Attitudes to Deafness (Bunting 1981) confirms that many aspects of deafness are little understood by the general public.

That class teachers, given their 'ignorance' of deafness, did not, generally speaking, feel greater anxiety about having a deaf pupil in the class, and that they were as favourably disposed as they were to having such a pupil, was probably related to their lack of awareness of the implications of deafness. (This is a matter to be discussed in more detail shortly.)

Clearly, however, the more knowledgeable teachers are about deafness and its implications the more they might be able to teach their deaf pupils effectively. My research supports the case made by other researchers (see Chapter 2) for devoting careful thought to the provision of appropriate in-service training for class teachers concerning the special problems and special needs of pupils with hearing losses. Competence in catering for the special needs of hearing-impaired pupils, and the development of favourable attitudes, is necessary if class teachers are to promote the effective integration of hearing-impaired pupils into ordinary schools.

Whilst approximately half the class teachers observed and interviewed were generally favourably disposed to receiving a hearing-impaired pupil into their class this does not mean that having deaf pupils in the class was completely unproblematic, even to those teachers. Indeed, in the minds of many class teachers there were several 'problem areas' associated with the teaching of hearing-impaired pupils. The major difference between those teachers who felt, on balance, favourably disposed towards receiving deaf pupils into their classes and those who felt, generally, more unfavourable, was that for the latter group the problems associated with having a deaf pupil in the class outweighed any rewards that might accrue from doing so. If hearing-impaired pupils are to be enjoyed rather than endured by teachers in ordinary classes it is necessary to understand what are these problems and to consider ways of coping with them.

Problems for Teachers Associated with Having a Hearing-impaired Pupil in the Ordinary Class

Resentment

A problem, referred to by only a minority of teachers, five in number, but which evoked strong feelings, and which was perhaps the most important factor underlying hostile or negative attitudes in them towards accommodating a hearing-impaired pupil, was the feeling of resentment at having a deaf child in the class for a substantial part of the school day whilst there was a teacher of the deaf full time in the school. These 'resentful' teachers, who all worked in a school with a unit for hearing-impaired pupils, were very conscious of the special problems associated with deafness and aware of the extra responsibility imposed by having in their class a pupil with a hearing handicap. They were also aware that the teacher of the deaf employed at the school was paid an extra allowance to teach deaf pupils, of whom there were a relatively small number in the school, eight in all. They felt, therefore, that they were having to carry an additional fairly onerous burden which, in their eyes, was primarily someone else's responsibility. The following examples of comments exemplify this resentment:

Junior teacher	'I don't see why when there's a fully equipped unit with a member of staff getting extra pay and a full-time classroom assistant that I should have to have a deaf child nearly all the time in my class.'
Junior teacher	'I don't see the point of bringing David all the way here in a special taxi just to be in my class nearly all the time.'
Junior teacher	'I do feel a bit resentful when there's Mrs Johnson with just a handful to deal with and I've got all these *and* a deaf one.'

Not all 'unenthusiastic' teachers felt as resentful about having a hearing-impaired pupil in their class as those cited above. It was certainly the case, however, that the problems most commonly referred to by both 'favourable', and indeed even by 'reasonably enthusiastic' teachers, related to the extra time and effort required to teach a pupil with special hearing difficulties caused by a hearing impairment.

Hearing-impaired Pupils Cause Extra Work and Take Extra Time

When teachers were hard pressed by the demands of a large class — often a class of children of mixed ability — and had an awareness that a deaf pupil entailed extra work, there was a tendency to regard a hearing-impaired pupil as 'yet another burden'.

Teachers who believed that they should provide for both the special needs of the hearing-impaired pupils and who also perceived that those with normal hearing have 'special' needs can be put in a dilemma: if the hearing-impaired pupil is given the extra time he is believed to need, other pupils may not be properly catered for. The presence of a hearing-impaired pupil in the class seemed to be more of a problem to those teachers who felt they needed to devote a considerable amount of extra attention to him in order for him to make the necessary progress. The following statements referring to profoundly deaf pupils typify this dilemma:

Junior teacher	'She needs a one-to-one relationship all the time. It's all right for PE and needlework, Julie can join in and know what to do just by looking, but not for academic subjects, not for someone as deaf as Julie. I've got a very wide range of ability in this class . . . no sooner have I set them work and got the whole class settled, than the bright group have finished and wanting more work. Yet to help Julie, I'd have to spend all my time with her, going over everything I've said and I just haven't the time.'
Junior teacher	'The problem is he needs so much time spending on him. I've 31 children you know; that means only two minutes per child. Now I spent 45 minutes the other afternoon reading with David because he couldn't do it himself — and the queue — it was terrible!'

Other teachers, whilst not expressing a view as strongly as those cited above, did make it clear that the deaf pupil competes for the teacher's time along with other pupils. For example:

Infant teacher	'I give as much extra help as I can but I've several slow ones in this class and I have to think of them too.'
Junior teacher	'I feel that all the children need me and have a right to my time.'
Junior teacher	'If I had him for basic subjects then the whole class would suffer.'
Junior teacher	'I can see that Susan is getting behind for some things and it worries me but what can I do? I can't turn my back on all the others.'
Junior teacher	'She needs a lot of help with her reading but if I gave it I'd only be teaching *her*.'
Secondary teacher	'I couldn't give them (unit pupils) extra time. I have to think of them all and they are all entitled to my time. It's what I'm paid for.'

For many teachers the need to devote extra time and effort to a hearing-impaired pupil was seen as an implication of having such a child in the class. This was perceived as a problem particularly when teachers felt under pressure from the demands of a large heterogeneous class. Where, on the other hand, teachers had small classes, or classes they regarded as in some way 'easy', they generally said that they felt happier about having a deaf pupil in the class. The following sample of such teachers' comments illustrates this standpoint:

Junior teacher	'I might feel differently (about having a deaf pupil in the class) if I'd 30. It makes such a difference only having 26.'
Junior teacher	'Yesterday I went over the history we've been doing with Julie on a one-to-one, and that was great. But the others *will* get on by themselves.'
Junior teacher	'If I'd not got such a good class I'd say "no chance!" (to having a profoundly deaf girl in the class). But they're marvellous as they just get on by themselves.'
Secondary teacher	'Fortunately it's a small class — only 21 — so it's easier to do a bit more for her.'
Secondary teacher	'I have to spend quite a lot of time with Kathy. There are such gaps in her knowledge. Fortunately it's a small group and they work well by themselves.'
Secondary teacher	'It's ideal at the moment because we've a small class and I can get around to anyone who needs extra help.'

The research findings suggest, then, that when class teachers are working in what they regard as favourable circumstances they are more willing to accept a hearing-impaired pupil into their class and to offer him extra help. What 'favourable working conditions' seemed to mean to teachers was having an easily manageable class. Teachers cannot, however, count on having classes that are small and easily disciplined. Thus, if educators want to facilitate the integration of hearing-impaired pupils, or indeed any category of handicapped child, it is likely to be necessary to take special steps to ensure that teachers have what they believe to be reasonable working conditions.

'Difficult' or large classes can be made more manageable to class teachers receiving handicapped children by making them smaller and/or by offering teachers the services of ancillary or support staff. Such measures formally acknowledge that a deaf pupil means extra work: they are likely not only to promote attitudes of goodwill among class teachers but also to encourage teachers to offer possibly much needed extra help to the integrated hearing-impaired pupil.

Communication Problems

What might seem to be an obvious difficulty for class teachers of hearing-impaired pupils is the problem of communication. Interviews with class teachers indicated that communication with deaf pupils was seen as a problem by some, though not all, of the teachers.

The spoken language of many of the deaf children featuring in the investigation was defective. In the case of a few children with profound hearing losses their speech was virtually unintelligible to the inexperienced listener. It was not surprising, therefore, that some teachers felt concern and anxiety about the difficulties they had in understanding the spoken utterances of their pupils. The kind of difficulty for teachers, caused by poor speech, was expressed very simply by a teacher referring to her profoundly deaf pupil:

Junior   'Julie, Oh Julie! I can't understand a word she says.'
teacher

Teachers did, however, seek ways of overcoming these problems. One teacher of a young, profoundly deaf junior girl, for example, tried to overcome the problem of not understanding the deaf child's speech by a strategy of pretence:

Junior   'I don't like to hurt her feelings, so I pretend to understand
teacher   and just hope that I've got it right.'

Some teachers found it useful to elicit the help of the deaf pupils' classmates who, possibly through closer informal contact and by being of similar age, had built up implicit understandings between themselves and the deaf pupil. The following citation typifies the position of such teachers:

Infant   'I'm pleased when she asks questions, but I often don't under-
teacher   stand what she means — the other children help, though. They
            seem to know through *intuition* what she's trying to say.'

Some remarks by another teacher indicate a similar gratitude for the assistance offered by normally hearing pupils in helping her understand the speech of a severely deaf girl, though she none the less found the situation awkward:

Secondary 'I do have difficulty understanding Gwen's speech sometimes
teacher   and this is embarrassing. Fortunately the girls seem more tun-
            ed in to her and can usually tell me what she's said . . . but
            it's still embarrassing.'

It would appear, then, that some teachers were worried because they
could not easily understand the speech of their deaf pupils and this, of
course, has implications for the integration of such pupils. Several
teachers, on the other hand, did not seem unduly perturbed that the deaf
children in their classes had defective speech. One infant teacher, for example, found the speech sounds made by her profoundly deaf young pupil
incomprehensible but this was not a source of concern or anxiety to her
as her comment reveals:

'I don't understand a word she says, of course, I'm not really sure that
she knows what words are . . . she just opens her mouth and out comes
a series of noises. But she doesn't seem to worry so nor do I.'

That pupils who had relatively serious difficulties in producing intelligible speech were not perceived as problems is interesting and perhaps
surprising, but is in line with the research findings of Bitter and Johnston
(1973), referred to in Chapter 2, which stated that:

deficiencies in the ability of the hearing-impaired child to communicate
was one of the problems least frequently stated by regular class
teachers.

The writers of the report suggest that a reason for communication not
being perceived as a problem by class teachers could have been that it
was too obvious to state. There may, however, be another reason why
the defective speech of hearing-impaired children does not cause as many
problems to some class teachers as might at first be supposed and this
is related to the asymmetrical relationship which exists between school
teacher and school pupil. Teachers generally have the authority to control the activity of their pupils, yet pupils are not expected, nor permitted, to give instructions to direct the behaviour of the teacher. Any
observer in classrooms is likely to find that many of the utterances teachers
direct at pupils have the objective of controlling actions rather than
eliciting verbal responses. To put it simply, teachers often speak without
expecting to be spoken back to. For this reason perhaps, a child who
does not speak much, or does not speak well, may for much of the time

be indistinguishable in many classroom situations from a pupil who speaks normally. The power differential, giving pupils restricted rights in conversations with teachers, is a general feature of school life at all stages of education and is thus a possible explanation of why some class teachers did not complain, or did not complain to a greater extent, about the defective speech of their deaf pupils.

A greater difficulty for class teachers receiving hearing-impaired pupils into their class, and a possible impediment to successful integration, was associated not so much with deaf pupils' speech but with their receptive language difficulties. Several teachers, particularly those who had a pupil with a more substantial hearing loss, experienced problems and even distress in explaining things and getting through to a hearing-impaired pupil. The following citations of teachers' remarks illustrate this problem of explaining:

Infant teacher	'Once she gets the hang of it, she's all right. It's getting her started that's the problem.'
Infant teacher	'I'm always having to tell her at great length what it is that I want her to do . . . and the annoying part is that it takes less time to actually *do* it than it does for me to explain to her what I want done!'
Junior teacher	'You can't talk to a profoundly deaf child as you would talk to a normal child of the same age. What you say just goes over their head.'
Junior teacher	'I'd say something like "get out your maths book", and a second later he'd say, "should I get out my maths book?" . . . it got on my nerves.'
Junior teacher	'For some things I have to explain and it takes a long time.'
Junior teacher	'With needlework and craft you can *show* her what to do, but I couldn't explain anything difficult for example in maths.'
Secondary teacher	'She does sometimes get hold of the completely wrong end of the stick.'

This sample of citations is sufficient to suggest that the difficulties deaf children have in understanding spoken utterances can be frustrating to class teachers and might possibly foster less favourable atittudes towards having these pupils in the class.

The most serious difficulty of all concerning communication related to the variability and uncertainty of response of the hearing-impaired pupil to the spoken word. Communicating relatively difficult ideas to children is, of course, a normal problem for adults and a familiar problem for teachers. Teachers know that merely making a statement and issuing an instruction is no guarantee that pupils will understand or grasp the point. Often teachers use the technique of getting 'feedback' from the pupil in order to know whether the message has been understood. When a teacher is dealing with a deaf pupil, however, there is a special difficulty precisely because the 'feedback' itself can be ambiguous: several teachers felt that there were occasions on which they were unsure whether or not their deaf pupil had 'got the message'. The following comments by teachers referring to their deaf pupils exemplify these problems of ambiguity and uncertainty:

Infant teacher	'I don't mind having her at all — she's no trouble. But I worry about *her* and whether she understands what's going on half the time.'
Junior teacher	'It's not a problem for me but I do worry for her. I think Alison is going to get very frustrated. I do quite a lot of "chatting" lessons, not too formal, but you know . . . and I'm sure she misses most of it. She smiles and laughs with the others, but I think she's just copying them. I can't be sure.'
Junior teacher	'I am getting worried about what he's missing. I just don't know what he gets out of it.'
Junior teacher	'Sometimes she's with me, and sometimes she's not — and I'm never sure which it's to be.'
Secondary teacher	'I'm not sure whether she understands or not in lessons. My only real check is through the written work — but she may have copied that.'

Uncertainty for the class teacher was found to increase when hearing-impaired pupils adopted strategies designed to indicate that they had understood what had been said, when in fact, they had not. (Strategies adopted by hearing-impaired pupils in ordinary classrooms will be discussed more fully in Chapter 7.) A frequently noted strategy, for example, was for pupils to nod and smile and say 'yes' to teachers speaking to them in the hope that their response would be found satisfactory. However, this response was often found to be unsatisfactory. Indeed, what teachers appreciated in a hearing-impaired pupil was a willingness to make it obvious when they had *not* understood what had been said or what was going on and a preparedness to come forward and ask questions during lessons. The following sample of comments by teachers typify this feeling of gratitude:

Junior teacher	'I'm glad when she asks. I don't mind a bit.'
Junior teacher	'Mark's very forthcoming. If he doesn't understand anything he'll come and ask.'
Secondary teacher	'I like it when they're outgoing. Then they're not afraid to ask questions.'
Secondary teacher	'She's very good. She will ask questions afterwards.'
Secondary teacher	'You can tell when she's not grasped anything, so that helps.'
Secondary teacher	'I feel I don't have to worry about Elizabeth because she'll *always* ask if she doesn't understand anything.'

It is clear from the above citations that when hearing-impaired pupils reduce the communication uncertainty for class teachers this is much appreciated, and relieves teachers of some of the anxiety associated with having a deaf pupil in the class. A willingness to ask questions when they had not understood characterised the classroom behaviour of some, though not all, of the hearing-impaired pupils featuring in the investigation. It is clearly worthwhile for teachers to encourage appropriate 'forthcoming behaviour' in all hearing-impaired pupils in ordinary classes. Such behaviour is likely to help foster favourable attitudes in class teachers towards receiving hearing-impaired pupils and thus promote their integration.

Breakdowns in communication, and ambiguity of communication, between class teacher and hearing-impaired pupil are, without doubt, situations which as far as possible, should be avoided if integration is to be effective. However, it would be wrong to assume that all communication failures were found to be a source of worry and distress to class teachers. Occasional misunderstandings were often perceived by teachers as a source of amusement rather than anxiety. These incidents, when they occurred, seemed in the eyes of the teachers, to add spice to everyday classroom life and encouraged warm attitudes towards deaf pupils. Two examples of incidents observed which had amused teachers illustrate the point. The first incident occurred during an English lesson in a junior school:

The teacher had wanted her class to do some written work around the proverb — 'Too many cooks spoil the broth.' In the oral discussion preceding the writing the teacher emphasised to her pupils that she did not want the proverb taken too literally, that is, she did *not* want to read accounts of small kitchens containing large numbers of people. Andrew, the deaf pupil, had paid close attention during the discussion and had understood a lot of what was said. He had failed to grasp, however, the central point made by the teacher. He simply did not catch the 'don'ts' and 'not's' contained in the teacher's instructions. Thus he wrote a composition entirely about cooks, kitchens and soup!

A second incident occurred during a maths lesson with top juniors.

The lesson was on 'shapes' and the teacher instructed her severely deaf junior pupil to find the shape of a parallelogram. Mark, the hearing-impaired pupil, rummaged through the 'shapes box' and after a few minutes of apparently fruitless searching returned to the teacher looking puzzled with the words: 'Miss, what shape's a pelican?' This misunderstanding caused pleasurable laughter when recounted to the whole class and in a sense enhanced his acceptability within the class.

However, examples of amusing communication difficulties such as the two cited above do not detract from the more serious problems associated with a deaf pupil's receptive communication. When deaf pupils in ordinary classes have persistent difficulties in following the oral part of lessons and in understanding teachers' instructions and explanations that is, of course, a problem for teachers as well as for the hearing-impaired pupils. It does not, however, necessarily mean that such hearing-impaired pupils should not attend ordinary classes, nor that they should be a source of anxiety and concern to their class teachers. It would seem desirable, though, that class teachers are made aware of the nature of the communication problems of any particular deaf pupil. This is especially important when the problems of communication are not immediately obvious and where there is uncertainty and ambiguity in a deaf pupil's response to the spoken word.

Low Academic Achievements and Uncertainty of Expectation

Allied to the possible communication difficulties of hearing-impaired pupils, and a factor which may impede the effective integration of such pupils into ordinary classes, is the problem of low academic achievement. Children who have been deaf since early infancy usually have both receptive and productive language retardation of varying degrees of severity. This linguistic retardation affects a deaf child's ability to read and write as well as his ability to talk. The average hearing-impaired pupil has, therefore, greater difficulty in achieving average academic attainments than do his normally hearing peers. (See the research evidence on the academic attainments of deaf pupils reported in Chapter 2, pp. 27–9.) Since pupils who are 'poor' attainers in school are generally thought to be a problem to teachers, it might be speculated that deaf pupils with low academic achievements are perceived as problematic by their class teachers and for this reason these pupils might be less willingly received into ordinary classes.

The evidence collected on the attainments of the hearing-impaired school-leavers who featured in the investigation is given in Chapter 7. In broad terms, the material indicates that hearing-impaired pupils were typically, though by no means inevitably, at the 'lower end' in terms of academic attainments.

Some teachers clearly did find the low academic attainments of their deaf pupils a problem. One teacher, for example, seemed to blame herself for the apparent lack of progress in a deaf pupil in her class as the following rather poignant remarks about her profoundly deaf pupil indicate:

Infant   'In all my eight years of teaching, I can honestly say that Mark
teacher   is my only failure. I don't feel I've got anywhere with him.
          I don't feel he's learnt a thing.'

Other teachers, whilst not necessarily blaming themselves, were none the less anxious about their deaf pupils' low attainments. The following comments illustrate this view:

Junior   'Now about Susan, I know Peter (unit teacher) said she was
teacher   doing well here but I'm not sure. When she started in my
          class she was in the top group for maths but as the work got
          more difficult so she has fallen further and further behind.
          She's ended up in the next-to-bottom group. Now it worries
          me when a child's not fulfilling her potential like that.'
Junior   'I don't know why Julie's (hearing impaired) here. She can't
teacher   do the work I set. She just copies from Sally's (normally hear-
          ing) book. And if I ask her questions about it, she often starts
          crying. I do feel it's not fair on her.'
Secondary 'I'm all in favour of integration, but they (unit pupils) get
teacher   left behind and it worries me when they can't keep up.'
Secondary 'Maxine's a worry to me. She was doing well in the first year
teacher   and now she's fallen behind. I don't know whether she doesn't

understand me or she can't hear me or whether she just can't write essays.'

The comments cited above suggest that for those teachers, the low academic achievements of their hearing-impaired pupils not only caused anxiety but appeared to threaten their self-conception as professionals entrusted with the task of imparting knowledge and developing pupils' ability to learn.

Not all the hearing-impaired pupils in the study were achieving 'well-below average' attainments. In the schools where normal attainments generally were below average, hearing-impaired pupils, as indicated earlier in the chapter, did not appear to teachers to be worse, or much worse academically, than other pupils. Often they were regarded as equal to or better than their normally hearing peers and this helped to create favourable and accepting attitudes in class teachers.

However, even when teachers were aware of the relatively low academic achievements of their hearing-impaired pupils they were not all disquieted or anxious. Indeed, most of the teachers who had 'low achieving' deaf pupils in their classes, accepted the situation with equanimity. This was mainly because they expected low attainments from deaf pupils and were grateful for modest achievements. This was particularly so when teachers felt that their deaf pupils were making some progress. The following statements of teachers are typical of these views:

Infant teacher	'I'm very pleased with Cheryl's progress. There are two or three in the class that are worse than her and they're not deaf.'
Junior teacher	'She does well considering her handicap.'
Junior teacher	'She's behind with her written work, but that's only to be expected in view of her language difficulties.'
Junior teacher	'She's way behind, but I don't mind so long as she's getting something out of it.'
Secondary teacher	'He's as good as some who aren't deaf.'

These comments suggest that some teachers, provided they believed they were making some contribution towards the academic progress of a hearing-impaired pupil, and that the child was getting some benefit by being in the ordinary class, felt it worthwhile to have a deaf pupil in their class.

It is interesting and significant that for many teachers, low attainments were seen as contingent upon deafness, and teachers adjusted their expectations accordingly. Often, if deaf pupils' achievements were within normal limits, even though at the lower end of 'normal', teachers were satisfied. Whilst it might be considered desirable that class teachers do not have such high expectations that a linguistically retarded hearing-impaired pupil cannot realistically meet them, it could be argued that the standards expected of a hearing-impaired pupil should not be too low, or too different from those expected of other pupils, if his integration is to have any meaning.

If a deaf pupil is not working to reasonably normal standards, nor adapting and responding to the stimulus of normal academic expectations, then he is not integrating into the ordinary class as a full member of it. However, what *is* reasonable to expect, academically, from any particular deaf pupil is very uncertain. Specialists in the field of education of the deaf are by no means agreed as to what are the appropriate linguistic and educational norms for the developing deaf child (Ross *et al.* 1982). It is, therefore, extremely problematic for those with overall responsibility for the education of deaf pupils in ordinary schools to advise class teachers in any accurate and detailed way as to what precisely they should expect, academically, from a deaf pupil: this is a problem which, at least for the present, seems unresolvable.

Inexperience of Deafness

Not knowing what to expect, academically, from a deaf pupil, and concern about deaf pupils' achievements, were found to be related to class teachers' inexperience of pupils with substantial hearing losses. Several teachers recalled apprehensiveness at the prospect of receiving a hearing-impaired pupil into their class, but experience of one or more deaf children seemed to allay their nervousness about their ability to cope. Often problems anticipated did not materialise. For example, a secondary teacher recalled his uneasiness at the prospect of having to communicate with a profoundly deaf girl about to be placed in his class, but, as his comment indicates, he was relieved to find his fears unsubstantiated:

Secondary   'I wondered what I'd do at first. I didn't think I'd be able to
teacher   talk to her, but really she's no problem at all. She seems to
                understand what I say.'

An infant teacher expressed a similar fear of being unable to cope with a severely deaf boy:

Infant   'I was dreading him coming, but now he's here, he's just like
teacher   any of the other children.'

This teacher came to the view that her deaf pupil had, in an important
sense, much the same inclinations and needs as other children in the class.

A junior teacher not only felt disquiet in anticipation of the arrival
of a severely deaf child but also felt concern during her early days with
him as her pupil. Her comment illustrates the point:

Junior   'I'm so *conscious* of him all the time. As soon as I get in
teacher   in the morning I'm aware of him and wondering if he's all
          right.'

These and other remarks that the teacher made indicated that the hearing-
impaired pupil was causing her considerable anxiety. Two or so months
later, however, the teacher was claiming:

It's going quite well now. I've got used to him and I don't worry about
him so much. He's coming on quite well actually.

For this teacher, experience of the hearing-impaired child alleviated the
fear that she was not competent to contribute to his educational
development.

The overall impression gained from my research into the attitudes of
class teachers was that feelings of fear and apprehension about coping
with a deaf pupil in the class were fairly common, but that these feelings
tended to dissipate after the pupil had been in the class for a short while.
This finding, which confirms other research into the education of handicapped children into ordinary classes (see Chapter 2), indicates that
familiarity with a deaf pupil is necessary if teachers are to develop
favourable attitudes towards him and thus help promote his integration
into the ordinary class.

That teachers, over time, felt more confident in dealing with a deaf pupil
does not necessarily mean that they were all competent in catering for
their deaf pupils' educational needs. Indeed, the comment of one secondary teacher about his severely deaf pupil suggests that getting used to
having a deaf pupil in the class can lead to a lack of concern for his special
needs:

Secondary teacher	'I was worried about him at first and was conscious that he was there, but now I just treat him like all the rest.'

For this teacher the fact that one of the pupils had a hearing loss had ceased to touch his consciousness.

Interviews with other class teachers indicated that several teachers were relatively unaware of the special educational implications of a hearing loss and because of this they perceived hearing-impaired pupils neither as a problem nor as an asset. A lack of awareness, or acknowledgement, on the part of class teachers that a deaf pupil has special educational needs has significant implications for the education of deaf pupils in ordinary schools.

Awareness and Recognition of the Educational Problems of the Hearing-impaired Pupil

No teacher who featured in the investigation was totally unaware that one of her pupils had a hearing loss. However, there were about 20 per cent of the class teachers who, for most practical purposes, regarded the deaf pupil in the same way as any other pupil. These teachers had neither 'favourable' nor 'unfavourable' attitudes towards receiving deaf pupils into their classes: in terms of the categories referred to earlier in this chapter, they were, on the whole, 'neutral' or 'indifferent' about having a hearing-impaired pupil in their class. A sample of the views of these teachers illustrates the position:

Infant teacher	'I don't think that I notice he's deaf. He behaves just like all the others.'
Junior teacher	'As far as Elizabeth is concerned, I don't think many people notice that she *is* deaf; she does everything that the others do and she's above average in ability.'
Junior teacher	'I don't take any special notice of him.'
Secondary teacher	'To tell you the truth I don't notice him much, he doesn't stand out in any way.'
Secondary teacher	'When I'm talking I'm not aware that she's deaf. I don't know whether I should be.'
Secondary teacher	'I only see the class once a week, so I don't really know her that well. She doesn't stand out to me.'
Secondary teacher	'The only problem with Joanne is remembering she is deaf.'

Awareness, or lack of awareness, of a pupil's deafness seemed to be related to the amount of contact a teacher had with the deaf pupil. Hence, 'unaware' teachers were more likely, though by no means inevitably, to be working in secondary schools where contact with any particular deaf pupil was infrequent. Consciousness of a pupil's deafness also seemed to be lower when the hearing-impaired pupil looked and sounded normal and was achieving reasonably normal academic standards. The comment of a teacher with a normal looking, clear speaking, moderately deaf infant pupil full time in his class typifies this lower awareness:

Infant teacher	'I don't notice he's deaf really. I didn't know there was a deaf child when I took over the class and I didn't notice he was any different.'

In addition to those teachers who barely noticed that one of their pupils had a hearing handicap there were a few teachers who made a special point of ignoring the fact that a pupil in the class was deaf. This position was justified on the grounds that there were plenty of matters to think about besides one deaf pupil. The following comments are typical of this stance:

Junior teacher	'I'm getting to the point where I just carry on regardless. You've got to train yourself. I can't think of him all the time.'
Secondary teacher	'I know that there is somebody deaf in the room, but most of the time I don't think about it — you can't!'
Secondary teacher	'I'm glad to have the unit pupils, but I think my first priority is to all the others. That's what I came here to do, so I try not to think about the deaf ones.'

Other teachers adopted a similar stance of 'paying no attention' to their deaf pupil(s) because they believed that these pupils, when in normal school classes, should be regarded as normal. The statement of a secondary teacher, referring to his pupils from the unit in the school, sums up this viewpoint:

Secondary teacher	'As far as I'm concerned when they're in here they're like normal pupils. I don't want them to stand out in any way.'

For some teachers, therefore, the fact that one or more of their pupils was deaf was a background awareness only occasionally brought to the forefront of their minds. Where teachers either did not perceive, or chose not to perceive, their hearing-impaired pupils as different from the others they were not likely to pay deliberate attention to catering for their special needs: it is this that is significant concerning the attitudes of the 'accepting but neutral' class teachers. In not regarding hearing-impaired pupils as significantly different from normally hearing pupils, and in not recognising the handicap of deaf pupils, teachers may often be overlooking crucial educational needs. There is a possibility that some teachers, unintentionally and unwittingly, may exacerbate the educational ill effects of the handicap of deafness by not offering deaf pupils appropriate positive discrimination.

Investigation of the views and attitudes of class teachers, then, towards having a hearing-impaired pupil in their class leads to the conclusion that such pupils are generally well received. As has been seen some teachers were barely aware that one of their pupils had a hearing handicap and, therefore, having such a pupil in the class was unproblematic for them. The majority of teachers, however, were aware that a deaf pupil represented a 'departure from normal expectations' but this did not mean that he was perceived by them as a problem: indeed, the investigation has revealed that many class teachers believed that deaf pupils were interesting and rewarding to teach. A small number of teachers received their hearing-impaired pupils rather reluctantly: the chief reasons underlying these less welcoming, less favourable attitudes, seemed to be either resentment or concern about having an additional teaching burden.

During the foregoing discussion, the aim has been to draw attention to those aspects of class teachers' views which are relevant to the integration of hearing-impaired pupils. Whether a class teacher regards a deaf pupil for all practical purposes as 'like any other'; as an onerous extra responsibility; as an interesting challenge; as a pupil with very specific learning difficulties; or as an unfortunate or disadvantaged pupil worthy of sympathetic special treatment, will almost certainly affect the way that teacher behaves towards him. Views influence behaviour but they do not prescribe actions in a simple, deterministic way. It is, therefore, not enough only to know teachers' views; it is important to know the kind of educational treatment and the types of accommodation that ordinary teachers are offering the hearing-impaired pupil in the ordinary class. The success or otherwise of a policy of integration depends very much on the amount and nature of attention a class teacher is prepared to give a handicapped pupil.

Class Teachers' Accommodations to Hearing-impaired Pupils

An important way in which the educational provision for a hearing-impaired pupil in the ordinary class varies is related to the degree of responsibility a class teacher is herself prepared to take for the pupil's educational development. The class teachers featuring in my investigation were observed to differ in the extent to which they were prepared to modify their normal practice of teaching in order to adjust to the special needs of hearing-impaired pupils. A possibly helpful way of conceptualising different types of accommodation is to use what I shall call 'a positive discrimination continuum'. That is, accommodations will be distinguished in terms of the nature and amount of extra and special help that a class teacher is prepared to give to the hearing-handicapped pupil. By means of the positive discrimination continuum the *essential* features of different types of teacher accommodation will be thrown into relief.

Type 1 — No Special Accommodations. At one end of the continuum was the teacher who was willing to accept a hearing-impaired pupil but *not* prepared to offer him special attention. Teachers such as these constituted approximately 25 per cent of those interviewed. For these teachers the handicapped child was welcome, but on a 'sink or swim' basis. Such a teacher made virtually no modifications to her teaching style, save perhaps to face forward when speaking and to ensure that the pupil was seated near the front. The teacher offered little or no positive discrimination for a number of reasons. For example, she may have been not interested in, or unaware of, the special educational problems caused by a hearing handicap.

As seen earlier in this chapter, several teachers came into the 'unaware' category. They were often committed to the belief that a handicapped child in the ordinary class was entitled to the same benefits as any other pupil in the class but no more. Teachers at this end of the positive discrimination continuum often espoused the notion that 'integration means equal treatment'. A junior teacher, referring generally to hearing-impaired pupils from a partially-hearing unit contained in her school, expressed this idea:

Junior
teacher

'Well surely you've lost the point of integration if you give them special attention. When they're in here I think they should be one of us, treated in the same way as everyone else. I don't want to give any special treatment.'

This belief was based on the idea that if a handicapped child cannot benefit from the normal facilities and provisions of the ordinary class then he has no right to be there. The view is underpinned by the idea that normalisation means normal treatment. Alternatively, a teacher offering no positive discrimination to a hearing-impaired pupil in the class may have been aware that a hearing-impaired pupil had special needs, but conscious also of the fact that she already had a large number of pupils with normal hearing who needed her time. The comment of a secondary teacher sums up this standpoint:

Secondary   'I can't do much for Maria because there are so many in the
teacher   class. Now if there were just 15, I could perhaps give her
             some special attention. I *am* conscious of her but I don't do
             anything.'

In such circumstances a class teacher may well feel that it is the specialist teacher of the deaf, and not herself, who should cater for the needs of the deaf pupil.

The extent to which class teachers *should* take responsibility for the special problems of hearing-impaired pupils in ordinary classes is a difficult matter to decide. One thing is certain, however, and that is that specialist teachers of the deaf need to be clear as to what is going on in the ordinary class. If a class teacher is offering no positive discrimination to a hearing-impaired pupil in her class, for whatever reason, specialist teachers of the deaf may have to offer considerable additional support.

Type 2 — 'Normal' Additional Help. The next step along the continuum gives us the class teacher who was prepared to offer a hearing-impaired pupil some extra help and who was willing to make some modifications to her teaching style, but the positive discrimination was limited. Approximately half the teachers featuring in the investigation were in this category. Most present-day teachers are accustomed to offering differential treatment to pupils, 'according to need', whilst at the same time adhering to the principle of 'being fair'. It is in the spirit of giving extra assistance to those who need it that many hearing-handicapped pupils received extra attention from class teachers. The position is stated clearly in a comment by a teacher referring to her severely deaf pupil:

Junior   'I have to help him out occasionally and perhaps sometimes
teacher   I give him extra attention, but then you'd do that for *any* child
           who was having difficulties.'

And by the following remark of a secondary teacher referring to partially-hearing unit pupils in the school:

Secondary 'They do get more help from me, I suppose, but that's because
teacher they're stuck. You always give more to the ones who are
stuck.'

Teachers at this point on the continuum were generally favourable towards receiving a hearing-impaired pupil into the class, aware of his presence and recognised that a deaf pupil has problems resulting from his handicap. Because they lacked specialised knowledge, however, they did not characteristically give a great amount of thought to the special educational problems caused by a hearing impairment. They did not, therefore, offer specialised help to their hearing-impaired pupils nor did they generally spend much extra time with them.

Type 3 — Considerable Positive Discrimination. A small but significant minority of teachers, just under 25 per cent, felt that they could and should devote careful thought and extra time to catering for the special needs of the hearing-impaired pupils in their classes. Teachers at this point on the positive discrimination continuum clearly felt that deaf pupils, because of their severe educational handicap, deserve 'priority' treatment. These teachers were often very sensitive to the educational problems caused by a substantial hearing loss.

The teacher who offered considerable positive discrimination to a hearing-impaired pupil made several modifications to her usual teaching style. Without necessarily sacrificing the interests of other pupils in the class such a teacher characteristically took a number of measures to ensure that the hearing-impaired pupil was kept abreast of the class work. For example, the teacher might take pains to speak more slowly and clearly, ensure that she was always facing the deaf pupil, write key words on the blackboard, offer a special blackboard summary of the main points of the lesson, make sure that all pupils' utterances were available during a class discussion by repeating the comment, and directing it towards the deaf pupil; check the hearing-impaired pupil's understanding of the material towards the end of lessons; ensure that the pupil had his hearing aid switched on and that his batteries were not flat, etc. Teachers who observed even some of these practices could be regarded as offering considerable positive discrimination. No teacher in this band of the spectrum of discrimination made every possible accommodation that there was to make to adapt to the needs of a hearing-impaired pupil. The adjustments, even sacrifices, that some teachers were prepared to make were, nevertheless, impressive. For example, one secondary teacher shaved off his beard to make himself more 'lip-readable' to his profoundly deaf pupil; another trimmed his moustache for the same reason. Some teachers gave up free periods to give extra tuition in subjects such as French, Commerce, Russian, English. Several devoted considerable periods of time during lessons to assist the hearing-impaired pupil in his understanding of the material.

Some teachers were very sensitive to specific problems caused by deafness. One teacher, for example, was well aware that her deaf pupil could not look at a textbook and listen to her voice at the same time and took steps to remedy the problem: she constantly kept a watchful eye on the hearing-impaired pupil, giving him direct cues as to when to look up and when to look down. A science teacher commented that she did not walk whilst talking; made sure the class was quiet before addressing them; explained things more carefully; always checked with the deaf pupils that they understood what to do; kept near to her hearing-impaired pupils when they lit Bunsen burners, 'because they can't hear the gas'. The list of examples such as those indicated is extendable.

A few teachers claimed that with experience of hearing-impaired pupils, and with continued practice at making adjustments to their teaching, they were able to routinise the special accommodations that they made. Teachers who routinise their special educational treatment of hearing-impaired pupils offer positive discrimination easily and without undue effort; they can make modifications to their teaching without needing to reflect about what they are doing. The following citations of comments by teachers reflect and exemplify a routinisation of special educational provision:

Junior teacher   'Whenever one of the unit children is in my class I automatically seem to do things like not talk to the board and speak up. I don't even know that I'm doing it.'

Secondary teacher   'When I set them an experiment I always check with Debbie and Amanda (phu pupils) that they know what they're doing. I've just got into that habit.'

If teachers can make accommodations to hearing-impaired pupils in the same taken-for-granted way that they offer educational help to other children in the class this is undoubtedly beneficial to hearing-impaired pupils as well as convenient to class teachers.

Clearly not all special help can be offered in an effortless way and not all the special needs of hearing-impaired pupils, or those of any other pupil, can be routinised in a simple way. Hearing-impaired pupils often have very time-consuming needs and it is almost always difficult to overcome that fact. Moreover, where special attention and extra help are given, unless care is taken, this can stigmatise the handicapped child in the eyes of other pupils. A few teachers were conscious of the idea that 'singling out' a pupil for special help would result in 'showing him up' in front of the whole class. This view is sensitively stated by the teacher of a severely deaf pupil:

Secondary 'I feel if I don't give her extra help she'll get behind but
teacher   on the other hand I don't want to give her too much attention
           and make her feel different from the others and single her
           out too much. I think you've got to get the right balance.'

Teachers at this point on the continuum were generally more knowledgeable than other teachers about deafness, and sensitive to the educational implications of the handicap. Whilst it might be unreasonable to expect all class teachers to be knowledgeable enough about the problem of deafness to make special accommodations to them in the first place, the fact that some class teachers were able to make a number of adjustments to their teaching to accommodate the special needs of deaf pupils implies that it might be possible, under certain conditions, for more teachers to offer considerable educational assistance to their hearing-handicapped pupils.

Type 4 — Excessive Positive Discrimination. In discussing the attitudes and practices of teachers who offered considerable positive discrimination towards a hearing-impaired pupil, it is implied that such action is generally beneficial to the educational development of the handicapped pupil. It is, however, possible to offer excessive discrimination. Class teachers may single out a hearing-impaired pupil for so much extra attention that he is made to feel too much of a special case within the ordinary class.

Two teachers only were observed to make rather a 'big production' of the presence of a hearing-impaired pupil in the class. Often with the best of intentions, these teachers drew too much attention to their hearing-impaired pupils. For example, during the lesson, one teacher kept referring to her profoundly deaf pupil in rather obvious ways. She would ask the pupil if she was 'all right' and excessively repeat items for her benefit. She also offered exaggerated praise for what appeared to be rather modest achievements. Another teacher spent a considerable amount of time with her hearing-impaired pupil, requiring other pupils to wait for long periods for their turn. She also used a great amount of gesture and exaggerated speech when talking to her hearing-impaired pupil. Both these teachers clearly over-dichotomised hearing-impaired pupils from those who can hear normally and so ran the risk of expecting different standards of work and behaviour from the two categories.

The above examples of behaviour of the two teachers in this final category serve as a reminder that positive discrimination can be taken too far and lead to undesirable results. If teachers react in ways that are rather too 'special', the deaf pupil, far from feeling integrated, may feel very much an outsider. Moreover, other pupils may develop patronising, belittling, and even hostile attitudes towards the 'special', 'over-favoured' deaf pupil. (The reactions of normally hearing and hearing-impaired pupils to the special attention given to the deaf pupil will be discussed in more detail in Chapters 6 and 7.) Those advising ordinary class teachers might perhaps take care to see that the process of positive discrimination is not overdone in the ordinary class and that the aim of integration is not, in this way, thwarted.

In classifying ordinary teachers' responses to the presence of a hearing-impaired pupil in the class, along what has been termed a 'positive discrimination continuum', the categories have inevitably had to be over-simplified in order to demonstrate their distinctive features. Teachers in the 'real world' do not behave in such a clear-cut fashion: they do not display quite such 'pure' responses to the presence of a hearing-impaired pupil in the class. There is no doubt, however, that elements of the responses observed and just described are to be found in the attitudes and reactions of ordinary class teachers who are currently receiving hearing-impaired pupils into their classes.

It is important to note that specialist help can be given, and is given, by some class teachers in the ordinary classroom. It is not the case, as is suggested by the rather simplistic models described on pp. 72–4 in Chapter 3, that specialist support for handicapped children is offered only by specialist teachers of the handicapped. Those in the specialist field of education of the deaf need, however, to be alert to the different responses of class teachers, and to the kinds of educational treatment that may be offered hearing-impaired children in ordinary classes. Awareness of different teacher responses and practices influences not only the nature of the advice that needs to be given to teachers by specialist teachers of the deaf, but also the amount of support that needs to be provided by the specialist services.

Some Possible Effects of Different Teaching Styles

So far in this chapter I have discussed the views teachers have concerning a hearing-impaired pupil placed in their class and reviewed the possible different ways they accommodate to his educational needs. As stated earlier, teachers of ordinary school classes, whether a hearing-handicapped pupil is present or not, are employed in the first place to serve the educational needs of pupils who are not deaf. A teacher's style of instruction, and organisation of learning in the classroom, will almost certainly, therefore, be primarily based on the assumption that her pupils have normal hearing. Teachers with a deaf pupil in their class may make various kinds of adjustments to their teaching in order to accommodate to his special needs, as previously indicated. There is, however, a limit to the extent to which class teachers can modify their principles and procedures in order to accommodate the needs of one, or a few, hearing-impaired pupils. The hearing-impaired pupil is required, therefore, to adapt to the many different situations that arise out of his teachers' characteristic teaching style and method of class organisation.

The number of different classroom contexts and teaching styles currently to be found in British schools is considerable. Teachers vary their pedagogic style according to the age of the pupils, the nature of the subject to be taught, the learning objectives, and their own personal customs and preferences. These variations of teaching style clearly have implications for the deaf child. It is not appropriate here to attempt to itemise all of the different teaching styles, or to discuss all the possible implications of different classroom practices for the deaf pupil. For a very useful account of the impact of the ordinary classroom on the hearing-impaired pupil at different stages of education, the reader is referred to Webster and Ellwood (1985). One or two examples, based on classroom observations, will be cited here in order to demonstrate how important it is to be sensitive to the effect different teaching styles can have on the ability of a deaf pupil to follow ordinary class lessons and thus benefit from his integrated education.

Perhaps most significant for pupils who are hearing impaired, is the way a class teacher communicates ideas. Ideas are mainly communicated through language, and teachers vary in their use of language in the classroom. They vary in the amount of speech they use and the extent to which they address the class as a whole. Teachers vary in their verbal fluency, the clarity and speed of their speech, the precision in their language, the extent to which they ask questions and check the understanding of the pupils, the amount of summarising, reformulating, editing and correcting of pupils' contributions, the explicitness with which instructions are given and new topics specified. Generally speaking, the more a teacher repeats or reformulates ideas in order to reduce ambiguity, the better it is for the hearing-impaired pupil, and indeed for other pupils.

Teachers also vary in their use of written material in addition to the way they express ideas orally. Generally, teachers who make much use of written material are likely to be particularly helpful to many deaf pupils. Material such as hand-out sheets, flash-cards and blackboard summaries benefit the hearing-impaired pupil by providing a permanent visual record of language in contrast to the fleeting, often imperfectly understood spoken word.

Teachers also differ in the extent to which they communicate information and ideas through technical aids such as sound and video tapes, TV and radio. A deaf pupil will almost certainly have special difficulties following the often poor quality sound from video and tape-recordings and he will not, of course, be able to lip-read the radio or a TV commentary.

The few examples given above serve to demonstrate that educators responsible for placing hearing-impaired pupils in ordinary classes need to be aware of the implications of different classroom practices on the deaf pupil so as to take measures to ensure that his prospects of being effectively integrated into the ordinary class are maximised. Clearly, class teachers receiving hearing-impaired pupils into their classes cannot be expected to abandon all instructional techniques which might cause problems for such a pupil because in doing so they might cause no less harmful problems for their normally hearing pupils. However, unless there is some awareness of the classroom situations which hearing-impaired pupils find difficult or impossible to cope with, it will not be possible to take any appropriate compensatory measures. Furthermore, it is important that teachers do not merely speculate about the types of classroom situations which might cause problems for hearing-impaired pupils. It is crucially important to get the 'consumer view' of integration. Deaf pupils themselves are in the best position to judge what does and what does not give rise to difficulties in following lessons and, therefore, they need to be consulted if appropriate accommodations and support are to be offered. The views of hearing-impaired pupils about their ordinary school experiences are discussed in some detail in Chapter 7.

This chapter has explored class teachers' reactions, responses, and accommodations to having a hearing-impaired pupil in their class. It has been demonstrated that teachers do not all share the same views concerning the presence of a hearing-impaired pupil and that not all teachers behave in the same way towards such a pupil. My investigation has clearly indicated that the way in which a class teacher — the 'managing director' of the classroom — responds to a hearing-impaired pupil in the class has critical consequences for his education and integration. Perhaps of equal significance for the integration of deaf pupils in ordinary schools, is the attitude and behaviour of the other participants in classroom life, namely, the normally hearing pupils: it is their responses and their behaviour which will be considered in the next chapter.

6 REACTIONS OF NORMALLY HEARING PUPILS TO THE DEAF PUPIL IN THE ORDINARY SCHOOL

The intention in this chapter is to examine and describe normally hearing pupils' perceptions of hearing-impaired peers in ordinary schools and to examine their behaviour towards them. A consideration of these matters is important because the way normally hearing pupils interact and associate with hearing-impaired classmates determines, in part, the success of integration policy: indeed, a primary goal of integration is to facilitate contact between handicapped pupils and their peers. Furthermore, the ability of the deaf child to adapt to the ordinary school, and to benefit academically from placement in ordinary classes, depends to a significant extent on whether other pupils are not only sympathetic to his special problems but willing to offer positive assistance. Merely placing normally hearing and hearing-impaired pupils side by side is no guarantee that there will be even basic contact, much less, significant social interaction between them.

The material in this chapter, based on evidence from my research, falls into three main sections. First, there will be an examination of normally hearing pupils' perceptions of hearing-impaired peers, that is, their ideas about the deaf and their sympathy, or lack of it, for children with substantial hearing losses. Second, the extent to which normally hearing pupils are prepared to accommodate the special needs of hearing-impaired peers will be looked at and also their willingness to offer their support and friendship. Finally, the factors underlying the way normally hearing pupils respond to, and interact with, hearing-impaired pupils in the ordinary school will be explored in some detail.

Normally Hearing Pupils' Perceptions of their Hearing-impaired Peers

An exploration of the prevailing perceptions of normally hearing pupils towards their hearing-impaired peers will provide important information and useful insights into the way hearing-impaired pupils are socially accepted and integrated into the ordinary school. I will begin by considering normally hearing pupils' sensitivity to deafness, and their ideas about the kinds of problems experienced by people who are deaf, because this has a bearing on the manner in which they accept and accommodate hearing-impaired pupils into their midst.

Normally Hearing Pupils' Sensitivity to Deafness

Many pupils displayed genuine concern and sympathy for their deaf peers: this applied at all stages of education. A number were able to put themselves in the position of someone who is deaf and imagine some of the difficulties confronting a deaf person. The following comments by pupils of all ages illustrate typical feelings and ideas:

Claire	7 years	'You can't understand really and you can't hear the music and you can't hear anything, and that's not fair because the other children can.'
Gail	9 years	'They're sort of in a little world of their own.'
Georgia	9 years	'Well you can't really join in any games at parties. You have to be able to hear the music.'
Jenny	12 years	'Awful, dreadful, I'd hate to be deaf.'
Gilbert	12 years	'You must be all closed in on yourself.'
Valerie	12 years	'You're apart from everybody.'
Angela	12 years	'It's awful — you can hardly hear yourself speak.'
John	13 years	'It sounds like Daleks speaking.'
Janet	13 years	'When you're having a laugh and a joke, they can't laugh because they don't know what the joke is.'
Karen	14 years	'It must be horrible to be deaf.'

In addition to being aware of general problems experienced by the deaf, several pupils were sensitive to some specific difficulties facing the hearing-impaired pupil in the classroom itself. The following sample of remarks from hearing pupils exemplifies the point:

Elaine	7 years	'You can't understand the teacher very well.'
Hazel	7 years	'She comes in the class and she starts talking because she can't understand.'
Suzanne	9 years	'They can't play the recorders because it

		hurts their ears.'
Gaynor	12 years	'If you're deaf you can't answer the questions because they can't speak properly.'
Angela	13 years	'The teachers . . . in the work . . . 'cos they can't understand what the teachers say.'

Generally, these comments of normally hearing pupils suggest that there is a certain amount of insight into the problems associated with the handicap and a good fund of sympathy for the hearing impaired. Furthermore, many pupils displayed some knowledge of the nature of deafness and the implications of different hearing losses. For example, most pupils were aware of the connection between a severe hearing loss and poor speech. The following remarks indicate that this is so:

Hazel	7 years	'When you're very deaf you always talk funny.'
Ross	7 years	'Sometimes Alison says a word and it doesn't come out right.'
Gail	9 years	'Christine can only say some words.'
Janet	12 years	'She's not completely deaf but she can't talk long.'

Though aware of the 'speech' difficulties of hearing-impaired children, normally hearing pupils characteristically appeared not to have much grasp of the fundamental, linguistic problems generally associated with severe hearing losses. On this matter they were often less well informed than the class teachers interviewed. The following comment of a ten-year-old boy sums up what many pupils thought about this topic:

Martin	10 years	'They just can't get the words out.'

The normally hearing pupils' lack of appreciation of the linguistic retardation that can be caused by a severe prelingual hearing loss and its consequences for academic development meant that they were not, on the whole, predisposed to equate deafness with any lack of intellectual capacity. Since most of the deaf pupils in many respects behaved in a 'bright' and 'alert' manner, this permitted judgements of 'normal ability' by other pupils, even though the school work of the hearing-impaired pupils did not always reach normal standards. Moreover, where hearing-impaired pupils showed good ability in particular spheres, other pupils were quick to notice it. The following comments from hearing pupils about hearing-impaired classmates exemplify the point:

Ross	7 years	'They might be deaf but they're not dumb. They're very good at their sums.'
Gail	9 years	'And Christine's clever. She's very good at drawing cats. She loves cats.'
Georgia	9 years	'Debbie can sew best of anybody.'
Gilbert	12 years	'We had a Maths test see, and guess who came top — Dale!'
Gaynor	13 years	'Even though she's very deaf, she's very brainy, ain't she?'
Angela	13 years	'When she first came here, even though she couldn't understand, she got *every* sum right and we tried for ages to do that but we couldn't.'

Of course not all the hearing-impaired pupils who featured in the investigation evoked such praise and commendation for their achievements from their normally hearing peers. Some deaf pupils, invariably those who were of lower intelligence, were frequently regarded by other pupils as a 'bit slow'. However, generally, comments from pupils suggested that on the whole normally hearing pupils had a generous but reasonably realistic view of hearing-impaired pupils' abilities and intelligence. There was no evidence that they felt that deafness or poor speech *per se* were associated with stupidity. If this is generally the case, it would seem that attitudes among modern British schoolchildren towards the deaf have improved compared to a century or so ago when deafness was almost invariably equated with dumbness.

Enquiries relating to pupils' knowledge of hearing aids revealed that here also normally hearing pupils were, for the most part, realistic in their appraisal of them. A popular fallacy among the hearing population generally is that hearing aids restore hearing and thus transform a deaf person into a hearing one (Bunting 1981). Yet the normally hearing pupils interviewed appeared to be quite perceptive on this point and were aware that hearing aids could not magically create perfect hearing. Some pupils were better informed on this matter than some of the class teachers. The following citations from normally hearing pupils at all stages of education on the topic of hearing aids were characteristic:

| Ross | 7 years | 'They help, but they still can't hear all that well. In this programme I watched, the lady |

		said if you were deaf this is how quiet it sounds, it's a miracle they can hear it. I can only just hear it.'
Karen	12 years	'Unless she knows when you're talking she can't hear you even when she's got her aid in.'
Tracy	14 years	'It makes them hear better but they can never hear like us.'

An explanation of pupils' understanding of the limitations of hearing aids may simply lie in the fact that their everyday experiences affirmed that in spite of wearing aids, deaf pupils had persistent and obvious difficulties in hearing what was going on around them. Furthermore, there was considerable interest among pupils of all ages in hearing aids, and this in itself may have led to a more realistic assessment of them. Most pupils had at some time played with and listened to sound through an aid. Many commented that things sound 'funny' or 'scratchy' through a hearing aid, and several pupils noted to their discomfort, that aids picked up and amplified background noises as well as speech. Thus, generally, the pupils seemed to be under no illusion that hearing aids restore normal hearing.

There was, however, one notable area of misunderstanding among normally hearing pupils concerning a hearing-impaired person's ability to compensate for his deafness, and that was to do with lip-reading. Many pupils, like their class teachers and indeed the hearing population generally (Bunting 1981), overestimated the value of lip-reading to the deaf person. They believed that deaf pupils could have an effective understanding of spoken language provided they were able to look at the lips of the speaker. (The idea that speech can be understood almost as well visually as aurally is, of course, erroneous. Not only do several sounds in English look alike, for example, p, b, m, but many are invisible or barely visible, for example, k, g, th, h, er. Moreover, at the normal rate of utterance it is extremely difficult to make sense and meaning through vision alone of the rapid, fleeting pattern of speech. There is no doubt that hearing-impaired children get important clues to the meaning of words by observing lips; their intent manner of looking at speakers' faces testifies to this. Thus whilst normally hearing pupils need to be aware of the importance of facing the deaf person whilst talking, it is important that they should not exaggerate the benefit he gets from the experience.) The following sample of comments from pupils of all ages indicates this misconception:

Samantha	6 years	'She can understand you when you talk . . . you lip . . . you talk . . . I mean you lip talk.'
Jeanette	6 years	'We do lip-reading together.'
Ross	7 years	'We look at her. If she can't hear us, she can see the movements of our lips.'
Diane	9 years	'She understands by reading the lips.'
Gail	9 years	'Christine mostly lip-reads — she can't hear you.'
Valerie	12 years	'If you are deaf you can *see* speech.'

An unfortunate consequence of believing in the paramount importance of lip-reading in comprehending the spoken word was that some normally hearing pupils underestimated the value to the deaf of *hearing* speech. Few children are totally deaf and all the hearing-impaired pupils who featured in the investigation had some residual hearing. Yet several pupils, particularly younger ones, were observed to 'mouth' words rather than vocalise them to deaf classmates. Some pupils reported this practice with pride in the belief that they were being helpful. A statement made by a seven year old serves as an example here:

| Sarah-Jane | 7 years | 'When we talk to Cheryl, we move our lips to the words.' |

If educators want to ensure that hearing children 'speak up' to their deaf classmates, then formal intervention may be necessary. A short simple talk given by a teacher of the deaf with examples of filtered speech (which simulates for the hearing the experience of deafness), with and without the visual pattern, could readily illustrate the need for a deaf person to be able to listen to, as well as to see, speech.

On the question of sensitivity to deafness, the evidence from the investigation suggests that normally hearing pupils on the whole feel sympathetic to those handicapped by a hearing loss, and also have some awareness of the implications of deafness. As outlined above, misunderstandings did occur, but the overall impression was that knowledge was incomplete rather than incorrect. It is significant, however, that many pupils were aware of the differences between themselves and hearing-impaired pupils and of the many difficult problems facing a deaf pupil in the ordinary school. This awareness influenced the way normally hearing pupils interacted with hearing-impaired pupils and the extent to which they made helpful accommodations to them.

Teasing and Victimising Hearing-impaired Pupils: the Perceptions of Normally Hearing Pupils

An awareness that a fellow pupil is deaf and has difficulty in understanding and producing spoken utterances will not necessarily lead the normally hearing pupil to feelings of sympathy and behaviour which will support the integration of hearing-impaired pupils. The perception of 'difference' in another pupil can lead pupils to make fun of or, even worse, physically attack that pupil. If deaf pupils are commonly ridiculed by other pupils because of their deafness this will set them apart from, rather than integrate them into, the ordinary school.

The evidence from the research findings reviewed in Chapter 2, based primarily on teachers' reports, suggested that the teasing and victimisation of handicapped pupils in ordinary schools was not in fact a problem, or at least not a serious problem. There is, however, a methodological problem in uncovering information in the sensitive area of teasing and bullying in schools, namely that asking teachers or pupils about it may not be sufficiently reliable or valid. Teachers are not always aware of the full extent of these practices and pupils are not always willing to admit to them. However, by talking to normally hearing pupils, hearing-impaired pupils and former hearing-impaired pupils, in addition to a large number of teachers, a serious attempt was made to obtain a fairly reliable picture of typical practices in this area.

Because teasing, victimisation, bullying, mickey-taking, etc. have a crucial bearing on integration, they are considered from the viewpoints of *both* categories of pupil in order to check whether there are significant differences of perception between the two groups. The views and feelings of the hearing-impaired pupils on being bullied or teased will be considered in Chapter 7. The views of the normally hearing pupils will be considered in this current chapter. The material considered in this chapter is based primarily on interviews and informal talks with normally hearing pupils supplemented by reports from teachers where this seems appropriate. On no occasion during my visits to schools did I witness any incident involving the teasing, making fun of or bullying a hearing-impaired pupil, so the discussion cannot draw on any personal observations.

One of the most serious forms of victimisation that can occur in schools is bullying. According to the normally hearing pupils interviewed, however, pupils in ordinary schools do *not* bully or seriously humiliate hearing-handicapped pupils. This point was confirmed by many teachers who were particularly anxious, in this context, to point out 'there was nothing like that here'. One or two teachers admitted that some pupils, invariably boys, were 'a bit silly' with some of the deaf pupils, but none believed this had any serious consequences for the hearing-impaired pupils concerned. Some pupils and teachers believed that 'being deaf' in fact meant that a pupil was *less* likely to be ridiculed or picked on by other pupils. Their reasoning suggested that whilst it is the case that children can be cruel, more often than not they draw the line at seriously mocking or humiliating a pupil who is obviously less fortunate than themselves. One twelve-year-old boy, for example, suggested that deaf pupils were immune from bullying at his particular school as his comment illustrates:

Gilbert   12 years   'Yes, there's a lot of bullies in this school. But they wouldn't go for the deaf ones, 'cos it wouldn't be fair.'

A certain amount of bullying is a fact of life in many secondary schools, but it would appear from interviews with normally hearing pupils that a hearing-impaired pupil is unlikely to be a target of such attacks. This finding is confirmed by Hegarty *et al*. (1981), who state:

To the best of our understanding negative incidents and patterns of relationships were comparatively rare. Some did occur but nobody regarded this as a major problem area.

There was evidence from my investigations, however, that deaf children were, on occasions, a target for mild teasing and name-calling. Examples of names given by normally hearing pupils to their deaf peers included: 'deaf lugs', 'deafie', 'ear aid'. Whether or not the awarding of a stigmatising label such as 'deaf lugs' is perceived as a problem by the hearing-impaired pupil himself is a matter to be discussed in Chapter 7. Generally, it is possible to see the phenomenon of name-calling in the wider context of normal pupil subculture. Nicknaming is a characteristic feature of school life as several normally hearing pupils interviewed pointed out. The nicknames they referred to sometimes bore a relationship to some physical characteristic, for example, names such as 'specky-four-eyes', 'lanky', 'shorty', 'brainbox', were used. These nicknames were frequently no more than humorous identity tags and because their use was so widespread they could be seen to indicate membership of the normal group rather than the reverse. According to the normally hearing pupils there was no intrinsic difference in a deaf child being called 'deaf ears' than in another being called 'specky-four-eyes'.

The practice of nicknaming might, however, be extended by pupils to include more elaborate forms of teasing. There were, indeed, some reports from normally hearing pupils that certain deaf pupils in the school were, on occasions, made fun of and played pranks on. The following comments from secondary pupils provide some examples:

| Gilbert | 12 years | 'Some of them mess about with Dale and Alison, like they swap their rulers.' |
| Valerie | 12 years | 'They pull their chairs away so they fall down.' |

In several cases the form of teasing had a direct bearing on the handicap itself. The comments below of pupils of different ages describe these types of practice:

Gail	7 years	'Some play "Deaf Unit" and put shoe laces in their ears, but I don't think that's very nice.'
Robert	9 years	'They pull their ears and wriggle them in front of him.'
Tracy	12 years	'I've heard, right, and I think it was Alison and Peter — they was over there near the doors and they was telling them to say like — "effing" words 'n that and giving them bad language.'
Karen	12 years	'The boys sometimes tease like, Sally-Anne at Register says "Yah", an' the boys go "Yaaah", sort of imitating her.'

As well as taking advantage of the fact that a pupil had a hearing loss there were also reports of pupils laughing at and mocking the inevitable communication errors, deviant vocalisations, and occasional strange noises made by some deaf pupils:

| Elaine | 7 years | 'Some of the children giggle — they giggle when she goes "grunt" — like a pig — "grunt, grunt".' |
| Jane | 8 years | 'Sometimes when we have a spelling test, you have to be silent and she shouts out and |

		the others giggle.'
David	10 years	'When she puts up her hand sometimes, she makes a funny sort of choking noise. Some of the boys think that's funny and they laugh.'

None of the pupils interviewed actually admitted themselves to laughing at or in any way making fun of a deaf pupil. Rather, their tone and words displayed pious disapproval of such practices. Whether they were all as saintly as they claimed to be was not possible to judge. However, there were reports of instances where the teasing of hearing-impaired children by some pupils provoked a counter response in others. The following statement of a junior pupil referring to a deaf classmate illustrates such a case:

Susan	11 years	'Sometimes I've seen children make funny noises behind his back and run away from him . . . but there's those that say, "Now, don't do that. That's not fair. He can't help being deaf".'

It is likely that some, if not most children, are aware of the poor taste and black humour which is associated with making fun of a handicapped child and this may act as a constraint on such behaviour. Several pupils expressed the view that 'It's not fair to take advantage of a handicapped child', and felt they should be protected from teasing or 'mickey-taking'. The following comments of pupils illustrate this view:

Susan	11 years	'Nobody would ever tease Mark about his hearing aid or being deaf or anything.'
Amanda	12 years	'No one would tease Joanne about her deafness — only about those things that anyone might get teased about.'
Stephen	13 years	'I don't think anyone gets at him — some of the boys mess him about a bit . . . Well like, if I said, well we were making fun of handicapped children, my Mum would say "What's the world coming to?".'
John	14 years	'No, we wouldn't tease them; not if they're handicapped. We do tease some people.'

The comment of Susan quoted above suggests that wearing a hearing aid could be a source of joking and making fun of the deaf pupil. However, interviews with pupils, as suggested earlier, indicated that most normally hearing children are very interested in hearing aids. Many pupils found these technologically sophisticated gadgets a source of fun rather than a resource for making fun. In one infant class visited a hearing aid was clearly something to be sought after rather than shunned. Having seen and played with the post-aural aid of the profoundly deaf girl attending the class, the pupils made a request to have a hearing aid for themselves! Radio aids held a particular fascination. With this type of aid, sound is transmitted from a microphone worn by the teacher to the receiver worn by the pupil by means of radio waves. It is, of course, the 'wireless' characteristic of these aids which makes them suitable for use in ordinary classrooms. A radio microphone can transmit sound for a distance of 30–100 m. This means that a teacher can leave a classroom but still be heard in that room on the radio receiver. This special feature of radio aids was on occasions a source of great amusement to pupils. *Many* hearing pupils gleefully reported incidents whereby a teacher would leave the classroom and forget to switch the microphone off. This meant that anything she said or did whilst in the corridor, Headteacher's office, staff room, ladies cloakroom, etc. could be heard on the receiver back in the classroom. Hearing-impaired pupils in possession of the radio receiver characteristically took great pleasure in allowing other pupils to 'listen in' to events outside. A further attraction of radio aids to hearing pupils lay in the fact that they closely resemble the 'walkie-talkie' sets used by the police. Jokes based around the familiar 'come in Delta 5' theme were common.

In summary, according to normally hearing pupils hearing aids do not, generally speaking, provide grounds for teasing or making fun of one who is deaf. The fact that hearing aids, unlike say, glasses or teeth braces, represent in the eyes of the pupils a form of reasonably advanced technology, may account for this.

In sum, then, the evidence from my investigation of the views of normally hearing pupils confirms the findings of researchers such as Hegarty *et al.* (1981) that handicapped children are not generally persecuted or seriously denigrated in ordinary schools. Some pupils claimed that they would be very reluctant to ridicule in any way a less fortunate pupil; others were prepared to protect a deaf pupil from what they believed to be unfair mockery and negative discrimination. The teasing and nicknaming experienced on occasions by hearing-impaired pupils was considered by pupils with normal hearing to be broadly equivalent to that endured by most other pupils and if this is the case, can be seen as integrative rather than segregating. It would, however, be unwise to draw firm conclusions about the presence or absence of teasing of deaf pupils in ordinary schools simply from the say-so of normally hearing pupils and teachers. The picture presented in this chapter, though faithful to the views of the normally hearing pupils interviewed, becomes more complicated when the feelings of the hearing-impaired pupils featuring in my investigation are taken into consideration. Thus, before making definitive judgements about the phenomenon of teasing and victimisation of hearing-impaired pupils in ordinary schools, readers should consider the evidence presented in Chapter 7.

Normally Hearing Pupils' Perceptions and Ideas about Integration

Given that normally hearing pupils on the whole have positive rather than negative attitudes towards hearing-handicapped peers and, given that they are generally sympathetic to deaf pupils, one would expect that they would be in favour of the policy of integrating the deaf into the ordinary school. Indeed, there seemed to be a general consensus among the pupils interviewed, that deaf children should be educated with others in ordinary schools. The following sample of comments from normally hearing pupils of different ages about hearing-impaired children in their school indicate an ideological commitment to the notion of integration:

Andrew	9 years	'I think it's nice for them to be with us because they can get used to what we say and what we do.'
Susan	10 years	'Why should he go to a special school if he can come here. He's doing very well.'
Tony	12 years	'They should be here to mix up with other people.'
Valerie	12 years	'. . . so they can lead an ordinary life.'
Jackie	13 years	'I think they should go to ordinary school just like everyone else otherwise they're different.'

Subscription to the broad ideology and acceptance of some of the practical implications of integration are not, however, the same thing. It is important to know whether pupils in ordinary schools feel equally enthusiastic about the above-average amount of help and attention received by many of their hearing-impaired peers.

Most pupils accepted and felt happy about the fact that class teachers might need to spend *some* extra time with a pupil with special needs. The following comments of normally hearing pupils on the question of extra help from teachers are typical:

| Jeanette | 7 years | 'I think the teachers should be kind to Alison because she's deaf.' |
| Tony | 12 years | 'I think the teachers should help the deaf children but not too much. It wouldn't be fair, just because they were deaf.' |

It would appear, then, that for most normally hearing pupils, it is more or less taken for granted that a hearing-impaired pupil has special needs and will require some extra help if he is going to cope in ordinary classes. The comment by Tony, quoted above, indicates, however, that some pupils might feel that this help should not be unlimited. Tony, for example, clearly felt that only *so much* extra attention should be given to a deaf pupil. Other pupils appeared to resent it if too much fuss was made of a deaf classmate. The conversation between two twelve-year-old secondary girls, Deborah and Amanda, cited below, concerning the special attention given to a deaf classmate by one particular teacher illustrates this point of view:

Deborah	'Mrs Harris — she's awful. She keeps saying to Joanne — "You deserve a medal you do Joanne. You have to work twice as hard as everyone else, you're wonderful." But when she says things like that she puts us down. She makes us feel we're not so good.'
Amanda	'And I think that's why some of the girls don't let her join in with them. They think she's petted and spoiled and given a lot of attention and that Joanne's big headed. But she's not.'
Deborah	'It's a shame really because the girls that don't really know her think she laps it up and that she gets away with things and that she's petted, but she's not really . . . it's only Mrs Harris.'

These comments suggest that over-attention to a 'special' pupil by a teacher may provoke pupils' annoyance and irritation.

Discussions with other pupils yielded further evidence that too many special concessions to deaf pupils, particularly if they took the form of more lenient treatment, offended their sense of justice. Some statements by pupils illustrate this feeling:

Peter	10 years	'If we're playing, we'd be in trouble — not them!'
Jenny	12 years	'Sometimes they get away with things — like if we don't hand in our homework then we're in trouble, but for the deaf ones the teachers don't say anything.'
Janet	13 years	'She doesn't get shouted at like us.'
Angela	13 years	'We always say "You're the pet" an' everything like that.'
Gaynor	13 years	'If *she* does anything wrong, OK. Well if it comes to us we always get shouted at for it.'

It can be seen from all the above examples that some forms of positive discrimination might result in pupils directing negative attitudes not just towards the teachers' conduct but the hearing-impaired pupils themselves.

Hearing-impaired pupils in ordinary classes are believed by many teachers to need some extra help, as seen in Chapter 5. Normally hearing pupils also accept in principle the idea that teachers may need to spend extra time with deaf pupils to enable them to cope with the lessons. None the less, it would appear that there is a fine line in the eyes of normally hearing pupils between offering some extra help, or special consideration and offering too many special concessions to a deaf pupil. Hearing-impaired pupils are seen by their normally hearing classmates as 'special', but not that special; as 'different', but not so different that they merit what might be seen as too much leniency and too many privileges.

It is clearly undesirable if class teachers' well-intentioned efforts to do the right thing by a handicapped pupil result in alienating other pupils from him and thus segregating him from the normal school community. Teachers may not be aware of any feelings of resentment on the part of normally hearing pupils because pupils are unlikely to tell teachers about them. It may well be easier said than done, however, for class teachers to cater for special needs in the ordinary classroom and at the same time be seen to be fair in the eyes of all other pupils. For example, a hearing-impaired pupil may be allowed to talk to a neighbouring pupil, even though the teacher is speaking, so that the deaf pupil might be informed of points he would otherwise miss. Yet all other pupils would be expected to remain silent at such a time. Furthermore, a teacher may in certain circumstances tolerate rule-breaking behaviour on the part of a hearing-impaired child on the grounds that she believed he was unaware of the rule in the first place. For example, a teacher may overlook the fact that a deaf pupil has 'disobeyed' her instructions if she believes that, because of his handicap, he had not heard that instruction in the first place. The danger is that these 'accommodating' acts on the part of teachers may be perceived as unfair privileges by other pupils, and are likely to hinder rather than help the social integration of deaf pupils into ordinary schools.

Interviews with normally hearing pupils indicated that, on the whole, their perceptions of deaf pupils were realistic and their attitudes friendly. Realistic views and attitudes were clearly conducive to the integration of deaf pupils into the ordinary class. That some pupils, some of the time, felt resentful that deaf pupils were allowed too much in the way of special concessions, did not prevent them from believing that on the whole deaf pupils, because of their handicap, merited special attention. That this is so is supported by the fact that normally hearing pupils themselves were found to be prepared to offer a number of accommodations to a deaf peer to help him cope in the ordinary class. It is this matter which will be considered next.

Accommodation Offered by Normally Hearing Pupils to Deaf Classmates

An overwhelming impression gained from observations in classrooms and from interviews with teachers and pupils was that normally hearing pupils' positive feelings towards hearing-impaired pupils were often translated into positive acts of friendship and constructive assistance. In any one class there were always one or more pupils willing to be helpful as well as friendly towards a hearing-impaired pupil. Class teachers frequently reported generous behaviour on the part of their pupils towards a deaf pupil. The following comments from teachers concerning their pupils' behaviour towards deaf peers are typical:

Infant teacher	'They're wonderful.'
Junior teacher	'They're very good with him.'
Junior teacher	'Gail is very kind to Christine. They all are really.'
Secondary teacher	'She'll always give Elizabeth a hand if she's stuck.'

Secondary   'One of the girls always takes her in hand and makes sure
teacher   she knows what she's doing.'

During periods of classroom observation, many instances were seen
of normally hearing pupils offering assistance of various kinds to a deaf
pupil. For example, by nudging elbows, tapping hands, touching arms,
pupils would 'cue-in' a hearing-handicapped neighbour as to when to look
up at the teacher, put their hand up, collect their milk, go to play, etc.
Normally hearing pupils also gave more specific support to hearing-
impaired neighbours to enable them to follow lessons, such as pointing
to a page/map/picture/diagram in a book, tracing their finger under the
words of a story, poem or any piece of written text in a book which was
being read aloud by the teacher. Several pupils allowed deaf classmates
to see their work in their notebooks and even on occasions allowed them
to copy such work. A further task performed by some pupils was that
of 'interpreting'. Using varying means of communication such as talking, whispering, mouthing, miming and gesturing, normally hearing
pupils reformulated classroom events so that they became more readily
available to hearing-impaired friends. The process of interpretation of
teachers' utterances also worked in reverse; many hearing children were
able to 'translate' a deaf pupil's incomplete or barely intelligible utterances
and convey the message back to the teacher. An interesting example of
'interpreter' work was found in one of the secondary schools visited:

> Two normally hearing twelve-year-old girls and their severely deaf
> friend, had, in their French lessons devised a special written code
> for the language based broadly on English phonology. The normally
> hearing girls translated the French teacher's spoken words into a code
> which the deaf girl converted into 'proper' French. In addition, dur-
> ing French dictation, these same girls helpfully 'wrote in the air' punc-
> tuation marks such as 'virgule', 'point', 'point d'exclamation' for the
> benefit of their deaf friend.

Such forms of interpretation are clearly helpful to hearing-impaired pupils,
and, as seen in Chapter 5, often much appreciated by class teachers.
   On occasions, deaf pupils actively sought assistance from a normally
hearing neighbour. Not once was such a request for help observed to be
turned down. Most support given, however, was spontaneous and unsolicited. Many of the normally hearing pupils acknowledged that they
occasionally or frequently helped a hearing-impaired classmate:

Suzanne	7 years	'Sometimes when the teacher says "Right, now everybody look this way" and Alison's still writing — I give her a nudge an' I say "Look at Mrs Barker".'
Susan	10 years	'I usually look across the table and make sure he's on the right page.'
Deborah	12 years	'After lessons either Amanda or I give her our books, so she can check she's got everything down.'

Touching and nudging, as referred to in the first comment above, were popular methods employed by normally hearing pupils to keep hearing-impaired associates alerted to significant classroom events. Some pupils, however, were prepared to modify their mode of communication in more elaborate ways to accommodate the needs of hearing-handicapped peers. Several pupils, of all ages, were able, apparently unreflectingly, to alter their communication style in order to facilitate mutual understanding. Observations in classrooms revealed a variety of special communicative devices, such as speaking up, speaking with greater clarity, slowing down the rate of utterance, facing the deaf person before speaking, using gesture and mime, exaggerating speech and, as mentioned earlier, mouthing rather than vocalising their words. The following sample of statements from pupils describe techniques they felt to be helpful in easing communication between themselves and a deaf classmate:

Jeanette	7 years	'We look at his face and don't talk fast.'
Ross	8 years	'We try to speak up when we talk to Cheryl. We don't speak very fast.'
Georgia	9 years	'We look at her. If she can't hear us she can see the movement of our lips.'
Gail	9 years	'You must remember to look straight at her, into her eyes so she can see your face. And you mustn't talk too quickly.'
Susan	11 years	'Sometimes you can talk with your hands.'
Janet	11 years	'Sometimes if you speak clearly to him it helps.'
Amanda	12 years	'If she can't understand you can act what you want to say.'
Jack	13 years	'He understands us by lip-reading and we talk a bit slow.'
Angela	13 years	'If you stand in front of her she can hear you.'

Observations of the reactions of hearing-impaired pupils to these different forms of communication suggested that generally they found these accommodations helpful and relevant to the needs of the immediate situation. Whether communication by gesture or silent mouthing is advantageous to the long-term educational development of auditorially deprived and linguistically retarded hearing-impaired school children is, of course, open to question. What is certain, however, is that the strategies worked out and developed by normally hearing pupils are used by them in the honest belief that they are helping a deaf classmate comprehend what they say and understand more of what is going on in the classroom.

If my observations in classrooms can be generalised, it would appear that among normally hearing pupils there is a willingness to convert kindly attitudes towards hearing-impaired classmates into friendly acts. Normally hearing pupils were found to be making an important contribution in serving the special educational needs of the hearing-impaired child in the ordinary classroom. The importance of this contribution should not be underestimated. In helping hearing-impaired pupils follow lessons normally hearing pupils act as valuable, perhaps invaluable, teachers' aides. Furthermore, in seizing opportunities for keeping hearing-impaired children in touch with classroom events generally, normally hearing pupils were seen to be helping to forge links and foster friendships between the two categories of pupil.

A question that arises in this context is the extent to which practical steps should be taken by educators to encourage 'pupil support' of the hearing-impaired pupil in the ordinary class. Is there any form of teacher intervention which will promote helpful and friendly interaction between hearing and hearing-impaired pupils? The research evidence cited in Chapter 2 is equivocal on this topic and therefore provides no firm answers to these questions. In view of this it is appropriate to consider *who* are the pupils that offer helpful and friendly support? Do they possess any special characteristics which predispose them to behave in this way? Comments from class teachers cited below suggest that pupils who in their view were 'mature', 'sensible', 'intelligent', 'sympathetic' or even 'domineering', were often the ones to take the initiative in assisting a hearing-impaired classmate:

Infant teacher	'She's that sort of girl. She likes to have someone to take under her wing.'
Junior teacher	'Kathryn is friends with Julie and helps her a lot. She's a really mature sort of girl.'
Junior	'I deliberately sat Cheryl on Ross's table. He's the nicest boy

teacher	I know.'
Junior teacher	'Well Sarah-Jane's rather a bossy type so she welcomes the opportunity to look after Alison. And she *is* helpful.'
Secondary teacher	'Amanda and Deborah are always helpful to Joanne. I think it's because they're intelligent and sensible.'

'Helpful' pupils were not, however, always categorised by their teachers as confident or sensible. Several teachers reported cases of 'befriending' pupils who had special problems of their own, and/or had something of an 'outsider' status among their peers. There were two instances of pupils whom teachers had at one time categorised as 'difficult' and 'disruptive' pupils befriending hearing-impaired pupils. These pupils had each 'taken on' a deaf peer as a friend and, much to the delight of their teachers, this very act seemed to improve the behaviour in school of these two pupils. The following statement of one of the teachers indicates that having a hearing-impaired pupil in the class had proved an asset because of the effect on the 'difficult' pupil:

Secondary teacher	'I'm really glad to have Debbie here. Since she's come Tracy, who used to be a real tear-away, has taken to looking after her and now she's almost a model pupil. I can hardly believe the change. Having Debbie's been a real success.'

Three other cases were reported by teachers of pupils who, prior to the introduction of a hearing-impaired child into the class, had been regarded not so much as disruptive but as 'isolates' — children who were having difficulty in forming stable social relationships with their peers. Each of these pupils had gravitated towards and befriended a deaf pupil, in all cases, according to their teachers, to their mutual benefit. One secondary girl who was thought by teachers to be a bit 'touchy' and 'awkward' had made a 'best friend' of a severely deaf contemporary, and as a consequence, both pupils had become more acceptable among others. Another 'slow learning' girl, aged seven, had become a close friend of a profoundly deaf girl and acted as her constant aide and interpreter during lessons, playtimes, assembly, etc. A third pupil, recently arrived from the Middle East, had, according to his teacher, some problems in 'settling down' in his new school. Once he had struck up a friendship with a severely deaf boy in the class, however, he seemed much happier, and the deaf pupil gained a helpful companion. It would seem, then, that for certain normally hearing pupils, the need to be needed is occasionally facilitated by the presence of a deaf pupil and might have particularly beneficial effects on their sense of well-being whilst in school. The above three examples illustrate the idea that integration is a complex notion: all pupils, if they are to be integrated into their schools, need to feel a sense of worth within the pupil community. Deaf pupils, by having special needs as well as possessing normal human qualities, can promote in other pupils a sense of self-esteem and feelings of belonging, and thus mutually enhance the integration of both categories of pupil into the school community.

It is apparent from the above examples that pupils who were found to be helpful to hearing-impaired classmates display a *variety* of characteristics, and this is likely to be generally the case. This being so it would be difficult to identify in advance pupils who could be relied upon to be especially supportive of a hearing-handicapped pupil. When a hearing-impaired pupil was deliberately placed next to a pupil or group of pupils with recognised sympathetic qualities and good sense, teachers felt it worked well. Most of the cited examples of befriending and helpful behaviour on the part of normally hearing pupils, however, occurred spontaneously without any formal intervention from the class teacher. The investigation, therefore, did not provide much support for the idea of formally introducing, say, a 'buddy' system, whereby a particular pupil is selected to take care at all times of a handicapped pupil in the ordinary class. It is probably more sensible to wait for 'supportive' pupils and 'befrienders' to emerge naturally. None the less, teachers should be sensitive to what is going on in terms of which pupils are befriending a hearing-impaired pupil and be prepared to monitor this behaviour. It is conceivable that 'unsuitable' pupils might choose to form a close acquaintanceship with a hearing-impaired child and offer inappropriate or inadequate support.

A possibly more useful form of teacher intervention might be to inform the pupils that a deaf child would be joining the class and instructing them to be as helpful, kind and co-operative as possible. This had occurred in several classes visited. How effective was this form of intervention, however, proved difficult to assess. Two junior pupils felt it was unnecessary to be told to be helpful, as their comments reveal:

| Ross | 9 years | 'We were told to be nice to the unit children but we like them anyway. Even before they came to our class we were always playing with them.' |
| Georgia | 9 years | 'It's not that you *have* to, but it's nice to be kind to deaf children.' |

These statements corroborate observations in ordinary classes that even pupils who had not been specifically encouraged to 'be nice to a deaf child' were just as willing to offer useful assistance, where necessary, to a hearing-impaired classmate. Specific teacher requests to hearing pupils to show special consideration to the deaf may, therefore, be irrelevant. It is doubtful, however, if such teacher intervention does any harm, and it may be a sensible precaution to ask pupils to be helpful and friendly to deaf children. I would suggest, further, that pupil support will almost certainly be enhanced, and made more constructive, if pupils are given information about deafness and some of the problems associated with it.

It has already been argued, from the evidence of the research, that normally hearing pupils generally have some understanding of the difficulties caused by having a hearing loss and that they feel sympathy for the predicament of a deaf child. None the less, their knowledge of deafness was on the whole incomplete and, therefore, open to improvement. At one junior school visited, which contained a partially-hearing unit, an illustrated talk had been given by a teacher of the deaf to each class in the school. The ordinary class teachers believed this to be particularly beneficial, and felt that such instruction had helped create a climate in the school which was more sympathetic to the special needs of the deaf pupils. Teachers thought that subsequent to the talks the pupils offered more constructive assistance to the deaf children. There is evidence, therefore, that pupils' interest in deafness can be stimulated through positive intervention and that steps can be taken to ease interaction between the hearing and the hearing impaired.

Normally hearing pupils' consciousness of deafness can, and perhaps should, be raised to encourage these pupils to offer maximum appropriate assistance to the hearing-impaired pupil in the ordinary class. It is, of course, also important that teachers are made fully aware of the potential that exists in the ordinary classroom for the educational support of special needs pupils. A little careful monitoring and encouragement of helpfulness among pupils can benefit the hearing-impaired pupil, and relieve the class teacher of some of the pressure of ensuring that her hearing-impaired pupil is coping with the demands of the ordinary class.

Factors Affecting the Attitudes of Normally Hearing Pupils Towards Hearing-impaired Peers

So far in this chapter there has been broad discussion of the ways in which normally hearing pupils perceive hearing-impaired peers and the ways they behave towards them. It would, however, be wrong to assume that all hearing-impaired pupils are accepted into ordinary classes in a uniform manner, or that hearing pupils perceive and react to deaf classmates in the same way no matter what the circumstances. Observations in classrooms confirmed not only that the attitudes and responses of normally hearing pupils to hearing-impaired pupils varied but also that there were discernible reasons for much of this variation. It is relevant, therefore, in the final section of this chapter, to examine the major variables influencing pupils' attitudes and their ways of interacting with the hearing impaired in the ordinary school. These are: familiarity with the hearing-impaired pupil; opportunities for association with the deaf pupil; personal characteristics of the hearing-impaired pupil and, finally, the age of the pupils. Each of these factors will be considered in turn.

Familiarity with Hearing-impaired Pupils

Normally hearing pupils' perceptions of deaf peers were affected by the extent to which they were familiar with handicapped pupils. The more accustomed normally hearing pupils were to the presence of deaf pupils in the school, the more the deaf pupils became accepted members of that school. Several teachers pointed out that, once established in a class, a hearing-impaired pupil attracted no special attention:

Infant teacher	'The children know he's deaf and wears hearing aids, but they don't take any notice now.'
Infant teacher	'Now they've got used to her they don't make any special fuss. They know she's deaf, but that's it.'
Junior teacher	'They used to be a bit wary of the deaf pupils but now they just take them for granted.'

These comments suggest that whilst the hearing-impaired child in the ordinary school setting may begin by being 'newsworthy', the novelty wears off over time. A similar conclusion was reached also by Hegarty *et al.* (1981) on the integration of handicapped children in ordinary schools. They state:

After a period of initial curiosity, especially in the case of very young children, and in regard to the physically handicapped and hearing-impaired, the presence in a school of peers with special needs was generally accepted as a matter of course.

That hearing-impaired pupils were accepted in the ordinary school is, of course, welcome news for those who consider social integration an important objective. A possible and less desirable consequence for a hearing-impaired pupil in being too much taken-for-granted by other pupils in the ordinary school is that these pupils will cease to offer the kind of helpful accommodations referred to in the previous section. If a deaf pupil is not regarded as special there is a danger that he might not be given special consideration. Observations indicated, however, that for the hearing-impaired pupils their being accepted as part of the normal scene and their being offered special concessions, could be, and usually was, co-extensive. The point can be illustrated with an example from a secondary school visited:

> A severely deaf girl, Gwen, aged 14 years, had been individually placed full-time at her local school. Gwen had established herself not only as an accepted member of the class, but as an inseparable part of a clique of girls, known amongst their contemporaries as the 'gang of three'. Gwen was so well assimilated into this small group that questions relating to her special status as a handicapped person met with some surprise, even hostility. One of the normally hearing members of the group in fact stated quite emphatically 'You know she's a *normal* girl, just like anyone else.' In spite of the girls' insistence on Gwen's 'ordinariness' observations in classrooms and reports from teachers both confirmed that Gwen's two friends treated her in a manner quite different from the way pupils in the school normally behaved towards one another. The two hearing girls offered Gwen a variety of special services such as 'interpreting' the words of the teachers, checking her notes, ensuring that she was doing the work expected, etc. What appeared to be happening in this situation was that special concessions and accommodations to the needs of the deaf pupil had, over a period of time, become routinised.

In the above example the perception of differences diminished but the special assistance did not. It would seem that the normally hearing pupils offered special help without reflecting on the matter. The comment of one of Gwen's friends sums up the situation: 'It just comes naturally. You don't think about it.'

The type of response from normally hearing pupils illustrated in the above example was further confirmed by observations in classrooms in different schools. Greater familiarity with the hearing-impaired pupil resulted in greater acceptance within the community of normally hearing pupils, but this did not mean that deaf pupils were expected to conform in every respect to the behavioural norms of non-handicapped children. If it is generally the case that special accommodations to the handicapped become routinised and that 'abnormality' is taken for granted by the 'normal' group, a very desirable situation exists from the point of view of integration. It means that differences are acknowledged but do not necessarily imply inferior status.

It is not claimed that all the hearing-impaired pupils who featured in my investigation enjoyed equal status with their hearing peers whilst receiving maximum special support from them. In any case, it would be incautious to generalise from a relatively small sample of pupils. However, observations in schools indicate that normally hearing pupils can offer normal experiences to the deaf and at the same time accommodate their special needs.

Associative Factors Influencing the Acceptance of Hearing-impaired Pupils

The extent to which normally hearing pupils can become familiar with hearing-impaired pupils and accept them as part of everyday school life depends, not surprisingly, on the amount of exposure of the one group to the other. Likewise, the nature of the interaction between the hearing-impaired and the normally hearing pupils is likely to depend, critically, on the opportunities for association available to the two groups. The hearing-impaired pupils who featured in the investigation varied, first, in the amount of time they spent in the ordinary class and second, as to whether they were placed in the ordinary school individually or as a group of similarly handicapped pupils. A general, if expected, conclusion resulting from my investigation, and one which confirms the research findings cited in Chapter 2, was that the more opportunities given the hearing-impaired pupil for interacting with normally hearing pupils, the more likely he was to be accepted into the normal group. The less time the hearing-impaired pupil spent in the ordinary classroom, the less likely he was to form close friendly relationships with normally hearing pupils, and the more likely he was to interact socially with similarly handicapped peers. There are good reasons why this should be so. Human relationships tend generally to form with those closest to hand. Pupils who perhaps travel in the same special bus or taxi to school, who attend a significant proportion of lessons together in the same special class or who have even at one time attended the same special school — all these pupils have a base of experience in common which is likely to draw them together. The tendency for hearing-impaired children who attended units to 'stick together' was noted frequently both by class teachers and other pupils. The following citations from teachers and pupils referring to unit pupils in their school confirm the point:

Secondary teacher		'They tend to keep themselves to themselves, even though the others are quite willing to be friendly.'
Gilbert	12 years	'They do stick together. I think there should be some people in the unit so that they can make friends with the others.'
Heather	12 years	'We like Sally-Anne but Tracy and Sally-Anne, they go off with Susan and the others who are deaf, so we don't get much chance to make friends.'

Many teachers believed that the unit system itself served to segregate hearing-impaired pupils from others in the school. The following comments of two teachers in schools containing units were typical:

Secondary teacher	'They (normally hearing pupils) tend not to take much notice of the unit pupils. I think it's because their home base is too secure — it's too close. It sets them apart from the rest of the school.'
Secondary teacher	'If he didn't have the unit to go back to and his deaf friends he'd *have* to mix more with the others.'

Where hearing-impaired unit pupils attended ordinary classes in small groups of two or three, there was, according to teachers, even less contact between deaf and normally hearing pupils. The following statement by a secondary teacher referring to two deaf pupils who attended her class exemplifies a view held by several teachers in similar circumstances:

Secondary teacher	'I don't think I've seen them ever have any contact with the others. And that's a shame because they (normally hearing pupils) would be quite willing to be friendly.'

Another factor common to most hearing-impaired unit pupils, and one which served further to segregate them from other pupils, was that most of them lived outside the catchment area of the school, sometimes a considerable distance away. This meant that there was less opportunity for hearing-impaired pupils to participate in extracurricular activities where relationships might be cemented and less opportunity for friendships to be continued after school hours.

It seems clear from the foregoing discussion and citations that situational factors, those that have been termed 'associative' factors, influence significantly the amount of contact and friendship that is possible between hearing and hearing-impaired pupils in the ordinary school. It would be wrong, however, to exaggerate the isolation of unit pupils from their hearing peers. Many of the hearing-impaired pupils who attended ordinary classes on an intermittent basis enjoyed friendly relationships with other pupils in the class. A few had formed very close relationships and had made 'best friends' from among the normally hearing group. It cannot be claimed, therefore, that the unit system is incompatible with acceptable levels of social integration of hearing-impaired pupils in ordinary classes. At the risk of over-generalising from a small-scale investigation, it does seem likely, however, that the unit system *per se* detracts from the total assimilation of hearing-impaired pupils into the ordinary class, and from full acceptance by normally hearing pupils. This view, of course, has considerable common-sense foundation. Any part-time member of a school class, whether handicapped or not, is likely to have marginal status within the class. Furthermore, where there are groups of hearing-impaired pupils attending a school the common feature of deafness is, in itself, likely to promote association within that group: it would be surprising if it were otherwise.

There is no attempt, here, to argue from the evidence of the research that *all* hearing-impaired pupils ought to be individually placed in their local school. There may, on academic grounds, be important reasons why a deaf child in the ordinary school needs the support that can be offered in a special class. Furthermore, as will be demonstrated in Chapter 7, some hearing-impaired children have a strong emotional need for the companionship of others with a similar handicap. However, the findings do suggest that whatever the advantages of the special class in the ordinary school, this type of provision will in itself tend to segregate hearing-impaired from normally hearing peers and act as a constraint on the formation of close association between the two groups.

Personal Characteristics of the Hearing-impaired Pupil Affecting his Acceptance in the Normal Class

An environment which facilitates interaction between hearing and hearing-impaired pupils is not, of course, the only factor determining patterns of relationships between the two categories of pupil. A facilitating environment may be a necessary condition for the promotion of friendship between normally hearing and hearing-impaired pupils but it is not a sufficient one. The personality, character, beliefs and interests of associating pupils greatly influences whether or not they like one another and form friendships. Thus, as for any other pupil, the individual personal characteristics of the hearing-impaired pupil will influence the way other pupils perceive him and how likeable they find him.

It is appropriate to consider first the feature that is common to all pupils with a severe hearing loss, namely, their difficulties of communication. On the face of it, it seems highly likely that the communication difficulties associated with the handicap of deafness would frustrate the maintenance of normal social relationships between hearing-impaired and normally hearing pupils. Indeed, discussion with normally hearing pupils indicated that, on occasions, interaction between themselves and deaf peers was strained. The following comments from normally hearing pupils testifies to this point:

| Georgia | 9 years | 'Well with Julie it's a bit difficult talking because she's deaf so she can't talk, not properly.' |
| Gaynor | 12 years | 'When you've stood there talking to her and she says "What . . . what . . . what . . .?", it gets on your nerves sometimes.' |

Comments from several pupils, however, suggested that in spite of the difficulties, efforts were made to be patient and to try to overcome the communication problem in one way or another. The statements of normally hearing pupils, cited below, exemplify some of the strategies adopted for coping when communication with hearing-impaired pupils became difficult:

Jeanette	7 years	'Karen can't speak very well so we can't always understand her — so we just play.'
Amanda	12 years	'You can be talking to her and you say something six times and still she doesn't understand. You get fed up but you try not to let it show.'
Jenny	12 years	'We do sometimes have difficulty understanding them, but we try and think about what they meant. We don't like to ask them to say it again as I think that makes it worse for them. That makes them feel they're not very good so we try to understand.'

The above examples illustrate the point that whilst interaction between hearing and deaf pupil might be affected by communication problems, sustained relationships are not necessarily prohibited.

Many of the hearing-impaired pupils had great difficulty in speaking fluently and intelligibly and in understanding the speech of others. None the less, there were examples at all stages of education of close friendships between normally hearing pupils and pupils with severe and profound hearing losses. This would seem to indicate that the ability to communicate normally is not necessarily a key factor in the maintenance of social relationships between school pupils. That this is so was also confirmed by examples of pupils with moderate hearing losses and less severe communication difficulties who had no 'proper friends' among the hearing group or who were even unpopular with them. This indicates that characteristics independent of hearing loss and communication handicap influence a hearing-impaired pupil's ability to be liked by others. Moreover, it suggests that deafness is by no means inevitably a 'master status' dominating the interaction between a hearing-impaired pupil and his peers. Several teachers reported, often to their surprise, cases of close friendships between normally hearing and deaf pupils. The following statements from teachers of the deaf about profoundly deaf children serve as examples here:

Unit teacher of the deaf	'Some of Cheryl's best friends are hearing — it's amazing.'
Unit teacher of the deaf	'You wouldn't think it's possible but Paul's best friends are in the mainstream.'

Several normally hearing pupils confirmed the existence of close, stable relationships between themselves and deaf pupils. The reasons they gave for being friends with deaf children were for what might be termed the deaf person's 'normal' likeable qualities. Thus, if a hearing-impaired pupil was regarded by others as amusing, or generous, or good natured, he, like any other pupil, stood a good chance of being popular with his peers. The following sample of statements from normally hearing pupils giving reasons for their choice of a deaf pupil as a friend, or for the general popularity of deaf pupils, illustrate the point:

Russell	9 years	'Everyone likes David. He plays a quiet game of football.'
Gail	9 years	'She's got a kind face, and she's never really rough. She's my best friend.'

Sarah	9 years	'All the unit children are nice. They're friendly and they play nicely — except the boys.'
Kathryn	10 years	'Julie's very nice and I play with her all the time. She let's me use her felt tips.'
Muhammed	11 years	'We like Mark because he tells jokes and he's very funny.'
Sandy	13 years	'Paul's great. He's really good at fighting.'

Hearing-impaired pupils who were less popular were also judged on the basis of 'normal' character traits. For example, one first year secondary boy was singled out by others in his class not because he was deaf but because he was 'rough', 'always messing about', and apparently inclinded to 'kick people'. A moderately deaf junior boy was unpopular among his age-mates for similar kinds of reasons. The following extract from a conversation between three seven-year-old boys about this pupil illustrates how his anti-social behaviour caused him to be unpopular:

Richard	'I don't really like Peter. He's always running around people and pushing them over.'
Andrew	'An' nicking things.'
Paul	'Like when you're eating crisps he'll come over and grab one — munch!'
Andrew	'When he's playing football he tries to kick people.'
Paul	'And he fouls everybody.'

Another example of unpopularity was of a hearing-impaired pupil, a 16-year-old moderately deaf girl, who was disliked by her normally hearing contemporaries because, in their view, she was 'standoffish' and 'unfriendly'.

Generally, observations in schools and talks with teachers and pupils suggest that the communication handicap associated with deafness was not as crucial to the maintenance of social relationships between deaf and normally hearing pupils as might be supposed. Pupils, on the whole, used the same criteria for liking a hearing-impaired pupil as they would for liking any other pupil. If it is possible to generalise from the investigation, it would seem that no hearing-impaired pupil, on the basis of hearing loss alone, can be 'written off' as incapable of integrating socially in ordinary classes. That the deafest of pupils in the study could form close and lasting relationships with others who were not deaf demonstrates the point.

The Age of Pupils and its Effect on the Integration of the Hearing Impaired

Finally in this chapter, consideration will be given to a factor which is undoubtedly relevant to the way hearing-impaired children are perceived and received by the normally hearing in ordinary classes, and that is the *age stage* of the pupils. Age is undoubtedly an important factor influencing the way children interact with each other. The manner in which five year olds, for example, behave towards one another is quite different from the style of interaction among teenagers.

Likewise the skills needed to be socially competent and acceptable at one stage of childhood are quite different from those required at another. The way children use language and communicate with each other changes dramatically as they grow older. This is, of course, particularly significant for deaf children. It is instructive, therefore, to examine characteristic pupil attitudes and behaviour towards hearing-impaired peers at each of the three major stages of education, namely, infant, junior and secondary.

Infant Stage. If one looks at the social environment of the infant school, it can be seen that young children possess many features which make the adaptation of the deaf child fairly easy. A brief observation of infant children confirms that this stage is a lively and active one. Psychologists have long emphasised that it is also an 'individualistic' and 'egocentric' stage in a growing child's development. Hadfield (1962) referring to four to seven year olds nicely makes this point when he says:

> It is an egocentric age in which the child is more concerned with himself and what he does than anything else. Sociability is at a discount.

Self-centredness is thought to be necessary at this stage in order for the child to develop an independence of adults. Clearly, young children do interact with each other, but up to the age of six or so, social relations tend to be rudimentary and ephemeral in comparison to later stages. Whilst young children are warm and friendly they are none the less self-interested. Indeed, Gesell (1970) suggests that a young child will use another child as: 'a pivot upon which the active player can turn'.

In talk as well as in play, the young child's individualistic character can likewise be discerned. When young children talk at length, even with other children present, it is almost as though they are talking to themselves. Tough (1973) suggests that:

In a way it seems that often the young child treats himself as the audience and parallels his activities with a rudimentary commentary.

Self-expression rather than the exchange of ideas seems, therefore, to be all important at this stage of development.

One quality closely associated with the egocentricity and individualism of the young child is a tolerance of human differences. Young children are open and friendly to anyone, and do not seem to be put off by such things as a handicap, or embarrassed by children such as the hearing impaired who have communication difficulties.

An explanation of the ability of young deaf and normally hearing children to get on so well together may lie in the fact that the hearing child, concerned more with his own expression rather than with the ideas of others, does not demand intelligent or necessarily intelligible responses to his remarks. One-sided 'conversations' are normal for young children. A deaf child's inability to verbalise fluently may not be noticed by a young contemporary, or at least not regarded as significant. An example observed was of a classroom 'conversation' between two six-year-old girls, one with normal hearing, the other profoundly deaf, with very limited ability to comprehend or produce understandable spoken language:

> The child with normal hearing was talking on the, to her, fascinating topic of whether she was going to put her coat on at dinner-time and where she was going to play; the deaf child was watching intently the face of her friend, occasionally nodding her head and alternating her expression from one of rapt interest, to mild surprise, to wide-eyed concern. It could be safely assumed from a knowledge of her communication problems that she was not understanding a word of what was being said. She certainly offered no verbal comment. The hearing girl, not deterred in the least by the lack of verbal responses or statements, kept up the flow of talk and, interestingly, when the occasion demanded, supplied *her own* responses to her statements and her own answers to her questions. Eventually the two girls left the classroom holding hands and giggling.

Clearly the non-verbal reaction of the deaf child did not seriously impair interaction nor preclude a relationship between these two girls.

Observations in classrooms generally confirmed that whilst young children do talk a lot they can also communicate easily and unselfconsciously in non-verbal ways. Several instances were witnessed of infant pupils making extravagant use of gesture, mime, mouthing, face contortions, etc. in order to communicate ideas to a deaf classmate. A six-year-old girl, for example, proudly proclaimed her prowess at communicating with her profoundly deaf friend, as her comment illustrates:

Samantha   6 years   'I'm friends with Alison and I have to talk "deaf language" to her. You turn your face so she can see you and we do lip-reading together and I can talk with my hands.'

In addition to attempting to convey ideas to a deaf child non-verbally, several normally hearing young children maintained rapport with deaf peers through a process of what psychologists might call 'phatic communication'. In other words, they were able to communicate feelings and emotions as well as ideas, through visual and tactile means. Examples of this type of communication included exchanges, glances, smiles, giggles, stroking arms, hugging and cuddling. Through this type of communication, young deaf children were able to keep in contact with others in the class without having to say anything.

In short, then, the infant stage of education has many advantages for the social integration of hearing-impaired children in ordinary schools. It is a time when normally hearing pupils are relatively unperturbed by the existence of a communication handicap in a peer. It is also, of course, a time when the hearing-impaired child himself is more likely to be unselfconscious and unembarrassed about his handicap. He does not suffer the inhibitions in making contact with others that older deaf children might suffer. The infant stage of education is, therefore, an appropriate time to allow the deaf and the normally hearing to learn to live with each other. However, whilst young deaf and hearing children may readily accept each other there are drawbacks on educational grounds to a policy of allowing hearing-impaired children to spend too much time among their hearing peers: it is appropriate at this point to draw attention to these disadvantages.

Whilst young children can communicate easily with each other it is arguable whether they provide good language models for each other. Experience of observing young school pupils talking to each other reveals a number of characteristic features which may not be conducive to the promotion of normal language development in children with substantial hearing losses. In the first place, young children often adopt strange postures when talking to each other. For example, they often do not stand up straight when they talk, they hold their heads sideways whilst speaking, they speak with their heads resting on their desks. They rarely face another child directly whilst speaking to him. They think nothing of 'conversing' whilst at the same time running about or searching in a cupboard. These observations confirm the view that young children act in parallel rather than in conjunction with others (Gesell 1970) and that interaction with others is 'egocentric' rather than 'social'. Second, the speech of little children is often indistinct. They sometimes mumble, talk behind their teeth, giggle whilst speaking, intersperse their talk with noises like 'aaaahhh', 'eeeeee', 'bbrrrr', 'zooooooum' and the like. These noises may have a communicative function, but they do interfere with the intelligibility of their words. Third, young children do not always obey the 'one speaker at a time' rule of conversation (Sacks *et al.* 1974); they sometimes interrupt other speakers and talk whilst others are talking, and this practice of course interferes with the intelligibility of their speech. And finally, the young child's talk contains many incomplete and, by adult standards, grammatically incorrect utterances. A normal five year old is only just in possession of all the structures of the English language, so it is not surprising that he makes some mistakes.

Children aged four to seven, of course, differ greatly in their skill at using language, and their verbal fluency will vary according to time and occasion. The following extract of a six-year-old boy, schoolmate of another boy with a moderate-to-severe hearing loss and placed full time in an ordinary infant school, illustrates how hesitant and unclear the spoken language of an infant-age child can be. Martin is conversing with a hearing-impaired classmate and another pupil from his class and is attempting to explain why he is not currently playing football:

Martin   'C — Cer — Cerz me, me Dad must 'ev — me Dad's took it away in the basket . . . he's . . . it's lost the ball outside . . . in the shed so . . . in the two sheds so I don't know where it is so I'm going to buy one at me birthday in August the fifth . . .'

This style of speech may not be characteristic of all six year olds, but it was reasonably typical of this young boy's spoken language in the particular situation. It seems improbable that this kind of talk would provide a good language model for a deaf child.

Thus, whilst young deaf children certainly learn much about the art of communicating generally from other young children, it is less clear how much useful linguistic experience they get from them. Furthermore, as already seen, young hearing children readily modify their style of communication to accommodate what they believe to be the needs of a deaf age-mate by using non-verbal strategies. This type of response, to be welcomed in one sense, is in itself unlikely to promote the development of normal oral language in the deaf child.

In sum then, there are many advantages at the infant stage of education for the social assimilation of children with a hearing handicap. There are, however, implications at this stage for the linguistic development of hearing-impaired pupils. Since it is on the quality of his language environment that a deaf child's own language development so crucially depends, educators need to be aware of the consequences of allowing a deaf child to spend all his time in the company of other young pupils. It may, for example, be necessary in the case of some young hearing-impaired children to withdraw them from the ordinary classroom for short periods in order that they might be given appropriate adult help in the development of their spoken language.

Junior Stage. Pupils at the junior stage of education possess several characteristics peculiar to this phase which have a bearing on the social integration of deaf pupils.

The pre-pubertal phase of development is held to be the time of greatest physical health. Children in junior schools are irrepressibly exuberant and energetic as Hadfield (1962) remarks:

> At this age boys and girls are so interested in life, so full of fun and vitality, so natural in their enthusiasms.

Play-time activities reflect the natural exuberance and vitality of this age-stage and many pastimes and games involve letting-off steam. Children rush about the playground, screaming and squealing for no obvious reason other than to discharge surplus energy. Opie and Opie (1969), writing about the games and play of schoolchildren, remark that:

> Some games are little more than statements of vitality. They have few rules, they offer small scope for subtlety because the options open to the player are few, and they make correspondingly large demands on the player's forcefulness.

It seems to be the case that the ability to participate in the 'rough and tumble' and the boisterousness of the play activities at this stage of life is, on occasions, more important than an ability to speak fluently and intelligibly. If this is so, then the implications for the social integration of deaf children are great: a hearing-impaired child, as well as any, can do a cartwheel across some grass, play 'Tag' or jump over a skipping rope. In contrast to the nursery-infant phase of individuality, there is more genuine co-operation at this stage, and children are more concerned about, and considerate towards, others. Junior children are typically not as self-centred as they were as infants, and are able to think beyond themselves; they are often capable of immense generosity, especially to those they consider less fortunate than themselves. Tears brim in their eyes when they think of children dying in India, orphaned in Asia, starving in Ethiopia. They willingly collect money for kidney machines or for the mentally handicapped. Their compassion frequently borders on sentimentality, but none the less the concern is there. One can expect, typically, therefore, that junior children will quite readily befriend a handicapped schoolmate.

A possible danger is that junior stage children might romanticise the problems of deafness and behave in a rather patronising manner, mothering, even smothering rather than allowing independent social development. Some examples of what could be regarded as 'protective' behaviour on the part of some normally hearing juniors, particularly girls, were observed in classrooms. Interviews with some junior girls did, also, reveal an element of pity and perhaps condescension in their attitudes towards hearing-impaired classmates. The following citation of part of a conversation between three eight-year-old girls about a profoundly deaf classmate suggests that she was regarded to some extent as a plaything:

Hazel	8 years	'All the children like her. She's nice to play with really.'
Elaine	8 years	'She's like a baby nice 'n cute.'
Mandy	8 years	'Yes, like a Teddy Bear.'

An example of over-protection that had developed into possessiveness is illustrated by the following extract of some talk between two nine year olds about their two profoundly deaf friends:

| Georgia | 9 years | 'She's (normally hearing) not very nice because Christine (deaf) sits next to Jane or Gail. Debbie (deaf) mostly should sit next to me, but Suzanne keeps dragging her to *her* place.' |
| Gail | 9 years | 'Suzanne sometimes tries to take Christine and Debbie away from us.' |

If integration is to be on the basis of mutual respect, it is important that teachers monitor the 'kind behaviour' of junior pupils towards a hearing-impaired peer and take steps to check, when necessary, over-protective behaviour and patronising attitudes. A way of helping the deaf pupil maintain equal status in the ordinary classroom is to ensure that he is not always at the receiving end of kindness and help. The deaf pupil might be given the opportunity to give as well as receive, and to show consideration to others.

Junior children readily make friends and friendships are vital to feelings of well-being and belonging. Friendships at the junior stage are typically much more enduring than friendships at the infant stage. Opie and Opie's (1969) work on the subcultures of schoolchildren suggests that the ability to talk fluently, and to express ideas with clarity, may not be as important a basis for friendship among junior schoolchildren as it is among adolescents and adults. Qualities such as 'looks', 'possessions', or 'amiability' may contribute more towards popularity among junior children than being 'interesting to talk to'. The following examples from Opie and Opie (1969) illustrate the point:

'Dulcie has got lovely hair, that's partly why I like her.'

(London schoolgirl aged nine)

'I like Brenda because she is very funny and very small. I also like Carol because when she has many sweets she always gives me some and she has lovely curly hair.'

(London schoolgirl aged nine)

My own observations in classrooms and interviews with pupils yielded comments from junior pupils which were strikingly similar to those of the Opies' schoolchildren. Here are two examples from junior girls who are talking about their deaf friends:

Georgia	9 years	'Christine's special. She's got a nice face and nice hair.'
Kathryn	10 years	'I like Mandy because she's got a nice smile and she's funny and she shares things.'

If junior pupils are not too concerned about the speech or eloquence of their classmates, then there is no special reason why a deaf child could not be selected as an acceptable friend by one who has normal hearing. If the deaf child has some pleasing personal attributes, then so much the better. The possession of nice hair, pretty eyes and an appealing smile may do much to compensate a girl who has poor speech. For boys, the ability to kick a football hard and accurately, fight fiercely, own a pocket calculator or a digital watch, may be more status-enhancing among peers than the ability to verbalise ideas. Thus if it is the case that junior children are 'competent, realistic, generous and fair' (Foster 1965) then they make ideal classmates for handicapped children, and greatly facilitate the adaptation of deaf children to the ordinary school.

It has been suggested above that junior children may use criteria other than the ability to talk well when choosing friends. This does not, of course, mean that junior children do not talk to each other and value the verbal exchange of ideas. The way junior children speak will vary from child to child and situation to situation, but some broad generalisations are possible. As the normally hearing child matures, so his speech and use of language more closely approximates that of an adult. The funny noises, incoherent, indistinct speech that is at times characteristic of the infant-age child has largely disappeared by the time children reach eight or nine years. Though still not as skilful as adults in monitoring their use of language, junior children, particularly older ones, are nevertheless capable of modifying what they say in response to particular situations. For example, they would be able to simplify or clarify, re-phrase or re-formulate utterances, or simply just 'speak up' for the sake of a deaf child.

Several junior teachers confirmed that many of their pupils made a special point of speaking up, and speaking with greater clarity, when talking to a deaf classmate. Pupils themselves acknowledged that they often monitored their utterances in accommodation to what they perceived as the deaf pupil's needs. The comments of junior pupils cited below have already been quoted earlier in this chapter for other purposes, but are repeated here because they illustrate the types of accommodations junior pupils are prepared to make when talking to a deaf child:

Ross	7 years	'We try to "speak up" when we talk to Cheryl and we don't speak very fast.'
Suzanne	7 years	'We look at her. If she can't hear us she can see the movements of our lips.'
Gail	9 years	'You must remember to look straight at her . . . into her eyes so she can see your face. And you mustn't talk too quickly.'
Janet	10 years	'Sometimes if you speak closely to him it helps.'
Susan	10 years	'If he doesn't understand you can sometimes help by making it simple.'

The above examples illustrate that, in contrast to younger children, junior age pupils are able to make modifications to their spoken language that are more directly related to both the communicative *and* linguistic needs of the deaf pupil.

Junior children will, of course, vary in the amount they say to deaf peers and also vary their use of language. But there is no question that normally hearing junior pupils will surround a hearing-impaired child with a constant flow of spoken language. Whilst teachers need to make sure that their normally hearing pupils do talk frequently and in a normal manner to hearing-impaired classmates, it is not likely that these pupils will need much encouragement. The exact nature of the contribution of normally hearing seven- to twelve-year-olds' talk to the language development of children with severe hearing impairments is not clear. Furthermore, we are not yet in a position to assess the relative merits for a deaf child of, on the one hand, the deliberate and controlled spoken language of informed and sensitive adults, and on the other, the less mature, less well-formulated, colloquial talk of the junior age schoolchildren. This is a complex matter and one which, I suggest, merits further research.

In sum then, socially, the junior stage of education is a good time for integration. Not only are junior pupils generous, open-minded and tolerant, they are also usually sensible, well informed, and quite capable of offering thoughtful, useful assistance to a handicapped peer.

Secondary Stage. It is at the secondary stage that many educators believe there will be the greatest problems for the social integration of the handicapped pupil. Normal teenagers, so it is argued, are less likely to be accepting and tolerant of pupils who are 'abnormal', particularly when the abnormality consists of a communication difficulty. It can be claimed almost with certainty that teenagers at this stage in their lives are more likely to suffer embarrassment in situations with which they feel unfamiliar. For this reason, along with others, teenagers often feel more secure if part of a gang or friendship group based on a common interest. It may well be the case that because of self-consciousness and embarrassment, teenage pupils are less able and willing to cope with a deaf fellow pupil if his speech is difficult to understand, his voice of unpleasant quality, and who cannot readily understand what is being said in the course of a normal conversation. This problem is intensified by the fact that verbal communication is of more functional social importance at this than at other stages of maturation. Characteristically, girls get together in huddles, and talk endlessly, so we are led to believe, about clothes, boyfriends, make-up, disco's, etc. Boys, especially younger secondary boys, still like to fight and to have a game of cricket or football but they also enjoy talking about soccer teams, racing drivers, snooker frames and such like. Adolescents with a marked hearing loss will have to struggle very hard indeed to keep up with these teenage conversations.

My observations in secondary schools suggested that some secondary pupils were indeed less tolerant than younger pupils of hearing-impaired contemporaries, and less willing to befriend them, communicate with them, or include them in their social circle. No pupil interviewed actually admitted to rebuffing or being unfriendly towards deaf pupils, but several reported that other pupils did behave in this way:

Deborah	12 years	'Some of the girls don't let her play with them. They can't be bothered to explain everything to her. You have to be patient with her.'
Gaynor	13 years	'Some people with them being deaf, they wouldn't entertain them to play with them. That's how some of them are, aren't they?'
Jack	14 years	'Some of the boys take no notice of him because he can't speak. We like him 'cos he's good fun.'

If these reports are typical of secondary pupils generally, then it would seem that there are certainly some hearing teenagers who find it difficult and problematic to enter a relationship with a hearing-impaired peer. However, a firm impression was gained that there were other secondary stage pupils who were willing to be helpful and friendly towards deaf pupils. Furthermore, as a result of general social and educative influences, many secondary pupils had acquired mature, sensitive and responsible attitudes towards deaf peers and the problems they experienced. The following comments of secondary pupils, for example, describing their behaviour towards deaf classmates illustrate a wariness of offering excessive pity because of the undermining effect that might have on the deaf pupil's view of himself:

| Kathy | 12 years | 'We like to treat them like anyone else really. If we are specially kind and give them special attention that might make them feel more different.' |
| Deborah | 12 years | 'You've got to be careful you don't say "Oh! |

you poor thing", otherwise she'll feel she's
not as good as us.'

| Janet | 13 years | 'We treat 'em as one of us. We don't feel sad for them because that makes them feel sad.' |

The degree of sensitivity displayed in these comments is rarely to be found
in younger pupils.

There are good reasons, therefore, why educators should not assume
that all normally hearing secondary pupils will find it beyond their means
to accommodate a pupil with impaired hearing. Observations in secondary schools indicated that hearing-impaired pupils continued to receive
support and helpful assistance in the classroom from other pupils, just
as they had done in the primary school. Furthermore, no secondary
hearing-impaired pupil was ostracised by others solely on the grounds
of his hearing handicap. Whether deaf pupils formed close friendships
with others in the secondary school seemed to depend far more on the
associative or personal factors already discussed, than on anything else.
There was a tendency in the two secondary schools visited which contained units for some of the hearing-impaired pupils to remain together
rather than seek friendships in the main school. But where deaf pupils
were placed individually in the secondary school they were fully
assimilated socially into the normally hearing group. It would seem,
therefore, that social integration at the secondary stage is possibly more
difficult for a hearing-impaired pupil than at other stages of education,
but it is by no means impossible. Because of self-consciousness and embarrassment deaf and hearing adolescents may find it more difficult to
interact. The fact that all teenagers, handicapped or not, have special problems of personal adjustment may serve to reduce mutual tolerance and
sympathy between the two categories of pupil. However, many hearing-
impaired pupils had the personal strength, buoyancy and capability to
be accepted by their peers, and many normally hearing teenagers accommodated them. The research in secondary schools showed quite clearly
that for every normally hearing pupil that is too embarrassed to talk to
someone who has problems in communicating, or whose vanity or other
motives prevent him from associating with a deaf pupil, there is likely
to be another who is confident enough and willing to take the trouble
to interact with a deaf person and make that interaction successful.

Conclusion

As emphasised at the beginning of this chapter, social integration is for many educators a major concern in the education of handicapped children in ordinary schools. There is a widespread belief that deaf pupils benefit from social contact with their normally hearing age peers. Some people fear, however, that far from enjoying the benefits of social contact in the ordinary school, many pupils with a hearing handicap will suffer bitterly because of it. Not only are they thought likely to fail to form normal peer relations, but they are thought liable to have to endure a range of negative experiences such as over-protection on the one hand, and victimisation and bullying on the other.

The evidence from my research into the responses of normally hearing pupils to hearing-impaired peers in ordinary schools gives grounds for optimism rather than pessimism with respect to the above matters. Generally, hearing-impaired pupils were accepted by their normally hearing peers, some of whom were prepared to offer helpful accommodations. Where hearing-impaired pupils were received less favourably by their classmates, this was related to features of their personality rather than their handicap. The factor which seemed to isolate hearing-impaired pupils most from their hearing peers was the existence of several other similarly handicapped pupils in the same school. The fact that many of the hearing-impaired pupils were placed in special units and attended ordinary classes on an intermittent basis served to segregate them from other pupils.

The unit system, whatever advantages it has for the personal, emotional and academic development of hearing-impaired pupils, tends to ascribe outgroup status to these pupils in the eyes of other pupils. Where groups of hearing-impaired pupils were placed in the ordinary school there was a greater tendency for them to be perceived by other pupils 'as a whole' regardless of individual differences among members of the group. The syndrome of being stereotyped was exemplified by the way many normally hearing pupils who featured in the investigation referred to the hearing-impaired pupils in the school as 'the deaf ones' or 'the unit children'. However, this is not to deny that on the whole, friendly relations existed between the two groups nor that enduring friendships were formed between unit deaf pupils and normally hearing pupils.

A high level of acceptance of hearing-impaired pupils in the ordinary school cannot be taken for granted. Social perceptions and attitudes are governed by many factors. We have seen, for example, how familiarity can lead to a more natural acceptance of the hearing-impaired pupil.

Knowledge about the implications of the handicap of deafness can result in more welcoming attitudes among normally hearing pupils and a greater preparedness to offer constructive support. It should be noted, however, that where teachers pay excessive attention to a hearing-impaired pupil and offer him too many special concessions, other pupils may feel resentful about the fact and become possibly less willing to be warmly disposed to that pupil.

In drawing attention to the factors which affect the responses of normally hearing pupils to the hearing impaired, the aim has been to offer educators information and insight which might enable them to promote accepting attitudes and friendly support for hearing-impaired pupils. This friendliness and support can, as has been demonstrated, be critical to the academic as well as the social integration of the hearing-impaired pupil in the ordinary school.

7 AN ORDINARY SCHOOL EDUCATION — THE RESPONSE OF HEARING-IMPAIRED PUPILS AND YOUNG ADULTS

Many of the formal studies on integration in education, discussed in Chapter 2, have focused attention on the attitudes of ordinary class teachers towards handicapped children and on the interaction between handicapped and non-handicapped pupils. Little work has been done on finding out how handicapped pupils themselves feel about being educated in the ordinary school or on the ways in which they attempt to cope in an educational environment which is not in the first place designed to cater for their special needs. Moreover, little or nothing is known of the views of handicapped people who have left school on their education in an ordinary school nor on how well they think this education prepared them for life in a 'non-handicapped' society. The purpose of this chapter, therefore, is to use my research evidence to examine the response of the hearing-impaired individual to an ordinary school education.

There were 50 hearing-impaired pupils featuring in my 1977/8 research, out of whom 40 were available for 'follow-up' interviews in 1983/4. Of the original number of 50 hearing-impaired pupils observed and interviewed in 1977/8, 15 had at some time attended a special school for the deaf. That a relatively sizeable proportion of hearing-impaired pupils featuring in the study had attended a special school was helpful in that it enabled those 15 pupils or former pupils to have a broader perspective on their experiences in ordinary schools.

The follow-up study was undertaken because I felt that evidence based on interviews with mainly older pupils, and deaf young adults who could reflect on past experiences at school and introspect about themselves in relation to others in the wider society, would supplement observations and 'in school' interviews and produce useful and interesting information on the meaning of integration from the hearing-impaired individual's point of view.

To assist the reader the material in this chapter is divided into three parts. In Part 1 hearing-impaired pupils' perceptions of their integrated education, the problems they experience in ordinary classes and the strategies they adopt to overcome special difficulties are described and discussed. In Part 2 the academic integration of the hearing-impaired pupils featuring in the study are considered by examining the pupils' academic attainments and their perceptions of them. In Part 3 the social integration of hearing-impaired pupils is explored through a consideration of their attitudes to normally hearing pupils in the ordinary school. In addition, and drawing on evidence from the follow-up study of former pupils, the ways deaf young adults see themselves in relation to the normally hearing world are examined and discussed so as to show whether or not they feel 'adapted to', 'assimilated within', of 'alienated from' the hearing-speaking society in which they live.

Part 1: PERCEPTIONS OF ORDINARY SCHOOL PLACEMENT

General Attitudes of the Hearing Impaired to Ordinary School Placement

My research evidence supports that of other writers (Anderson and Clarke 1982; Dale 1984) that on the whole handicapped pupils prefer ordinary to special schools. At both stages of the investigation the hearing-impaired pupils or young people who had views on the matter were, on balance, positively in favour of attending an ordinary school. Those who were not in favour were not negative about ordinary schools: it was simply that they were unable to express an opinion one way or another about a preference for ordinary over special schools. This was because they were either too young to have formulated an opinion or because they had no personal experience of special schools *and* had not thought about this form of provision as an option for themselves. Characteristic responses of this latter category of pupil to questions concerning placement in a special school were: 'I can't talk about that really'; 'How would I know?' or 'I can't imagine what it would be like'. It is, of course, not surprising that younger pupils, or pupils accustomed to a particular type of school, were unable to envisage a completely different type of educational environment.

Reasons given by hearing-impaired pupils for preferring an education in an ordinary school were expressed primarily in terms of the idea that 'normal' schools promote 'normality'. This notion is summed up by a moderately deaf school-leaver who claimed:

Paul   17 years   'I like being in a normal school 'cos you're treated like a normal person.'

Similar reasoning led several deaf youngsters to a criticism of special schools, namely, that they produce 'abnormality'. The following comments of severely deaf young people exemplify this attitude:

Joanne	12 years	'I don't want to go to the deaf school because then you'd be different from everyone else.'
Gwen	14 years	'I wouldn't want to go to Riverbank[1] (special school for hearing-impaired pupils). I don't like all the fuss.'
Sally-Anne	17 years	'I wouldn't like to have gone to deaf school. I'd rather be with normally hearing people. I think I've grown up with them and I don't think I could be stuck away and get into the life-style of a deaf person.'

An aspect of 'normality' of the ordinary school particularly appreciated by many hearing-impaired young people was its speech and language environment. That deaf pupils were surrounded by people who were talking normally helped them, so they believed, to acquire normal speech and language themselves. Special schools, on the other hand, were thought by many deaf people to be disadvantageous because they encouraged the use of simplified English or sign language, neither of which was regarded as 'normal'. The following comments are representative of views on these matters:

Cheryl	13 years	'I think it's better for me to go to a proper school so I can speak good. If I'd stayed on at the deaf school they still might give me baby words.'
Peter	16 years	'I nearly went to a deaf school at Runton. I didn't want to go because I didn't want to be taught sign language. I'd rather speak and I'd rather be with people that can hear and I didn't want to be with people that never say anything and just use their hands to talk.'
Susan	17 years	'At deaf school you'd be worse than you are 'cos they don't usually speak there and I'd

---

1. Names of the schools, places and names of teachers throughout the book have been changed in order to preserve anonymity.

| | | probably be just the same.' |
| Julia | 21 years | 'It was better at normal school because everybody talking and I like talking best.' |

Those like Julia and Cheryl cited above, who had previously attended a special school, also tended to believe that the normal academic standards of the ordinary school were more challenging and that on the whole this was a good thing. The following comments of profoundly deaf young people who had attended special school typify this viewpoint:

Paul	13 years	'At deaf school — too easy. Here work a little bit hard — but better hard.'
Heidi	15 years	'Here you have to work not like at deaf school where the work was very easy — all deaf children wasting their time playing the fool.'
Kathy	21 years	'It was really difficult. At the deaf school you could understand the teachers, not like hearing school but the work was very easy, too easy.'

Among those pupils who had previously attended a special school there was a strong feeling that the ordinary school had higher status: transfer to 'proper school' was seen as a form of promotion. The following statement by a severely deaf junior school pupil characterises this point of view:

| | | |
| Mark | 11 years | 'They said to my Mum, "I'm sorry Mrs Sutcliffe but he's so clever he ought to go to ordinary school", so that's why I'm here.' |

In addition to believing that the ordinary school offered them more 'normal' status and more enriched linguistic and educational experiences the majority of deaf pupils and young people, regardless of previous educational background, welcomed the opportunities the ordinary school offered them for social interaction with 'ordinary' pupils because it gave them the chance to broaden their range of social contacts beyond the deaf group:

| | | |
| Peter | 9 years | 'I play with Gary and Mark; I don't just like to be with the unit ones all the time.' |

Susan	12 years	'I don't just like the deaf. I like to mix with hearing children.'
Maria	18 years	'It's good to be in the ordinary school because we can get used to the hearing children and they can get used to us.'
Nicky	19 years	'You learn more off the normal hearing.'

The several reasons given by the above hearing-impaired pupils and young people for preferring placement in an ordinary rather than a special school can perhaps be subsumed under one all-important reason, namely, that the ordinary school offers a better preparation for life beyond school. That placement in the ordinary school facilitates adaptation to the hearing-speaking adult world was believed and stated to be the case by many of the hearing-impaired pupils, and confirmed by the young deaf people who had left school. The views of the latter are, of course, particularly important as these deaf young adults were not merely *speculating* about life after school. The following statements by hearing-impaired young people who had left school and were thus in the 'outside world' illustrate the reasons for preference for the ordinary school:

Joanne	17 years	'(At special school) you end up in an enclosed group and then when you come out you're starting all over again, just like you've been in prison. At least I was in the thick of it all the time. I have no great revelation coming to me. Being in a hearing school I was terribly unhappy but it made me tough. It made me independent and it means that I had nearly every shock that could be coming to me. There won't be many more to come.'
Maxine	18 years	'I've had to learn to stand on my own two feet. I found it difficult being really surrounded with hearing people. Deaf people, well you get so used to it. But, there's not that many deaf people standing at the bus stop, going into the shops all the time. The outside world is covered in hearing people.'
Maria	18 years	'At the Victoria (special school for the deaf) they're very deaf and they do sign language and the teachers give them a lot of

sympathy, but when they get out in the world as it is now they're not going to have the sympathy, because nobody's going to want to know them and also they're not going to be able to understand them.'

Kathy   22 years   'You're learning how to cope with the outside world, with what ordinary people are like. With being with them you feel that you should be with them, because otherwise when you go outside, you don't know how to speak to a normal person.'

The comment of Joanne's reminds us that even though life in the ordinary school might be perceived as difficult by some hearing-impaired individuals it is none the less preferable to the easier but over-protected environment of a special school. The 'medicine' of ordinary school life might at times taste nasty, but most of the hearing-impaired pupils and young people had faith in its 'curative' properties.

Thus, the hearing-impaired pupils and young people who participated in both the earlier and later interviews either took for granted their placement in the ordinary school or in broad terms expressed positive views about it. What is interesting and significant is that for these deaf pupils and young people 'normalisation', or at least 'near normalisation', was considered to be an appropriate goal in their education. There seemed to be a universal desire among those interviewed to adopt the behavioural norms of the normally hearing in order to be able to adapt to, and be accepted by, hearing-speaking society. These young people, whether or not typical of deaf young people in this country as a whole, wanted to talk as normally as possible, understand the speech of normally hearing people, achieve as near normal as possible academic standards and become socialised into the ways of normally hearing society. They believed that receiving an education in an ordinary school best helped them to achieve those objectives. They hoped that by being in a normally hearing school, some 'normality' would rub off on them. This does not mean that they were ashamed or embarrassed about being deaf nor that they lacked a sense of deaf identity. As will be seen in Part 3 of this chapter, many had a firm awareness of themselves as deaf people. However, none questioned that they needed to conform to the expectations of the normally hearing if they were to cope in what they saw as an indisputably hearing-speaking society.

On the basis of the study I would tentatively conclude that ordinary schooling is popular among hearing-impaired pupils and young people and generally preferred to an education in a special school. However, it is, of course, possible that since I did not interview a sample of pupils or ex-pupils of special schools, I am not presenting a universal and comprehensive picture of the views of British deaf young people with respect to ordinary vs. special schools. I interviewed only two hearing-impaired pupils attending special schools. These were pupils who were attending ordinary schools in my earlier investigation and had been later transferred to a special school for the hearing impaired. Their transfer to a special school occurred because they were judged not to be coping in the ordinary school. My interviews with these two pupils, secondary girls, were far from satisfactory in that I found it very difficult to communicate with either of them. With one profoundly deaf 13 year old thought to have 'other problems', there was no meaningful exchange. With the other, a moderately deaf 'slow learning' girl, I managed to establish that whilst she had been happy at her ordinary junior school, she believed that a normal secondary school would have been 'too hard' for her. These two girls may, or may not, be typical of the special school population as a whole. In any event, I would be reluctant, on the basis of those interviews to draw any conclusions at all on the views of special school pupils about their education. No doubt had I interviewed a number of special school pupils, some positive views about an education in a special school would have been found. Some research on this topic in the future would, therefore, be interesting and valuable.

This evidence, then, suggests that hearing-impaired children and young people educated in ordinary schools want, in the main, to conform to the social and academic norms of those schools. This does not mean that they all do so competently and with ease. Many of the pupils and young people encountered a variety of different kinds of problems in the ordinary school and the more important of these will now be examined.

Difficulties Experienced by Hearing-impaired Pupils in Ordinary Classes

The data presented and discussed in this section come primarily from observations of deaf pupils during ordinary class lessons and from interviews with pupils whilst they were still at school. Generally speaking, it was those pupils currently attending school who were more aware of the day-to-day problems of ordinary school life and who, therefore, had more to say on this topic but included are comments from former pupils where they make a contribution.

The majority of hearing-impaired pupils were very conscious that many of the difficulties they experienced could be directly related to their hearing loss. The classroom problems most frequently referred to were noise and the difficult situations arising from different styles of teaching.

Noise

All the hearing-impaired pupils who featured in my investigation had hearing losses which were substantial enough to necessitate the wearing of hearing aids. One feature of hearing aids is that they amplify all the sounds in the environment, not just the ones one wants to hear. They do not, in other words, have the capacity of the human ear to discriminate say, the speaker's voice from background noise unless the former is much louder than the latter. Furthermore, a hearing aid amplifies 'loud' sounds as well as other sounds, so that if noise levels are high this can cause discomfort to the hearing aid wearer. In the ordinary classroom, which has received no special acoustic treatment, background noise and reverberation is not 'damped down' so that even normal classroom noise will cause problems of interference for the pupil wearing a hearing aid. (In fact none of the classrooms visited had any such treatment.) When noise levels are high, as is often the case when 30 or more youngsters are gathered together in one room, the problem is exacerbated. The following sample of comments from hearing-impaired pupils confirms the discomfort and even distress experienced in noisy classroom conditions:

Andrew	11 years	'When Mrs Pollitt goes out of the room sometimes, it's very noisy and then it hurts my ears.'
Richard	11 years	'I hate it in the classroom when there's too much noise . . . it confuses me.'
Mark	11 years	'I try not to let the noise bother me. I keep it inside me, but once one afternoon it gave me such a bad headache, I had to go home.'
Maria	12 years	'I don't like it when everyone shouts. When they shout it goes loud and it sounds like one thing.'
Sally-Anne	12 years	'It makes me dizzy.'

These comments illustrate that classroom noise can be disturbing psychologically and even physically to the hearing-impaired pupil in the ordinary class. Several deaf pupils referred also to the way background noise, amplified through their hearing aids, interfered with their ability to grasp what the teacher or other pupils were saying:

David	9 years	'When all the children are talking at once I can't hear what anyone says.'
Richard	11 years	'When someone moves the chair I sometimes miss what the teacher is saying.'
Sally-Anne	12 years	'Sometimes I hear the children outside doing games and I can't hear what the teacher says.'
Peter	16 years	'It's background noise that's the main problem. I can't turn that down. When there's a very noisy atmosphere and people are talking I can't tell what the hell anyone is saying.'

The problem of background noise in the ordinary classroom is to some extent overcome when radio aids are used. Not all of the hearing-impaired pupils who featured in the investigation were fitted with such aids and it was those pupils without radio aids who experienced the greatest problems of background noise. However, even when radio aids were in use, the problem of noise interference did not disappear altogether. Several pointed out that the radio microphone used by the teacher picked up the noise of 'clothes' rub' as well as the teacher's voice. Moreover, a few pupils commented that where teachers wore jewellery around their necks, the sound of jangly beads and chains hitting against the radio microphone fed much unwanted noise into their radio receivers.

It is doubtful if the problem of noise in the ordinary classroom can ever be entirely overcome for the hearing-impaired pupil. Full acoustic treatment of all school classrooms is not a realistic objective, particularly in the current economic climate. The problem of interfering background noise and reverberation can be alleviated, if not overcome, by equipping classrooms with soft furnishings such as thick curtains and carpets, but again this involves financial expenditure.

It is helpful for hearing-impaired pupils if there is a quiet atmosphere in the ordinary class but it is probably unrealistic to expect a class full of lively children to remain quiet all the time. Furthermore, not all teachers are able to achieve, or even want, a classroom of silent or near silent children. Perhaps all that can be done is to make class teachers and normally hearing pupils aware of the way noise causes problems for a hearing-impaired pupil and encourage sensitive and helpful accommodations. For example, pupils could be encouraged not to shout when a hearing-impaired pupil is close by; teachers might be persuaded to aim for quiet rather than noisy working conditions in their classes; teachers could be asked not to wear such items as clunky necklaces when using a radio microphone.

Different Teaching Styles

Some teaching styles and teaching situations proved problematic and difficult for deaf pupils to cope with. A situation that several hearing-impaired pupils found difficult if not impossible to cope with was 'class discussion' or 'question and answer' sessions. Deaf people generally have difficulty not only in selecting sounds but in locating them. Thus, if a number of people are gathered together participating in a conversation or discussion, it is difficult for a deaf person to locate each speaker in time to focus on his face and so gain necessary clues to meaning from lip movements and facial expression. When a teacher is addressing the class as a whole, eliciting answers to questions and inviting comments and ideas from her class, the pupils speak from a number of different positions in the classroom. That the hearing-impaired pupils found this type of pedagogic situation hard to cope with is illustrated by the following comments on this style of teaching:

David	9 years	'It's awful then 'cos I don't know what the children are saying.'
Richard	11 years	'When all the boys and girls talk I can't understand it. I just look at the teacher and I can understand something.'
Alison	12 years	'When the children talk I couldn't hear anything. When the children shout out, I can hear them but not the teacher.'
Gwen	14 years	'No. No chance. I don't understand a word.'
Lisa	15 years	'I used to try to look round and see who was talking, but I couldn't so now I don't try.'
Paul	17 years	'I got a bit fed up like when we was in the classroom and started a discussion and there was quite a few girls in there speaking really low and sometimes I can't hear a word they were saying. I was just losing the discussion altogether. I didn't know what they were talking about so I couldn't join in.'

It is worth noting here that where there is verbal exchange between the teacher and a number of pupils radio aids do not have a particular advantage. Radio receivers are fitted with 'environmental' microphones so that it is possible for a pupil with such an aid to pick up sound from different parts of the classroom. However, the radio aids' environmental microphone does not enable the hearing-impaired pupil to locate sound any more easily than if he were wearing an individual aid.

A possible way round the problem of locating pupils' verbal contributions in class is for teachers to repeat or reformulate the ideas after each pupil has spoken. This solution is referred to by Richard, cited above, who perceived that the best he could do in this type of situation was to face the teacher and hope she gave sufficient commentary on what was being said to enable him to follow the lesson. If, during question-and-answer times, teachers can repeat or make explicit pupils' oral contributions, this might not only greatly benefit the hearing-impaired pupil, but also offer useful reinforcement of ideas to all pupils in the class. As stated in Chapter 5, some teachers adopt the technique of repeating and/or reformulating pupils' contributions 'naturally'. It is clearly a feature of teaching style which might be encouraged in all teachers when hearing-impaired pupils are placed in ordinary classes.

Another pedagogic technique available to school teachers which might lead to problems for the hearing-impaired pupil is what might be termed the 'lecture' style. Here the teacher gives expositions and explanations of ideas, for example by reading from a book or by speaking spontaneously, without inviting comments from pupils. This method of teaching is still fairly commonly used in many British classrooms, particularly with older pupils: it is one which I observed being used many times during the course of the investigation. It does not, of course, present the hearing-impaired pupil with the problem of locating different speakers, but none the less, several pupils found the 'lecture' style of teaching difficult to cope with. Anyone with imperfect hearing has greater than average difficulties in listening to a lengthy monologue, and that many hearing-impaired pupils found it a strain to concentrate when the teacher 'talked a lot' is exemplified by the following sample of their comments on this matter:

Mandy	10 years	'Sometimes, when the teacher reads out a story or something like that then I don't get a word of it.'
Mark	11 years	'When Miss Hampton talks a lot I can't keep up my concentration — it just goes.'

Georgina	15 years	'When the teacher goes on and on and I don't know what they say. And then sometimes they say, "Right, now you know what to do . . ." and I haven't a clue what to do.'
Susan	17 years	'I tried to lip-read but after a while it makes my eyes water.'
Gwen	20 years	'If I didn't know what was going on I had absolutely nil idea of what I was doing. You can go half-way through a lesson and she'll say "now put all that on paper", and I'd say "what?" You know, absolutely baffled and I'd get really mad because I hadn't heard a single thing of it. Yet I couldn't stand having to really concentrate continually all through the whole lesson.'

Observations of hearing-impaired pupils in classrooms where teachers were lecturing or reading from a book indicated that these pupils frequently 'switched off' from the situation. This was evidenced by behaviour such as staring out of the window, looking up at the ceiling or down at the floor, fiddling with objects on their desks such as pens, pencils, rulers or even trying to distract another pupil. Of course, no child has an unlimited attention span and no pupil concentrates all the time on what the teacher is saying. The evidence, however, suggests that hearing-impaired pupils have greater difficulties than the 'average' pupil in attending to and following a teacher's lengthy utterances. It might be advisable, therefore, when teachers make use of the lecture technique, which is invaluable on occasions as a means of getting information across to pupils economically and efficiently, that they take special steps to ensure that the pupil has understood what has been said. It might be necessary, for example, for teachers to go over points individually with a deaf pupil or delegate another pupil to do so.

A further type of difficulty reported by several hearing-impaired pupils occurred when they were required not only to listen to the class teacher but also pay attention to something else as well, such as a map, diagram or worksheet on their desks. The problem is summed up succinctly by the following comment of a severely deaf secondary pupil:

| Joanne | 12 years | 'I just can't do it when I have to look at Mr Lomax and look at the book and watch the |

blackboard. I just can't do it.'

Similarly the taking of dictated notes is difficult for hearing-impaired pupils because it requires them to look, listen and write more or less at the same time and this is expressed forcibly in the following statement by a severely deaf secondary school girl:

Gwen 14 years 'I have a lot of problems with dictating now. A lot of teachers do dictating now instead of writing on the board and it drives me mad!'

It is in these kinds of situations that class teachers may need to keep a watchful eye over a hearing-impaired pupil and repeat points and statements where necessary. Alternatively normally hearing pupils can be encouraged to offer support to a hearing-impaired neighbour in these difficult situations.

A further feature of teaching style which can have crucial consequences for the ability of hearing-impaired pupils to cope in the ordinary class is the manner in which a teacher speaks. According to the comments of deaf pupils and former pupils, teachers varied in terms of the clarity and loudness of their speech, in their lip-readability, their accent, and their apparent ability to stand still and face forwards when speaking:

David 9 years 'She speaks low.'
Richard 11 years 'Sometimes she mumbles her words.'
Michael 13 years 'He speaks to the blackboard.'
Paul 13 years 'Speak too fast.'
Julie 20 years 'There was one or two teachers with a moustache and a habit of putting their hand up to their mouth or they speak quiet.'
Gwen 20 years 'The French teacher was the funniest because she was Welsh. So it's difficult enough understanding a foreign language let alone a Welsh accent with a foreign language!'

By no means all teachers were criticised for the way they talked. Nevertheless, it is perhaps a necessary safeguard to advise all teachers receiving hearing-impaired pupils into their classes of the special receptive communication problems of these pupils and of the need to guard against certain ways of talking. It is, of course, unreasonable to expect a teacher to change her accent, but she might be tactfully persuaded to speak more distinctly, less quickly, or a little louder. It is a difficult and delicate matter to advise teachers to change well-established habits which have apparently not hindered their teaching in the past. But if hearing-impaired pupils in ordinary classes are to be given the maximum opportunity to under-stand what teachers say then 'rules' such as speak clearly, stand still whilst talking, do not speak whilst writing on the blackboard must be observed by class teachers.

Finally, in this section on the difficulties experienced by hearing-impaired pupils, attention will be drawn to problems associated with a pedagogic technique which has become increasingly popular in the modern British classroom and that is teaching through the use of sound and video tapes. These aids offer obvious advantages to teachers in enabl-ing them to broaden the experiences of their pupils and to make topics 'come alive'. The problem for hearing-impaired pupils, however, is that the quality of sound on tape and video recordings is rarely equal to that available 'live' in the classroom. Thus it was not surprising that many hearing-impaired pupils and former pupils reported difficulties in follow-ing TV commentaries and tape-recorded material, as the following com-ments illustrate:

| Mark | 16 years | 'Sometimes in English you need to play a lot of tapes, you see, and you would have to write about it. Well that was my worst point. You see because the teacher would say "sit in front of the class", but even if I sit in front of the class, it makes no dif-ference at all.' |
| Elizabeth | 17 years | 'I had to listen to a lot of tapes and I can't hear the tapes. I can't lip-read the tapes.' |

Several pupils observed in classes were obviously struggling to follow TV programmes on, for example, glaciers or Victorian England, or to follow tapes of French question forms or on different musical instruments. Again there are no clear-cut solutions to these problems other than sen-sitising class teachers to the difficulties involved for hearing-impaired pupils when these educational aids are in use, and in encouraging them to take special measures to ensure that the material has been understood.

It is clearly the case from what has been revealed that hearing-impaired pupils are likely to experience several kinds of problems in ordinary classes and as a consequence are often unable to follow, or only able to partly follow, the lessons. This, of course, is a serious matter and comments such as the following from severely and profoundly deaf young people reflecting on their past experiences in ordinary classes give grounds for concern:

Mark (severely deaf)	16 years	'I really had to concentrate and I couldn't do the work and then I wouldn't always understand.'
Joanne (severely deaf)	17 years	'There weren't enough hours in the day to do catching up on all you'd missed.'
Susan (severely deaf)	17 years	'I often missed what the teacher was saying.'
Paul (profoundly deaf)	18 years	'When teacher talk I got nothing, not at all, nothing.'
Julia (profoundly deaf)	21 years	'Sometimes I didn't understand a thing — no idea.'

It is significant that it was mainly older pupils and former pupils, especially those with more substantial hearing losses, who were prepared to admit to failure in understanding ordinary class lessons. Younger children were less eager to reveal their lack of understanding, possibly because they believed such confessions might lead to trouble, humiliation or unwanted special attention, or even simply that they were not aware of what they had missed. If it is generally the case that hearing-impaired pupils are reluctant to admit to problems in following ordinary class lessons, it would seem to be particularly important that both class teachers and teachers of the deaf are vigilant about monitoring how much a deaf pupil is taking in whilst in the ordinary class.

Despite the special problems and difficulties revealed, a firm impression gained both from talking to and observing hearing-impaired children in ordinary classes was that most of them were following something of what was verbally going on at least some of the time and some of them quite a lot of what was going on most of the time. There were several kinds of lessons such as games, PE, cookery, needlework, painting, etc. for which a hearing impairment does not constitute a major handicap. Furthermore, in the more 'academic' lessons, pupils generally spend much time working individually at their desks or tables from books of worksheets. Here again, provided the pupil knows what he is supposed to be doing, a hearing loss does not in the immediate situation represent a serious disadvantage.

The research evidence presented here thus challenges the impression given by McCay Vernon (1981), referred to in Chapter 2, that deaf children in mainstream classes understand 5–20 per cent of a lesson at most. The evidence also questions the view presented by Montgomery (1981) that the difficulties experienced by hearing-impaired pupils in mainstream classes are of such magnitude that they become 'very disturbed', later to be the 'clients' of priests, policemen and social workers. None of the pupils observed or interviewed appeared to be completely unable to cope with lessons in ordinary classes, nor did they believe they were the only ones to have problems with their work. As seen in Chapter 5, class teachers were often willing to take measures to ensure that deaf pupils could cope with the lesson material. Furthermore, as demonstrated in Chapter 6, normally hearing pupils frequently made helpful accommodations to deaf classmates in order to keep them in touch with what the teacher was saying and instructing. Moreover, difficulties that presented themselves to hearing-impaired pupils in the ordinary class were sometimes circumvented or at least alleviated by certain strategies and ploys they themselves had devised. These 'strategies for coping' will be considered next.

Strategies Employed by Hearing-impaired Pupils for Coping in Ordinary Classes

It is important for two reasons to be aware of characteristic ways in which hearing-impaired pupils attempt to overcome the special difficulties which confront them in the ordinary school class. First, knowledge of the responses of deaf pupils to difficult situations in ordinary classes is necessary if teachers are to identify when problems are occurring so as to offer appropriate and beneficial support to these pupils. Second, teachers need to know whether strategies which hearing-impaired pupils believe are helping them cope with the challenging demands of the ordinary class are, in fact, promoting their overall educational development. Clearly those strategies which impede rather than foster the education of hearing-impaired pupils in ordinary classes will need to be discouraged.

All pupils in schools must learn to behave and respond in accordance with the expectations of teachers and other people in school. Indeed, the process of schooling involves a considerable curbing of children's 'natural' inclinations and desires and entails presenting them with intellectual and other kinds of challenges which they may find difficult to meet.

A hearing-impaired pupil who has problems in school is not essentially different from any other pupil, and he is likely to resort to many of the strategies for coping which are typically employed by 'normal' pupils. Nevertheless, a hearing-impaired pupil is likely to have problems of a special kind over and above those experienced by 'normal' pupils and may, therefore, need to find ways of coping with those special difficulties.

'Conforming' and 'Passing for Normal'

Some of the special strategies adopted by hearing-impaired pupils in ordinary classes were undoubtedly motivated by a desire to conceal their handicap and appear to be conforming to the normal demands and expectations of the ordinary classroom. Goffman (1968) has pointed out that persons with what he termed 'spoiled identity', such as those with a physical or mental handicap, typically make special efforts to 'pass for normal'. In other words, they attempt to conceal from others those personal features which 'spoil' their identity. What is significant about the strategies observed in use by hearing-impaired pupils in ordinary classrooms which could be described as attempts to 'pass for normal' and appear to conform, was that generally, they were *not* conducive to the promotion of the deaf child's educational development. It is particularly important, therefore, that educators responsible for the education of hearing-impaired pupils in ordinary schools become acquainted with these ploys.

Hiding Hearing Aids. A strategy used by several hearing-impaired pupils in an attempt to cover up their handicap was to keep their hearing aids out of the view of others in the class. A hearing aid is, for most hearing-impaired people, the only visible symbol of the handicap. Thus in the minds of many hearing-impaired pupils who otherwise look 'normal' it is the hearing aid which confers on them a 'deviant' status. Several pupils had made obvious efforts to conceal post-aural aids beneath their hair and body-worn aids in skirt or trouser pockets. A possible disadvantage of having an aid in the pocket is that the microphone is to an extent shielded from the sounds in the environment that it should amplify. Furthermore, other objects in the pocket can feed unwanted noise into the microphone.

Radio aids, issued to many pupils were less easy to conceal. These aids have not yet been miniaturised in the way that individual aids have. At the time of the earlier investigation, the receivers of the aids worn by hearing-impaired pupils were black boxes measuring about 8" x 4" × 2" which had to be worn on the chest. Several pupils found these aids both cumbersome and stigmatising. This sentiment is illustrated by the statement of a moderately deaf teenager:

Julie   13 years   'With the big box you can't hide it under
                                 your jumper. It's always there and heavy.'

Pupils of secondary school age in particular seemed reluctant to wear
radio aids. Four instances were witnessed of secondary pupils keeping
their radio aid in its box, apparently 'forgetting' to put on their receiver
and to hand over the radio microphone to the class teacher. Teachers gave
several reports of hearing-impaired pupils pretending that their aids were
broken or had for some reason 'gone missing'. Thus both through observation and by report, there were many examples of attempts to avoid using
radio aids in spite of the advantages these aids generally offered hearing-
impaired pupils in ordinary classes.

That some hearing-impaired pupils did not want their handicap on
display was regarded as irrational by several teachers who claimed that
other pupils were well aware of who was deaf and who was not. As one
secondary teacher stated, referring to the unit pupils in the school: 'I don't
know why they try to hide their aids; everyone knows they're deaf.' Furthermore, as seen in Chapter 6, in the eyes of normally hearing pupils,
radio aids provided a source of interest and fascination and could be seen
therefore as, on some occasions at least, enhancing rather than reducing
the wearer's status among his peers. Thus the earlier research indicates
that there is a discrepancy of perceptions about hearing aids between the
two categories of pupil, hearing-impaired and normally hearing. Several
of the former group felt embarrassed and self-conscious about their aids
whilst the latter found them interesting and pleasurable. It might be
helpful, therefore, if teachers and parents could make reluctant hearing
aid users aware not only of the general benefits of use but also of how
acceptable these aids are in the eyes of other pupils. (It may be the case
that the concealment or non-use of hearing aids is now less of a problem. The follow-up interviews in 1983/4 indicated not only a greater
willingness on the part of hearing-impaired pupils to wear hearing aids,
whether personal or radio aids, but also there seemed to be less embarrassment about making these aids visible. This issue will be discussed
more fully later in this chapter when attitudes to hearing aids are examined. If attitudes among hearing-impaired pupils have become more
positive over the last four of five years, then this, of course, is to be
welcomed. It is still worth pointing out, however, that the hiding or non-
use of hearing aids is a possible strategy available to hearing-impaired
pupils in order to conceal their hearing handicap and one to which teachers

need to be alert.) It hardly needs emphasising that every effort should be made to ensure that pupils with substantial hearing losses wear appropriate hearing aids in order that they get maximum possible opportunity to grasp the spoken word.

Pretences at Understanding. That the hearing-impaired pupil has greater than average difficulty in understanding, or fully understanding, what teachers say is a point that needs no underlining. The struggle to comprehend classroom events and to follow lesson material is problematic for the hearing-impaired pupil in two major ways. First, any persistent lack of understanding of what has been said and of classwork generally can be a constant reminder of educational failure and is, therefore, likely to be demoralising for a pupil. Second, to be seen by teachers and other pupils to be uncomprehending of what is happening in the classroom can be both demeaning and humiliating. A tactic commonly adopted by many hearing-impaired pupils in order to avoid these feelings, was to pretend to understand. For example, teachers, when attempting to check the understanding of a deaf pupil with a questioning glance and a remark such as: 'Are you all right Alison?', or 'Did you get that David?', would often evoke enthusiastic 'nods', 'yesses' and 'smiles' from hearing-impaired pupils. Yet closer observation of these pupils often revealed that this positive acknowledgement of understanding was not always justified. Several instances were witnessed of a hearing-impaired pupil, having assured the class teacher that he was 'all right', turning to a neighbouring pupil for help or sitting pondering the blank page of an exercise book. Some hearing-impaired pupils and ex-pupils admitted that on occasions they feigned understanding to avoid special attention or disapprobation. They put up appearances 'for the sake of a quiet life' as the following comments reveal:

Susan	12 years	'I don't like to say I didn't get it because I might get told off and the teacher'd make a fuss.'
Gwen	14 years	'Sometimes I say "yes" even when I don't understand, otherwise they (teachers) might think I'm stupid,'
Deborah	17 years	'Sometimes I didn't crack on that I don't know what they've said . . . I hated them knowing. I'd just let them carry on the conversation and hope I'd get what she's on about.'

A willingness to 'fob off' the teacher rather than attempt real understanding can, of course, have serious consequences for the educational progress of the hearing-impaired pupil. Furthermore, where deliberate ploys are used to deceive the teacher, the process of teaching a hearing-impaired pupil becomes more ambiguous and uncertain. As already seen in Chapter 5 some class teachers found it difficult to ascertain whether their hearing-impaired pupils had understood the lesson or not, and this was problematic for them. It might, therefore, be helpful if specialist teachers counselling hearing-impaired pupils made them aware that they are making life difficult for their teacher by pretending to understand, and of course, in the long run, making life difficult for themselves.

A further strategy, used by several hearing-impaired pupils for giving the impression that they were following the words of their teacher was to put up their hands in response to teachers' questions even though they could not supply the answers. Teachers commonly invite oral participation from pupils, and those who wish to be seen in a favourable light are usually very keen to raise their arms as a sign of enthusiasm for the topic. Pupils who never put up their hand run the risk of being thought by teachers to be either inattentive, lazy or stupid. On many occasions pupils, both with normal hearing and hearing impairments, were observed to raise their hands, yet, when confronted by the teacher they were unable to produce the answer. Typical responses when 'caught out' were: 'I've forgotten'; 'I forgot the question'; 'I can't remember'. Whilst this strategy was common to both categories of pupil, the impression gained was that some hearing-impaired pupils used this tactic more frequently than their hearing peers in an attempt to display to their teacher that they were following the lesson. Again, this is a ploy to which educators need to be alert.

Copying the work of a fellow pupil is another tactic designed to deceive the teacher which was observed in use by both normally hearing and hearing-impaired pupils. The strategy of copying in order to appear to satisfy the demands of teachers must date back to the earliest days of schooling. Were it not for the fact that teachers can usually see through this ploy it is doubtless a strategy that would be used more often by the uncertain or lazy pupil. The evidence from the investigation suggests that the strategy of copying is resorted to by hearing-impaired pupils to a greater extent than would be expected of the 'average' pupil. Several teachers made special mention of the practice and the following comments of two primary school teachers referring to profoundly deaf pupils who attended their classes are typical:

'The way I know she hasn't understood the work is that she always has in her book exactly the same as Elaine.'

'She can paint well, but she always, but always, does what Gail (normally hearing) does. If Gail does a butterfly, then Christine does a butterfly; if Gail does a snowstorm, then we get a snowstorm from Christine.'

Several hearing-impaired pupils and deaf young people admitted to copying from others when uncertain of what they should have been doing:

Kathy	15 years	'I have been known to copy what the girl next to me has written down. It stops the teacher making a fuss.'
Maria	16 years	'Sometimes when I don't know what to do, like in Commerce, I just look at what the girl next to me has put down and I write that down.'
Mandy	17 years	'Sometimes I ask my friend to help me. I borrow my friend's work and I copy it.'

It is not necessarily harmful to the educational progress of a deaf pupil to copy from another pupil, especially if in so doing that pupil acquires a written record of lesson material which he has failed to grasp orally. However, when copying serves only to cover up for a lack of understanding of what has been taught then teachers need to be aware of the fact and take steps to curb the practice in the interest of the pupil.

'Pretending to understand' is a strategy that might well be anticipated from pupils with communication problems who want to stay 'out of the spotlight' in classrooms. It is, however, possible for hearing-impaired pupils to do the converse, that is exploit the hearing handicap and pretend not to understand for some self-interested purpose. Only one instance was found where this ploy was used persistently, but it seems worth drawing attention to it because the consequences of its use could be seriously detrimental to a pupil's progress. The instance of the use of this strategy came from a secondary school severely deaf girl who admitted some time after leaving school that:

Gwen	20 years	'I wasn't one for working hard. I did awful at school — I had to decide in my fourth year whether to work hard and try to get my "O" levels or not bother. So, I thought if I work and I don't get them, then I've lost out all round. So I didn't bother. And everyone thought it was through me being deaf. I played on it. The fact is you see I could do it, very easy, and I did it. I sort of went around looking puzzled . . . they didn't realise how crafty I was.'

Given that this particular pupil failed all her 'O' levels it would appear that 'craft' had allowed her to get away with not doing school work with the inevitable educational consequences. Though 'playing on the handicap' may be an uncommon ploy for hearing-impaired pupils in ordinary schools to adopt, none the less, teachers ought to be alive to its possible use.

Playing Up. A strategy, also involving some cunning, available to all pupils needing to draw attention away from their difficulties with school work is to 'play up'. This strategy was observed in use by three hearing-impaired pupils. These pupils, all boys, were regarded by teachers as poor at their work, a problem which was undoubtedly enlarged by an unwillingness to pay attention in class. Examples of behaviour observed included flicking pellets across the room with a ruler, talking to or joking with a neighbouring pupil, wandering around the classroom instead of settling down to work, provoking other pupils by poking them, 'pinching' items from other pupils' desks, fiddling with, and making noises with, their hearing aids whilst the teacher was talking. The three pupils were successful in evoking the annoyance of their respective teachers and in acquiring descriptions such as 'very naughty' and 'disruptive'. The strategy of perpetually 'playing up' in class was almost certainly going to have a detrimental effect on the progress of these pupils. Hearing-impaired children have enough educational problems as it is, without losing time in school by deliberately not paying attention to their work. That only three pupils out of the sample of 50 persistently adopted such strategies is perhaps reassuring. It is important, however, that educators are aware that the tactic of 'playing the fool' is available to the hearing impaired — as indeed to other pupils — and that special attention needs to be paid to the problems underlying this type of behaviour.

Generally, it would appear that those strategies used by hearing-impaired pupils for coping with the demands of the ordinary classroom which can be subsumed under the heading 'attempting to pass for normal' do not, on the whole, facilitate the educational development of those pupils using them. Whatever short-term gain to self-esteem a pupil may achieve by concealing his hearing aid, or pretending to understand the lesson material, the long-term academic integration of hearing-impaired pupils will be successful only if every effort is made to enable them to understand lessons in ordinary classes. This will inevitably involve helping the deaf pupil feel confident enough not to want to try to conceal his handicap and the problems that arise from it.

Hearing-impaired Pupils' Acknowledgement of their own Special Needs

By no means all the strategies for coping employed by hearing-impaired pupils could be described as deceptive or educationally harmful. Where hearing-impaired pupils feel confident enough to acknowledge their special difficulties and needs in the ordinary class they characteristically adopt sensible and helpful strategies. The major methods used by hearing-impaired pupils which were conducive to their educational development and which might be successfully emulated by hearing-impaired pupils in ordinary classes elsewhere will be outlined next.

Compensatory Activity Outside the Classroom. One way of overcoming special difficulties with school work is to work harder. Some deaf pupils, particularly older ones, claimed that they did extra work such as rereading worksheets and textbooks outside school hours in order to keep up with lesson material. Those who were prepared to spend extra time on their school work were, according to their teachers, more likely to keep up with 'normal' academic standards. Such pupils generally acknowledged that their handicap held them back academically but claimed that this had spurred them to greater efforts with school work:

Susan	17 years	'I think I've had to work harder because of my deafness. I was always at home doing homework till late.'
Joanne	17 years	'I had to do a lot of catching up at home.'
Heidi	22 years	'I did a lot of reading at home. I found that reading a lot of books help me with lessons.'

Many pupils and ex-pupils, however, did not see the need to work more diligently than the 'average' pupil and this suggests that there is a case for encouraging all hearing-impaired pupils to do some extra school work in out-of-school hours. Of course, deaf children like any other children, need time for leisure and recreation. Nevertheless, given that pupils with a hearing-impairment have a serious educational handicap, any activity which helps compensate for this disadvantage might profitably be encouraged.

Any pupil is likely to find it easier to do extra school work at home if he is given encouragement and indeed positive help from his parents. Several hearing-impaired pupils found this kind of support invaluable as the following sample of comments illustrates:

Dale	12 years	'If I can't do my sums or I can't understand something I ask my Dad to help.'
Elizabeth	13 years	'My Mummy and Daddy help me with my work and I find the work less hard.'
Lorraine	13 years	'I don't know what I'd do without my Mum. She looks through what I got for homework and explains to me some things I didn't understand before.'
Deborah	13 years	'I'd be lost without my Mum and Dad helping me.'

It is generally agreed by those concerned with the education of hearing-impaired children that there are not enough hours in the school day to give these pupils all the tuition they need to cope with their academic work, develop language, improve speech, and enlarge general knowledge. Thus, help from parents or possibly older siblings in the education of deaf children is a resource that where possible might beneficially be exploited.

Many teachers believed that the home environment of a hearing-impaired child was a significant factor underlying his educational progress. My investigation did not include interviews with parents and, therefore, there was no first-hand information about the type of educational support they were giving or were prepared to give. Indeed research into this matter would be useful. There are, however, *a priori* reasons for believing that it might be the case that more parents of hearing-impaired children would give more help if they were fully aware of its significance. At present educational provision for the hearing impaired does not allow many resources to be devoted to advising and counselling parents of school-age children. In fact, most parent guidance services in Britain are directed towards the pre-school hearing-impaired child. It seems reasonable to assume, therefore, that parental support is an educational resource that has not yet been fully tapped. More consideration might be given to making a reality the ideal of 'parents as partners' in the education of the hearing-impaired schoolchild.

Seeking Help from Neighbouring Pupils. Doing extra work and seeking help outside the classroom are two ways of compensating for difficulties with school work but were options chosen by considerably less than half the hearing-impaired pupils interviewed: 'within-classroom' strategies were more commonly selected. One such tactic was to seek the help of a nearby pupil. Many of the hearing-impaired pupils and young people freely admitted that if they had a problem with their school work, they regularly and often routinely sought the help of normally hearing friends and neighbouring pupils. The following sample of comments of hearing-impaired pupils and young people of all ages illustrates this technique for coping:

Christine	9 years	'In Mrs Jones' class when I sit next to Gail and I ask her help me.'
Maria	12 years	'Often when I don't understand what to do, I give the person next to me a nudge and say "What do I do?".'
Cheryl	13 years	'My friend helps me, Tracy. She sometimes . . . she sits next to me, she tells me what's going on . . . "What page is it?" She tells me "44" like that. She has a book and she points her finger under the writing for me.'
Heidi	15 years	'The other girls help me. Sometimes I ask them — sometimes they just help me anyway.'
Peter	16 years	'I mean my mates, they're very helpful. They'll try and help me out sometimes — they help me to understand.'
Gwen	20 years	'If my friend hadn't been there I wouldn't have had the foggiest idea what was going on and I'd probably have had blank books to this day.'

The comment by Gwen suggests that on the spot help from a normally hearing friend might be critical to the successful integrated education of some hearing-impaired pupils.

Generally, seeking help from normally hearing classmates was the most frequent 'support' strategy used by hearing-impaired pupils, and one found by many of them to be invaluable. Not all deaf pupils, of course, welcome the help or surveillance of other pupils. The following comments of two deaf secondary pupils illustrate their need to devise their own individual ways of coping:

| Richard | 11 years | 'I try to do things by myself if I can, Sometimes if I ask someone I get it more wrong.' |
| Joanne | 12 years | 'I always sit by myself in the lessons because I don't want to be bothered with anyone sitting next to me. It makes me confused. I prefer to work things out in my own mind.' |

Clearly 'other-pupil' assistance should not be foisted on a hearing-impaired pupil unnecessarily. Nevertheless, as seen from the comments of both hearing-impaired pupils in this chapter and normally hearing pupils in Chapter 6, there exists a pool of assistance in any classroom among normally hearing pupils which many hearing-impaired pupils find extremely helpful. It would seem advisable, therefore, to encourage hearing-impaired pupils, particularly those who are shy and unforthcoming, to seek such help when required since it is likely to be freely and willingly given.

A further positive step which might be taken by teachers to encourage hearing-impaired pupils to seek help from neighbouring pupils would be to facilitate or contrive situations in which the hearing-impaired child is able to offer help to a normally hearing classmate. Observations and interviews suggested that the giving of help in lessons was not all in a one-way direction from normally hearing to hearing-impaired pupil. A few deaf pupils were pleased and proud to be able to state that they, on occasions, could give helpful assistance with class work to friends and neighbours. It must surely be the case that deaf pupils' feelings of self-worth, confidence and independence will be enhanced if they are able to give as well as receive help. It may well be worthwhile for teachers to be aware of hearing-impaired pupils' special strengths as well as their problems and to try to create situations where a deaf pupil can contribute to those with normal hearing.

Seeking Help from Teachers. Another important source of assistance and support for the hearing-impaired pupil in the ordinary class is, of course, the teacher herself. Hearing-impaired pupils varied in their willingness to ask teachers to help them with their difficulties. Some pupils had no inhibitions about seeking clarification of points from teachers even though this might mean making several trips to the teacher's desk during the course of a lesson. Other pupils, however, were less willing to draw attention to themselves and their difficulties and reluctant to 'bother' the teacher. The following sample of comments from hearing-impaired pupils and young people illustrates the contrasting viewpoints:

David	9 years	'If I don't know what to do, Miss Hampson will always help me.'
Mark	11 years	'Mrs Taylor says I'm to go to her if I don't understand, so I do and she helps me.'
Lorraine	13 years	'You feel stupid if you keep going up to Miss Peters and saying "I don't understand". I try to work things out for myself.'
Paul	13 years	'Mrs Growley is very kind but I don't like to go to her too much otherwise she might get angry.'
Peter	14 years	'The teachers always say "Right does everybody understand?" I can just put my hand up and ask him to explain it to me again. That's all you have to say. I'm not going to muck 'em about 'n do that when I can't do it.'
Susan	17 years	'I'd first try to work it out for myself, then I'd ask whoever was sitting next to me and then if they didn't know I'd ask the teacher. But that was a last resort. I didn't really like bothering the teacher too much.'

Fears such as those expressed above by Paul and Susan that they might be a nuisance to teachers if they sought extra help were not, according to the evidence from my interviews with teachers, generally justified. Most teachers stated that they welcomed requests for help from hearing-impaired pupils. Explaining or re-explaining points to a hearing-impaired pupil helped teachers feel they were making a genuine contribution to his educational progress. Requests for help from a hearing-impaired pupil reduced the uncertainty and ambiguity associated with teaching a pupil with a receptive communication handicap, which, as Chapter 5 demonstrated, was on occasions a problem for teachers. If a hearing-impaired pupil could be relied upon to ask questions when confused or uncertain teachers would be relieved of the responsibility of constantly checking his understanding. This is particularly important for teachers of large classes who have many pupils and a range of educational needs to think about.

That most teachers said they were happy to receive requests for help from deaf pupils in their class does not of course mean that they wanted to have their time monopolised by a hearing-impaired child. As seen in Chapter 5 teachers vary in the amount of extra or special help they were prepared to offer a hearing-impaired pupil in their class. Not all class teachers saw the need, nor could spare the time, to give much special attention to the deaf pupil. Thus the reluctance of some hearing-impaired pupils to seek help from teachers might in some cases be based on a *correctly* perceived idea that teachers do not want to devote too much of their time to just one or two deaf pupils in the class. Thus, despite what many teachers said, it might have been the case that in some classes, if hearing-impaired pupils had sought more special attention, they would have been regarded by their teachers as 'nuisances'.

Notwithstanding that it is unreasonable to expect that hearing-impaired pupils should have excessive attention in the ordinary class, the seeking of help from teachers is undoubtedly a strategy that is necessary if these pupils are to make satisfactory educational progress. It would seem from both the comments of deaf pupils and class teachers that on balance hearing-impaired pupils should be encouraged rather than discouraged from seeking such help. It might be useful to point out to hearing-impaired pupils that provided they are not unreasonably demanding requests for teacher help will not only benefit them but in all probability will help the teacher in *her* work.

Fear of being a burden to class teachers was not found to be the only reason why some hearing-impaired pupils were reluctant to ask for help from their class teachers. The comments of hearing-impaired pupils suggests that not wishing to draw attention to themselves and their special status in the presence of other pupils with normal hearing acts powerfully to inhibit requests for extra help. Many deaf pupils and young people acknowledged their difficulties and special problems but resented being 'shown up' in front of other pupils. These hearing-impaired pupils did not like to ask for special help, nor did they welcome too much unsolicited special attention. They preferred to remain ignorant rather than be the focus of 'too much fuss'. Despite this a certain amount of positive discrimination in the ordinary class may well be crucial to a deaf pupil's educational development and, therefore, it is important that he has positive attitudes towards special attention and extra help.

Hearing-impaired Pupils' Attitudes to Positive Discrimination

The hearing-impaired pupils who did not, generally speaking, welcome having attention drawn to their special problems in the ordinary class did not conform to any age or hearing loss category. The following statements of hearing-impaired pupils and young people of different ages and degrees of hearing loss illustrate the 'anti-positive discrimination' viewpoint and some of the reasons for pupils holding such views:

Mandy (severely deaf)	10 years	'Oh no . . . too much fuss. Don't like it, no. Too much fuss.'
Heidi (profoundly deaf)	15 years	'I hate it when the teachers say "Are you all right over there? Do you need any help?" It makes you feel stupid.'
Alison (moderately deaf)	16 years	'I don't like it when the teacher comes up to me because I get shown up. I don't like it.'
Elizabeth (moderately deaf)	17 years	'When they repeat everything and say "Did you hear that?" and you know you have to . . . all the class have to wait for you. I don't like that. You know when they're pointing out in front of everyone "And where are the two deaf girls?"'
Mandy (severely deaf)	17 years	One teacher, she used to drive me up the wall, 'cos she'd make a fuss and the other people are watching you and they think "Hmmm" — you know, they probably think I'm teacher's pet.'
Joanne (severely deaf)	17 years	'I was plucked out of the class and shown off to everybody. I didn't feel different until everybody told me . . . I was made to feel like an intelligent goldfish or something like that. They made me feel like a curiosity — "You know, she's learnt to

walk and talk. Isn't she doing well!" It ex-
asperates me that. It's very patronising.'

For these pupils special attention from class teachers served to publicly
emphasise their handicap in a way that was unacceptable to them. It was
evident that with some people on some occasions their perception of their
academic needs was overridden by a desire to be left alone by class
teachers. Reasons given for not wanting extra or special help from the
teacher, as can be seen from the citations, include not wanting to be made
to feel 'different' or 'stupid' in front of other pupils and not wanting to
appear to be getting special privileges or favouritism from the teachers.

Not wanting to appear to be the 'teacher's pet' is perhaps not an
unreasonable standpoint given the views concerning favouritism expressed
by normally hearing pupils cited in Chapter 6. In Chapter 6 it was seen
that some normally hearing pupils did indeed feel resentment at what
they perceived to be unduly favourable treatment accorded by teachers
to deaf pupils.

By no means all the views elicited from hearing-impaired pupils and
young people were so inimical to having extra help and special attention
from the teacher. The following comments from hearing-impaired young
people demonstrate the point because they show appreciation when the
extra help is available and complain when it is absent:

Julie (profoundly deaf)	15 years	'My form tutor, she very nice. She help me a lot. I like it when they help me.'
Mark (severely deaf)	16 years	'They more or less treated me like a normal pupil really but they never got me after and said "Did you get everything?" No nothing like that. I think it would have been better because sometimes I did miss out on the work, if you get what I mean.'
Paul (moderately deaf)	17 years	'The teacher knew like you was deaf so they spoke up a bit louder for you, plus they let you sit at the front. They give you a bit more than they would like you was normal.'
Paul (profoundly deaf)	18 years	'After teacher explain to me — all right.'
Nicky (severely deaf)	18 years	'Some of the teachers were very helpful; some weren't. I tell you what if I were at school now I'd complain like to my deaf teacher, but at school you know, you're a

bit scared of what's going on. Like my Maths teacher, he didn't help me at all.'

Julie   20 years   'There were some teachers who checked
(moderately deaf)   if you understood afterwards and I ap-
                                preciated that because you didn't have to
                                worry about it then.'

Kathy   22 years   'It didn't make me feel odd or anything
(profoundly deaf)   when the teachers helped me. I appreciated
                                it.'

Since differences of opinion among the hearing impaired about special educational attention in the ordinary classroom do not, according to the evidence, appear to be related to hearing loss, or even to apparent need for special help, then clearly personality factors such as their degree of self-consciousness and/or feelings of adequacy are relevant. It is also the case that there are 'ways' and 'ways' of offering special help to any 'special needs' pupil in an ordinary class. Some ways are likely to be more acceptable than others to all the pupils in the class. For example, the class teacher who does not draw too much public attention to a deaf pupil and his special needs is less likely to provoke feelings of resentment concerning the amount of special attention given to the deaf pupil and also be less likely to embarrass him. That unobtrusive support is preferred by deaf pupils to attention which makes them feel special or abnormal is indicated by the following comments of a number of deaf pupils and young people:

Andrew   11 years   'Sometimes they treat you like an ordinary
                         person. Sometimes they're a bit kind.'

Alison   12 years   'I like it when the teachers are kind to me
                         but I don't like it if they make too much
                         fuss.'

Elizabeth   13 years   'I want to be treated as normal, but if only
                         they'd understand!'

Mark   16 years   'I wouldn't like too much special attention
                         during lessons. It's just I would have ap-
                         preciated if they say come to me afterwards
                         and just quiet-like said "Did you miss out
                         anything?" And if I did I could have told
                         them.'

Paul   17 years   'The teachers, they'd help you out and
                         make sure I was all right, but then they'd

treat me normal. I don't want anything
special.'

The comment by Elizabeth indicates a certain amount of ambivalence among deaf pupils towards special attention given by class teachers. This ambivalence, along with the differing views of hearing-impaired pupils on positive discrimination in the ordinary class, highlights the basic dilemma in integrating deaf pupils, namely, that it is logically impossible to treat pupils with special needs 'normally' and at the same time cater for their special needs. On the one hand, it is recognised that the hearing-impaired pupil in the ordinary class is likely to need some special attention from the class teacher if he is to make adequate educational progress. On the other hand my research findings indicate that too much special attention can, in the case of some deaf pupils, have an undesirable effect on their self-conceptions and their view of themselves in relation to others. In the light of these findings efforts might be made to sensitise teachers to the kinds of feelings that a hearing-impaired pupil might have when he is singled out for special attention in the ordinary class and to encourage teachers to be careful to offer extra help sympathetically and unobtrusively. Furthermore, hearing-impaired pupils might usefully be helped through counselling to accept more easily their special difficulties and to have greater confidence in themselves in spite of their problems. That some pupils were happy to receive special help from teachers indicates that positive discrimination in favour of the hearing-impaired pupil will not necessarily in itself be perceived as stigmatising.

Ordinary Class/Special Class Placement: Full-time Integration/ Part-time Integration: Hearing-impaired Pupils' Preferences

The discussion so far in this chapter has been confined to hearing-impaired pupils' perceptions of their experiences in ordinary classes and has not dealt with their perceptions of experiences in special classes. This is because the focus of the study was on the integrated education of hearing-impaired pupils and not on what happens in the separate special class. However, the majority of hearing-impaired pupils who featured in the investigation were placed in units within ordinary schools and spent some proportion of their school time in a special class with a teacher of the deaf. Only a small percentage, 12 per cent (six pupils), were individually placed in a neighbourhood school. Whilst it was not the purpose of the investigation to make a detailed comparative study of, say, unit provision vs. individual integration, none the less many of the hearing-impaired pupils and young people who were placed in a unit expressed views as to whether they preferred to be in the special class or the ordinary class and whether or not they liked to be in a school alongside a number of other pupils with hearing impairments. (As stated in Chapter 3, as a by-product of the investigation a summary of the educational and social advantages and disadvantages of different forms of integrated provision was produced — see Appendix 1.) Similarly, those pupils individually placed full time in their local school had ideas and opinions about being the only deaf pupil in their school. It is appropriate, therefore, to present and discuss the views of the hearing-impaired pupils and young people on these aspects of their educational placement. As stated in Chapter 3, educators responsible for the integrated education of hearing-impaired children have different ideas about what constitutes an optimum education for deaf children in the ordinary school and this accounts for the wide variety of practices of integrated education for the deaf. Some 'consumer' feedback, therefore, at least about some different types of integrated provision shoud be of practical benefit to educators.

The majority of hearing-impaired pupils featuring in the investigation, 88 per cent (44 pupils), were placed in units. These pupils spent 60–90 per cent of their school time in ordinary classes but they all spent some time in a separate special class with a teacher of the deaf. Some of these pupils had, in their earlier years of schooling prior to the investigation, spent all, or nearly all, of their school day in a separate special class.

Just as viewpoints varied, for example, concerning special attention from class teachers, so did hearing-impaired pupils' opinions differ about the relative merits of being in ordinary and special classes. A large proportion of the 44 pupils stated that they enjoyed their time spent in the special class. The following sample of comments from unit pupils and former unit pupils refers to their time in the special class and reveals that they found the academic work easier to cope with when taught in a small group by a teacher of the deaf:

Cheryl	7 years	'Here it better. I like it with Mrs Settle. I can do the work.'
Christine	9 years	'It's easy, the work.'
Sally-Anne	12 years	'It's nice and quiet in here. You can do your work better.'
Lorraine	13 years	'You understand the teacher better in the unit — it's not so hard.'
Deborah	13 years	'The teacher understands us better.'

Paul	18 years	'Miss Payne help me with my lessons. It help me a lot.'
Susan	18 years	'I believe it helped me particularly with class work. I appreciated the help I got from unit teachers. I couldn't always catch everything in lessons. I wouldn't have minded spending more time there.'
Kathy	21 years	'They help me most in the unit. I think English and Maths ought to be in the unit all the time, because in the unit I could understand them easy.'
Julia	21 years	'I would like to spend more time in the unit. It was easier.'

The views quoted above suggest that not only did these deaf pupils believe they understood their academic work better when taught in the unit, but also that the unit provided an invaluable support service for their work in ordinary lessons. Several pupils and young people were very positive about the unit for social as well as educational reasons. In the unit they were with other children whom they knew well and with whom they shared the common problem of having a hearing handicap. This for some reason was very reassuring. The following statements from hearing-impaired pupils and young people illustrate their feelings:

David	9 years	'Here you're with your friends.'
Cheryl	13 years	'It's smashing here, you're with everyone you know.'
Elizabeth	13 years	'I like it in the unit best because then I'm with Debbie and Lorraine.'
Susan	17 years	'I liked to be in a school where there were others who had the same problem as me — it reassured me that I was not the only one.'
Julia	21 years	'I hate to be the only deaf person in school. I feel lonely.'

Thus, among some of those who had attended ordinary schools with units there was a belief in the need for relationships with others who were similarly handicapped.

That positive views were expressed by most of the interviewees about the time spent in the special class does not mean that they would have liked to be in the special class all the time. Nor does it mean that deaf pupils and former pupils had no reservations about being educated in the special rather than the ordinary class. Many hearing-impaired pupils and young people had mixed feelings about receiving their tuition in a unit. Discussion with these pupils clearly demonstrated that it was possible for them to appreciate the special tuition offered in the unit, and the comfort and security of being in a small, special class, and yet at the same time be critical of some of the disadvantages of this form of provision.

Pupils gave a number of reasons for disliking units. For example, that the school and unit were generally some distance from the pupils' homes caused several problems in the opinion of some deaf pupils. These problems included the long journey to school, the stigma of leaving home and arriving at school in special transport, and not being able to attend their local school with their neighbourhood friends. Other criticisms of unit provision were: over-protection both academically and socially; over-surveillance; a relative lack of challenge and stimulus; and separation from normally hearing friends. The following statements, mainly, though not entirely, from older pupils and those who had left school, exemplify these problems:

Maria	12 years	'I like it in the ordinary class, because you can look out of the window and think your thoughts.'
Alison	12 years	'I don't like going on the mini bus really because it makes me feel I've had an accident. And the people see me in the coach and they stare at me and I don't like it. The children in my road look at me.'
Peter	14 years	'I come here in a taxi, I hate it. I don't like travelling every morning — every morning — every night — it's awful.'
Maria	16 years	'One advantage of the ordinary class is that teachers don't spend as much time on a thing as Mrs Hope (unit teacher) would. But I've got used to it now. The thing is in the ordinary class you have to *think* more about the work. I think that's better, getting your brain working.'
Peter	16 years	'I prefer to be in the ordinary class, really, because I'm with other people that haven't got the problems, so that helps me a bit better. I try to overcome the problem.'

Dale	16 years	'I like being outside best but it's easier inside.'
Mandy	17 years	'At the phu I did tend to go to Miss Payne for help, not the class teacher. I think it made me a bit lazy.'
Michael	18 years	'I could've walked to school with my friends and come home for dinner. I come from a different area, you know what I mean. They're snobs round there, 'cos they all talk about you know and this lad's got this and this lad's got that and a swimming pool at the back of the garden and that.'
Nicky	18 years	'If I'd gone to my local school, like, I could have hopped over the fence and been there in three minutes. And I'd got to know a lot of people from round here like.'
Maxine	18 years	'When I go to secondary school I was mostly into the hearing classes. I realised I didn't understand some things, but it helped me. And I got independence with the hearing people.'
Darren	17 years	'Of course for the five years at Grove Park school we (unit pupils) all stuck together, we all sat together, we all went around together and not meet the others.'

The comments cited above illustrate that older pupils and those who had left school were more willing to criticise their schooling than younger ones attending school. This is almost certainly because older pupils, and particularly those who have left school, are more able to stand back from the situation, reflect on their experiences and with their more mature understanding and awareness, offer critical comment. Moreover, those who no longer attend school are less afraid to 'speak out' about their education because they are no longer subject to the school's authority.

The research evidence just quoted and discussed concerning units refers to types of unit provision where the hearing-impaired pupils spent most of their school time in ordinary classes. There were pupils, however, who in their earlier years of schooling had had the experience of being educated full time, or almost full time, in a segregated special class. These hearing-impaired pupils and former pupils unanimously condemned the separate special class both on academic, social and personal grounds. The following sample of observations by older secondary deaf pupils and young people who had left school illustrates their position:

Alison	16 years	'That's wrong. They should never have done that — kept us away from others.'
Paul	17 years	'I think that at Sandway (segregated special class) it softens you up a bit so when you go out, you're not used to it. I think it softens you up. It's a bit too protective. And the thing was, I didn't get on with my teacher but where else could I go?'
Nicky	18 years	'It was terrible when we were cooped up with Mr Stanley (unit teacher) all the time. I didn't get to know no one and my Maths was dreadful.'
Kathy	22 years	'We were put in with the hearing for art — OK — music, games. But it's the proper lessons we need and that's where we should be — with the hearing children and it keeps us on the same level. It doesn't pull us down. The teacher wasn't teaching us what we needed and then again we were all different ages so we all had to learn differnt things and I don't think the teacher could cope with that you know. And I was teaching the others which wasn't doing me any good.'

These pupils felt over-protected, over-surveilled, under-stimulated, deprived of the opportunity for contact with normally hearing pupils, and in some cases 'trapped' with one teacher for several years with whom they did not 'get on'.

There is probably no escaping the problem of over-protection associated with separate special classes. Some hearing-impaired pupils, because very young, linguistically retarded, or having other handicaps, may well need this special protection. However, the views of 'straightforward' deaf pupils and former pupils cited above, throw considerable doubt on the wisdom of selecting segregated special class provision for the majority of hearing-impaired pupils in ordinary schools.

Those pupils or former pupils who were individually placed in their local schools, of course, had no experience at all of being educated in a special class. Discussion with these pupils suggested, however, that they might have appreciated being in a school where there were some other deaf pupils. It is significant that all but one of those who were individually integrated expressed a wish to know someone else who was deaf. There were only six such pupils in my investigation and, therefore, it would be unwise to draw firm conclusions from such a small sample. However, that five out of six felt some regret about not knowing anyone their own age who was deaf is a finding that cannot be discounted too easily. The one who did not see a need for deaf friends, a moderately deaf top junior girl, had a very low sense of awareness of her deafness. She attached no more significance to the fact that she wore a hearing aid than that her best friend wore glasses. The other five individually integrated pupils who felt some need for contact with someone similarly afflicted with a hearing loss were more aware of their deafness. The views of all five will be given to demonstrate the nature of their feelings on this matter. The citations all derive from the later interviews; the ideas and feelings of these older pupils and former pupils are similar to those expressed during the earlier investigation; their comments, however, reflect greater maturity and richness of expression:

Kevin	11 years	'Well I've got a friend now, Kathy. She's only seven but she lives near where I live. We're both deaf.'
Andrew	16 years	'I would like to have a friend who was deaf just for a bit of help and knock around with and go to places 'n that. We could talk about how we're going on. They have a problem and I've got over it, passed it and I can tell them what to do, sort of thing, and they could tell me if I had a problem they've got over.'
Mark	16 years	'Yes, I would like a deaf friend. I think if I did we could become good friends and we could have shared each other's problems, because we would know each other you see. It would probably have been better.'
Joanne	17 years	'It would have helped me especially when I was younger to have other deaf children to identify with. I think at some stage to have somebody else there who was deaf my

		own age . . . I think it would have helped to chat to, to pine to, like me, not somebody identical but somebody who had something of the same problem as me.'
Gwen	20 years	'I don't know anyone who is deaf and at least I'd have someone to talk to if I did get mad. I wish I did know someone.'

That these deaf young people expressed a need to know someone deaf like themselves does not, of course, mean that they would have preferred to be educated in a unit or in a special school. Neither does it mean that they felt isolated or alienated from the world of the normally hearing. Their comments do seem, however, to point to a possible drawback of full-time individual integration for the deaf. It may be necessary for educators to take steps to compensate for this drawback of not knowing someone else with a similar handicap by putting individually integrated deaf pupils in touch with one or two other children of similar age and handicap.

In general then, that there was a mixture of views, and indeed mixed views, among the hearing-impaired pupils and young people about their educational provision in ordinary schools underlines indelibly the view that educators cannot do everything for all pupils all the time and that there are indeed simultaneously inherent strengths and weaknesses in different types of integrated provision. That these dilemmas cannot easily be resolved is demonstrated by the lack of consensus among hearing-impaired pupils and former pupils about different types of placement. Given that hearing-impaired pupils have views on the matter, though, it might be worthwhile, particularly with older pupils, for educators to consult with them further and discuss also the pros and cons of different forms of provision. An appreciation and understanding of a pupil's views might be useful to educators when deciding the educational programme for that deaf pupil in the ordinary school.

PART 2: ACADEMIC INTEGRATION

As seen in Part 1 of this chapter the kinds of strategies hearing-impaired pupils select in order to cope in the ordinary classroom, for example copying the work of neighbouring pupils, seeking help from the teacher, playing up, etc. can be seen as a measure of how well or how badly adapted a pupil is to the ordinary class given that he has a hearing handicap. The 'well-adjusted' hearing-impaired pupil, it can be argued, is one who adopts 'sensible' strategies for coping in the ordinary class, that is, those which will help and not hinder his academic development; one who appreciates positive discrimination because he knows it is likely to be to his educational benefit. Perhaps a more objective way of judging whether or not a pupil is coping effectively in the ordinary class — is successfully integrated — is in terms of the level of his academic attainments. Now, as explained in Chapter 4, it was beyond the scope of the research objectives to make a detailed study of the educational attainments of the hearing-impaired pupils: this would have involved extremely time-consuming procedures of assessing each pupil on measures such as reading ability, speech intelligibility, maths attainments, etc., but the follow-up study did open up the possibility of some comparisons of educational attainments. The public examination results of all those hearing-impaired pupils who had completed five years of secondary education, 38 in number, were collected and recorded. (This number includes eight hearing-impaired young people who featured in the 1977/8 investigation but not in the follow-up study. The examination results of these former pupils were obtained from school records.) It was thus possible to compare the academic attainments of these 38 pupils with national norms of pupil achievement.

The Academic Attainments of the Hearing-impaired Pupil: Evidence of Normalisation?

It can be seen from Table 7.1 that the attainments of the subject group of hearing-impaired pupils fall below the standards achieved nationally by their age peers.

It might be concluded from the data in Table 7.1, therefore, that these deaf pupils were not fully educationally integrated because not academically 'average'. However, there are several points to make in respect of these attainments which should make the reader wary of drawing quick, firm conclusions to this effect from the data.

First, given that deafness is a fundamental educational handicap and given the almost inevitable retarding effect that a substantial hearing loss has on language development and the acquisition of knowledge, it is probably unrealistic to expect the academic and intellectual achievements of hearing-impaired pupils *at the age of 16 years* to match those of normally hearing 16 year olds. This is likely to be the case wherever deaf

Table 7.1: A Comparision of Formal Academic Attainments at Age 16 Years of 38 Hearing-impaired Pupils who Featured in the Study with National Attainments for All Pupils

	5 or more GCE 'O' levels	1-4 GCE 'O' levels or CSE Grade 1	1 or more CSE other grades	No graded result
Attainments of school pupils in England 1981/2[a]	28.4%	27.4%	35.6%	9.6%
Attainments of 38 hearing-impaired pupils 1979-84 who featured in the study	–	31.5%	39.9%	29.6%

Source: a. DES 1984.

pupils are educated and however much positive discrimination they receive. Second, relating more specifically to the subject group of 38 hearing-impaired pupils, nine of these, albeit a small proportion, had received the earlier part of their education in a special school. In each case placement in a special school at the age of five years was considered to be the most appropriate provision. Therefore, the ordinary school was not the only educational environment affecting the achievements of these particular pupils and hence not the only influence on the overall attainments of the hearing-impaired group. Third, in the case of hearing-impaired pupils who attended the secondary school in LEA 'C' (see Chapter 4), whilst they did not on average achieve national norms, they were, according to the school records, none the less, equalling or nearly equalling the average standards of attainment within that school. Fourth, as was pointed out by the teachers of the deaf working in the two secondary schools with units, there was a tendency, certainly between the years 1978–81 when jobs were more plentiful than since that time, for some of the hearing-impaired pupils to leave school before taking public examinations. This was a deliberate strategy on their part, generally supported by their teachers, to 'beat the rush' into the job market in the summer when the majority of 16 year olds left school. According to the unit teachers, a few of these hearing-impaired pupils could have been predicted to get formal educational qualifications had they stayed on at school and sat the public examinations. Finally, a matter of relevance is that whilst the attainments of the hearing-impaired pupils were, overall, below the national average, they were, arguably, not substantially lower than national norms of achievement. If it is agreed that this is so, then the picture presented by my investigation of the academic standards of hearing-impaired pupils in ordinary schools does not confirm the findings of, say, Conrad (1979) who reports that hearing-impaired pupils, wherever placed, attain *well* below the levels achieved by the school population as a whole.

Clearly, the results of my study, however interpreted, offer educators no cause for complacency. So long as deaf pupils are failing to reach their educational potential sustained efforts are needed in order to improve standards. Informal talks with the teachers of the deaf responsible for the overall education of those pupils featuring in the investigation indicated a belief that many of these pupils were underachieving in the sense that their attainments did not match their intelligence. A few hearing-impaired pupils, according to their specialist teachers of the deaf, produced results at the age of 16 which were 'disappointing', given that they were considered to be 'bright'.

The results from my survey of the academic attainments of some of the hearing-impaired pupils featuring in the investigation confirm the need for positive discrimination in favour of deaf pupils in ordinary schools if those pupils are to be given the opportunity to fulfil their educational potential. A form which this positive discrimination might take is extending the time period of compulsory education for deaf pupils. An extension to a leaving age of, say, 18 years, with appropriate financial allowances made to the pupils, could provide valuable 'catching up' time for deaf pupils. It is gratifying that Sir Keith Joseph, Secretary of State for Education, recently (BATOD Conference, 10 November 1984) acknowledged that educational development was slowed down by a hearing impairment and that the question of allowing deaf pupils extra time for their education should be considered.

Hearing-impaired Pupils' and Young Peoples' Perceptions of Their Academic Attainments

The findings of my own research investigation do not, of course, refute the findings of other investigations into the academic achievements of deaf pupils which are to the effect that such pupils do not attain as well as normally hearing pupils, other things being equal. A substantial hearing loss imposes serious limitations on a pupil's ability to succeed at school. That this is 'objectively' the case does not mean that hearing-impaired pupils 'subjectively' feel a sense of injustice because their hearing loss has held them back academically. It seemed to be interesting and important, therefore, to discover whether the deaf pupils who featured in the investigation believed that there was an association between hearing loss and educational retardation and whether they felt that this was unfair.

The evidence based on the 1983/4 interviews with 40 hearing-impaired pupils and former pupils indicates that their opinions were divided on this topic. Sixteen believed that their deafness held them back academically. Not all of these, however, felt this to be a matter of serious regret. Some examples will be cited of comments from these hearing-impaired pupils and young people which characterise their views and feelings:

Mark	16 years	'It has held me back a bit, I'm sure.'
Andrew	16 years	'I think so really. If I could hear I can know what's going on a lot and I can revise for a test or whatever much better.'
Mandy	17 years	'I've not done as well, no, but I've done alright. I'm not bothered.'
Joanne	17 years	'I could be so much better if I were not deaf and I feel frustrated about that.'
Paul	18 years	'If I not deaf I go to university. My brother go to Birmingham University.'
Kathy	21 years	'No, I not do well at school. I don't talk easy and it's not worth it. I can't do the English.'
Kathy	22 years	'Well, that's a hard one. I never thought really. Yes, I suppose it did — but I'm not unhappy with what I did at school.'

Reactions from among these interviewees varied from frustration to irritation to a tolerant acceptance of the fact that had it not been for their hearing loss they would have done better at school. It was rather surprising, given the 'objective' fact that deafness has a detrimental effect on educational attainments, that more of these young people did not feel more embittered, unhappy or resentful. What was even more surprising, however, was that 21 out of the remaining 24 made no connection between their hearing loss and their academic attainments, even though in some cases these attainments were very low. (The remaining three interviewees could not give an intelligible response on this matter.) They were either ignorant of the link between a severe hearing impairment and linguistic and intellectual development or they did not believe that in their case it made any difference to what they achieved. It was not that these deaf young people were unaware of the day-to-day problems caused by their hearing loss, as seen in Part 1 of this chapter, but rather that there was little or no consciousness of the long-term effect of a substantial hearing loss on educational progress. The following are some examples of statements which typify this lack of awareness:

Christine	14 years	'I don't know.'
Alison	16 years	'No, I don't think so. If I didn't listen in class my friend would tell me what the teacher'd said . . . I do as well as the others.'
Elizabeth	17 years	'I'm not very clear really. I never bothered with school work. I didn't think about getting qualifications.'
Lorraine	17 years	'I don't think it can have made a difference 'cos I do just as well as anybody else.'
Julie	20 years	'I did all right — according to my brains. I don't think I'd have done better just for being hearing.'
Gwen	20 years	'I *could* do the work. I just didn't want to.'

A broad conclusion, therefore, that can be drawn from my interviews with hearing-impaired pupils and former pupils on their feelings about the relationship between a hearing loss and academic attainments is that most of them were either unaware of such a relationship or were not unduly concerned about it. This finding perhaps seems surprising given how 'well-known' it is among educators of deaf children that even a mild hearing loss can cause educational retardation and that a severe or profound loss can greatly affect a child's linguistic, intellectual and hence academic attainments. Furthermore, hearing-impaired pupils in ordinary schools might be expected to be particularly aware of their academic differences from pupils with normal hearing given that they are in the milieu of normal standards.

An explanation of why many hearing-impaired pupils do not know about the effects of deafness on educational achievements may simply be that no one has told them of this and they have been unable to deduce it for themselves. The same probably holds true for some pupils who are deemed to be 'socially disadvantaged' or 'educationally deprived'. Unless the identity tag and all its alleged implications are made explicit to such a pupil he will probably remain ignorant of the effects of his home environment or deafness on his educational attainments. Given that many of those who featured in the investigation were not, in terms of public examination results, very far behind pupils with normal hearing, and rarely the worst in the class, it was presumably relatively easy to sustain the view that a hearing loss was on occasions an irritating classroom difficulty rather than a major educational handicap.

It might perhaps be considered desirable that hearing-impaired pupils do not feel embittered or resentful that their deafness represents a serious educational handicap. Some people might welcome the idea that deaf pupils feel so 'normal' that they are not aware of this significant difference between themselves and other pupils with normal hearing. It could be argued, however, that it might be beneficial if deaf pupils were more conscious of their disadvantaged position when it comes to getting those valuable and much prized education goals — formal academic qualifications. An awareness that a permanent and substantial hearing loss represents an educational set-back which remains with a deaf pupil for the whole of his school career might be a necessary condition for motivating him to compensate for this disadvantage in some way. A stronger realisation of the academic implications of the handicap of deafness may persuade some hearing-impaired pupils to work harder and to make a special effort to, say, improve their ability to read and acquire information through reading; to be more positive about seeking help from others such as parents, teachers and other pupils; to welcome more wholeheartedly special attention and extra help from teachers.

The extent to which teachers should raise the consciousness levels of their deaf pupils concerning their educational handicap is, of course, problematic. Teachers of the deaf, for example, may not want to draw too much of their deaf pupils' attention to the gravity, in educational terms, of their handicap for fear of depressing them or making them feel stigmatised. Any counselling of hearing-impaired pupils along these lines would need to be tactful and sensitive. None the less, in the case of some, or perhaps all deaf pupils, it may be unjust *not* to point out to them that they start school with a disadvantage which persists throughout their education. Therefore, if they are to stand an equal chance of succeeding at school, extra efforts on their part as well as on the part of their teachers are required. That this point may need to be made more explicitly to hearing-impaired pupils is borne out by the evidence presented earlier in this chapter that many of the interviewees did not see any special reason why they should spend more time on homework, on extra reading, etc. A deaf pupil is unlikely to make extra effort unless he sees the need to do so.

It has already been suggested that if hearing-impaired pupils do not achieve normal academic standards then they could be perceived as not completely 'normalised'. The findings of my investigation, however, if generalisable, suggest that many, though not all, hearing-impaired pupils in ordinary schools, despite having the yardstick of 'normal' academic standards plainly available to them, do not have a strong sense of their academic 'abnormality'. (It is, I believe, significant that most of the hearing-impaired pupils and former pupils featuring in the investigation were not as aware of nor perturbed by their 'abnormality' as some of the research evidence cited in Chapter 2 suggested (see pp. 35–7). They were certainly not as disturbed about their 'failure' to reach normally hearing standards as the 'anti-integrationists' have argued (see Chapter 3, pp. 65–8).) Paradoxically, it would seem that if hearing-impaired pupils were made more aware of their 'difference' from others in relation to the attainment of academic success, they might be better motivated to aim for higher standards, work harder, and thus achieve more 'normality' in the long run. This demonstrates yet again that there is a distinction between the process of normalising and the ultimate goal of 'normality'.

Part 3: SOCIAL INTEGRATION

In this final part of Chapter 7 consideration will be given to what some people would regard as the crucial goal in the education of deaf children, namely, the integration of the hearing-impaired individual into the wider society. One of the major reasons given for educating hearing-impaired pupils in ordinary schools is that it accustoms these pupils to the hearing-speaking world at a very early age and, furthermore, that it gives at least some of those with normal hearing the chance to come to terms with others who have a hearing handicap. The amount of contact between hearing-impaired and normally hearing pupils in ordinary schools and the quality of the relationships is, of course, important in itself but perhaps it is even more important as a basis for the later integration of the hearing-impaired individual into adult society. Using evidence from my research, therefore, the nature and quality of interaction between hearing-impaired and normally hearing pupils will be examined from the viewpoint of the hearing-impaired pupil. Then a consideration in broader terms will be made of the perceptions of the hearing-impaired individual concerning his sense of social identity, that is, his view of himself in relation to others in the wider society. The discussion on this matter will draw heavily on the evidence derived from interviews with deaf young people who have left school and who are, so to speak, 'in society'.

Relationships with Normally Hearing Pupils

As already seen, one of the principal reasons given by hearing-impaired young people for preferring an education in an ordinary rather than a special school was for the opportunity to meet and mix with normally hearing pupils. Interviews with hearing-impaired pupils and young people and observations in classrooms led to the broad conclusion that on the whole deaf pupils had satisfactory relationships with their normally hearing peers. The extent to which they interacted and made friends with normally hearing pupils varied quite considerably from pupil to pupil and it is illuminating, therefore, to examine the different responses.

The interviews with older pupils and young adults, 1983–4, proved invaluable in supplying deeper insights into the social relationships of deaf pupils in school. Their ability to reflect on and articulate the social aspects of ordinary school experiences was far greater than that of younger deaf children. Furthermore, since it is generally believed that social relationships between handicapped and non-handicapped pupils become more problematic as children grow older, it was particularly beneficial to draw on the experiences of hearing-impaired individuals who were currently experiencing, or who had just recently experienced, life in school during the 'difficult' adolescent phase.

At both stages of the research the hearing-impaired pupils came into three broad categories in respect of their relations with other pupils in the ordinary school. At one extreme were unit pupils who interacted minimally with normally hearing pupils and selected all their friends and close associates from the deaf group within the school. Then there were unit hearing-impaired pupils who had reasonably close association with both normally hearing and hearing-impaired pupils. At the other extreme were unit pupils whose friends were drawn predominantly from those with normal hearing and who strove as far as possible to separate themselves from other deaf pupils in the school. Also included in this category are the deaf pupils who were individually integrated into their local school and who had no choice but to select their friends from among the normally hearing group.

Those individuals who claimed to mix only with other deaf pupils in school were very much in the minority: there were only two out of the 50. Typical of their reports on their social experiences during the secondary stage are the following comments:

Julia	21 years	'I only go with deaf at school. I didn't
(severely deaf)		bother with hearing. I prefer to go with
		deaf, it's easy with them.'
Janet	22 years	'At school I only had deaf friends — no
(moderately deaf)		hearing. I didn't get on as well with them
		so it wasn't really good.'

A further two deaf young people with profound hearing losses were very close to the position of Janet and Julia in that their friends in school were selected predominantly from among the deaf group. Typical statements referring to their secondary school years demonstrate this to be the case:

Julie	15 years	'I know some who are hearing — not a lot.
		My best friends are deaf.'
Heidi	22 years	'I had one main friend who was hearing.
		The rest were deaf ones.'

The moderately deaf person, Janet, who mixed only with other deaf pupils, came from a deaf family and this might explain why she felt more at ease at school with other deaf pupils. The three others who mixed almost exclusively with other deaf pupils had manifest communication difficulties. This might in part explain why they preferred on the whole to be with other people with a similar kind of problem.

Common sense might suggest that, generally, pupils with the greatest hearing losses and least intelligible speech would be more likely to avoid contact with the normally hearing because of awkward and possibly embarrassing communication problems, and that those with the least hearing losses would have the most contact with the normally hearing. This, however, was not entirely the case. In the next and largest category of hearing-impaired pupils, that is, those who had several deaf and several normally hearing friends, there were six profoundly deaf pupils. All of these six pupils had obvious communication difficulties in that they often did not understand 'first time' what was said to them and they had speech which was deviant in several respects. Some examples of their comments will illustrate their capability of sustaining relationships with normally hearing peers:

Cheryl	13 years	'I've three best friends really. There's
(profoundly deaf)		Alison (deaf) and Tracy (normally hearing)
		and Sharon (normally hearing). We all go

		together in a group and talk about things going on.'
Christine (profoundly deaf)	14 years	'I've got some very good friends in my form.'
Kathy (profoundly deaf)	21 years	'Most of my friends at school were hearing and I could understand them easy.'

These comments indicate that communication problems between deaf and normally hearing pupils were not an insurmountable barrier to the development and sustaining of social relationships. It would seem that hearing loss *per se* is not the only factor governing the ability of deaf pupils to make friends with normally hearing pupils. Other factors may well include personality. The comment of one profoundly deaf young person suggests that she believed her outgoing personality helped her become incorporated into the hearing group at school:

Kathy	22 years	'I can't help being friends with people. I can't help it. At school I didn't play so much with the deaf ones — well, only now and again. I played with the hearing ones. I used to throw myself into it.'

That qualities such as 'personality' and 'self-confidence' were critical to the nature and quality of deaf pupils' relations with normally hearing classmates was confirmed by many teachers.

Another factor which emerged as significant in facilitating social relationships between hearing-impaired pupils and normally hearing pupils was the degree of commitment to the ideal of 'normalisation' on the part of deaf pupils. This commitment seemed to propel some hearing-impaired pupils to make an effort to contact and be friends with other pupils with normal hearing. The comment of a severely deaf secondary pupil exemplifies this commitment:

Alison	13 years	'I want to stay with the hearing people all the time because I want more listen, you know, and talk properly. Better to get with hearing people.'

A wish to become more 'normal', as seen earlier, was an important factor underlying many hearing-impaired pupils' preferences to be placed in ordinary rather than in special schools. Given such a desire for normality it is more likely that a hearing-impaired pupil in an ordinary school will be well motivated to associate with those who are 'normal'.

Variations in the relative amount of contact hearing-impaired pupils were found to have with normally hearing peers, and variations in the nature and quality of those relationships, did not just depend on the personal qualities of the deaf person. Opportunities for association between the two groups were clearly of great significance for friendship formation. The more opportunities there were for a deaf pupil to mix with the normally hearing, the more likely he was to select friends from among the normally hearing group. That this was so is illustrated by the following statements of unit pupils who spent less and less time in the special class as they progressed through their secondary school:

Peter	16 years	'Most of my mates are hearing. I used to knock around with Dale and Alan but now with me being in the ordinary classes more I'm with the others more.'
Lorraine	17 years	'I went around at first with Debbie (unit) and Elizabeth (unit). Then in the fourth year and in the fifth year I went around with girls who weren't in the phu.'
Maxine	18 years	'Me and Amanda were very close friends because we've always been together in the phu. When I was more in the hearing classes I had more friends who was hearing.'

In the final category of hearing-impaired pupils, that is those who mixed for the most part with normally hearing pupils, were those deaf pupils placed individually in their local school and who of course, had, in school, no choice but to select friends and acquaintances from those who had normal hearing. The only alternative for these deaf pupils would have been to have no friends at all in school. None of the six individually integrated hearing-impaired pupils could be said to be socially isolated. All six reported that they had close friends in school and that this was so was confirmed both by teachers and normally hearing pupils in the respective schools. There were also some unit pupils, 15 in all, who had options as to who to form relationships with yet who tried as much as possible to dissociate themselves from the other deaf pupils in the school. It would seem that these pupils identified with the normally hearing group either because they aspired to be 'normal' or because they felt they were 'normal'. Comments such as the following illustrate these preferences:

Peter	14 years	'I don't need to knock about with deaf people — all my friends are hearing.'
Richard	16 years	'All my friends have normal hearing. I don't think of being with deaf people — I've nothing in common with them.'
Alison	16 years	'All my friends are out of the unit, definitely out. I've quite a few friends, I like to be with hearing people because I don't really like people knowing I'm deaf.'
Mandy	17 years	'I never felt I had to have anybody deaf around me. I like to be with hearing people.'

Pupils such as these resented their 'unit' identity tag and were trying as much as possible to shake it off.

Thus, the willingness and ability of the hearing-impaired pupil in the ordinary school to interact with and form close social relationships with normally hearing pupils might depend on any one or more of a number of factors. These factors include the type of educational placement, the hearing-impaired pupil's hearing loss and ability to communicate orally, his personality, the strength of his ideological commitment to be seen as 'normal'. These different variables might combine in a complex way to influence or facilitate the extent to which hearing-impaired pupils in ordinary schools associate with those who have normal hearing. No hearing-impaired pupil found it impossible to interact at some level with normally hearing classmates. The majority of deaf pupils mixed regularly with normally hearing pupils and often made friends with them. These findings in relation to the feelings and perspectives of hearing-impaired pupils and young people are paralleled by those reported in Chapter 6 where social integration was examined from the point of view of the normally hearing pupil. In Chapter 6 it was demonstrated that there was no shortage of normally hearing pupils willing to be sociable towards, and friends with, hearing-impaired classmates.

That there were, in the main, good relations between hearing-impaired and normally hearing pupils should be encouraging to those wishing to promote integration policies in education. This is not to deny, however, that in the eyes of the hearing-impaired pupils and young people, there were on occasions some problems in their relations with the majority group in the ordinary school. The two major 'problem areas' referred to were difficulties of communication and being teased or in some way made fun of.

Difficulties of Communication

The majority of hearing-impaired pupils and young people were aware that on some occasions they had communication difficulties when interacting with the normally hearing in school. These communication difficulties could cause them shame, embarrassment and frustration. Several hearing-impaired pupils referred to occasional feelings of frustration when attempting to communicate with hearing peers. The comments of severely and profoundly deaf secondary pupils cited below illustrate these feelings:

Alison	12 years	'An' I say it sometimes *ten* times and she (normally hearing) goes "What did you say?" and I say it again and she doesn't get it and I get fed up when that happens.'
Susan	12 years	'I get angry sometimes when I say "What?" to my friends and they say, "Never mind, forget it!".'
Cheryl	13 years	'Sometimes they talk so fast. I'm not getting it.'
Deborah	13 years	'Usually I'm very quiet 'cos I'm frightened when I'm with the hearing girls and won't say it right and they'll laugh.'

Generally, however, these problems were not so severe as to cause persistent suffering and humiliation. A common response is typified by the following words of a severely deaf young person:

| Sally-Anne | 17 years | 'You have to learn to live with these problems when you're deaf.' |

Accepting communication difficulties as an inevitable consequence of a substantial hearing impairment was a characteristic reaction from the hearing-impaired pupils.

There was a minority of hearing-impaired pupils who appeared not to perceive 'communication' with normally hearing age-mates as problematic. Two of these pupils were moderately deaf, spoke intelligibly and seemed to be able to follow and comprehend the speech of others quite easily. These two were, presumably, thus being realistic in their appraisal of their ability to communicate with the normally hearing. There

were two other pupils, however, who were profoundly deaf and who claimed to have 'no problem' when communicating with their normally hearing peers. Given that there were many other pupils with less severe hearing
losses readily acknowledging communication difficulties there seemed
to be good reason to query how 'problem free' these pupils really were.
On enquiry their teachers did in fact confirm that these pupils did not
communicate easily with their normally hearing classmates. These two
pupils were disattending to what were probably very serious communication difficulties rather than facing up to the harsh reality of the problem.
Indeed a common way of coping with life's problems is to pretend they
do not exist. Again, this underlines the need for hearing-impaired pupils
in ordinary schools to be helped to come to terms with their handicap,
appreciate their limitations and understand their strengths. Pushing problems 'under the carpet' is no solution.

Problems of communication are an inevitable consequence of deafness
and can never be entirely eradicated. When hearing-impaired pupils enter
into social relations with their hearing peers, patience and tolerance on
both sides are necessary if communication is to be sustained. Mutual
accommodation in inter-communication is, I suggest, essential to the process of harmonious interaction between the normally hearing and the hearing impaired. The interviews with both categories of pupil, whilst indicating some problems caused by intolerance and impatience on both
sides, also revealed a certain amount of mutual accommodation in respect
of communication.

Reactions to Teasing and Name-calling

In the report of discussions with teachers and normally hearing pupils
in Chapter 6 concerning teasing and name-calling of hearing-impaired
children by normally hearing pupils, they claimed that whilst these practices occurred, they did not take place on a wide scale nor to any serious
extent. This conclusion was reached solely from their point of view. It
is essential, however, to examine the reactions of hearing-impaired pupils
themselves to being teased and called such names as 'deaf lugs', and
'deafoes'. It is one thing for normally hearing pupils and teachers in ordinary schools to make light of the teasing of deaf pupils; it is another
for the recipients of ridicule, however mild, to share that view.

Discussion with hearing-impaired pupils and young people revealed
that there was a discrepancy of perceptions between the hearing impaired
and the normally hearing on the issue of teasing and name-calling. Many
of the hearing impaired reported that not only was teasing more
widespread than the reports of teachers and normally hearing pupils had

indicated, but also that it caused more pain and emotional upset than others believed. Just over two-thirds of the deaf pupils and young people reported that teasing, even bullying, was or had been a feature of their school lives. Of these a significant minority claimed to have been 'very upset' through being made the target of 'micky-taking'. Here are some examples of their comments which illustrate the depth and strength of feelings:

Alison	12 years	'They keep making fun of me. They say "You're deaf", and they go "aah, aah, aah . . ." and I don't like it. It's horrible.'
Julie	15 years	'When I was first at this school, they pulling me, calling me names, "rag-bag", "deaf ears". I sometimes cry because they called me names and I get very upset and very angry with them.'
Joanne	17 years	'I was bullied and teased and I got hit. There was one child who used to swear at me and went out of his way to pass by and say "you deaf git". He systematically pushed me about and called me a "deaf git".'
Paul	18 years	'At school, lot of bullies call me names "deafies", "daft", pull my hearing aid. I just walk away but make me very upset.'
Julia	21 years	'I got quite cross. I got quite upset about it. When they made fun of me I got my temper up. It used to upset me a lot.'

The comment of Julie cited above supports those made by other hearing-impaired pupils that they are more likely to be teased and made fun of during the earlier years of secondary school than at any other time. Few complaints about teasing or bullying were made by primary age hearing-impaired children. At the other end of the age-scale, many secondary pupils and former pupils believed that as young people progress through secondary school they become more reasonable and sensible and, therefore, less likely to ridicule deaf pupils. They believed, furthermore, that as normally hearing pupils become more famliar with peers with hearing impairments, so they were more tolerant and accepting of them. There was also the view that, over time, the novelty of making fun of deaf children and their communication difficulties wears off and most normally hearing pupils, therefore, cease the practice. These viewpoints are exemplified in the following statements of hearing-impaired pupils and young people:

Andrew	16 years	'They don't make fun of me a lot now. When they found out I was hard of hearing some of them started making fun of me. They started calling me names. They just started laughing when I couldn't hear a thing. But they don't do that no more. I suppose they got used to it.'
Sally-Anne	17 years	'One or two called you names at first and it's got on my nerves, but it all stopped as we grew up in the school.'
Deborah	17 years	'It was just when we were younger. You got older — no one bothered when they got used to you.'

Some of the hearing impaired believed that by reacting to teasing in a particular way, that is by studiously ignoring it, they were able to 'train' normally hearing peers to discontinue the practice. The following examples of comments illustrate this view:

Maria	18 years	'Right at the beginning they did — just making fun of you behind your back and you know they was doing it. But you just ignore them and it gets them so annoyed that they pack it in.'
Heidi	22 years	'Whenever they called me names I took no notice, so they stopped. They get fed up with it.'

The practice of ignoring teasing was commonly used by hearing-impaired pupils, not just as a mechanism for inducing the 'micky-takers' to discontinue their activities, but as a way of coping with this potentially problematic feature of school life. The comments of a moderately deaf young person sum up this position succinctly:

Julie	20 years	'I used to get called names but it went in one ear and out the other — simple as that.'

A few deaf pupils claimed to use more aggressive tactics to ward off teasing:

Mark	11 years	'He calls me "deafie, deafie", but he's got glasses so I say "circle eyes", "circle eyes".'
Mandy	17 years	'Nobody called me names — they wouldn't dare, 'cos I'd punch 'em.'
Joanne	17 years	'By 13 I discovered I had a tongue and I stood up for myself. I felt rebellious, hurt and angry and I started to give as much as I got.'
Michael	18 years	'Yes, there was a lot of that. They call me "deaf-lugs" and things like that. I had a lot of fights at school, because of that. I gave 'em my fist — that put a stop to it.'

Hearing-impaired young people, thus, varied in the way they felt about teasing and in their behavioural responses to it. Some clearly 'took it to heart' more than others and were less able to 'shrug it off'. Some claimed to become visibly distressed and angry when teased; others ignored it; others fought back. There was some consensus, however, about the belief that it was almost invariably a minority of normally hearing pupils who indulged in the practice of 'mickey-taking'; boys — 'just a few of the boys' — seemed to be particularly culpable in the eyes of hearing-impaired pupils. That there were only a few teasers or name-callers served the purpose of enabling some hearing-impaired pupils and young people to attribute special qualities of character and mind to those particular hurtful pupils. For example, a few of the hearing impaired believed, as their comments indicate, that certain boys would torment them in class in order to direct attention away from the fact that they could not cope with their own work:

| Kathy | 14 years | '*They* can't do the work so they play and call *us* names.' |
| Joanne | 17 years | 'I think the children took anything out of me that they couldn't cope with.' |

According to the perceptions of deaf pupils such as these, name-calling was a consequence of normally hearing pupils scapegoating the hearing-impaired category of pupil in order to cover up their own inadequacies. Several hearing-impaired pupils demonstrated an ability to rationalise being teased by normally hearing classmates by attributing to the teasers moral or intellectual weaknesses. The following comments of hearing-impaired secondary pupils about their hearing 'tormentors' illustrate the point:

Caroline	13 years	'They're mental! Sometimes when they annoy me I just turn round and say "What's wrong with you, are you mental?"'
Lisa	15 years	'They say silly things but I just say "they're daft".'
Janet	15 years	'It's only the stupid ones who mess us about.'

The practice of shifting deviance away from themselves towards those harassing them allowed some hearing-impaired pupils to avoid feelings of humiliation at being teased.

Whilst the majority of hearing-impaired youngsters believed that their tormentors were 'cruel', 'unkind', 'stupid', etc., a few believed that some of the blame lay with deaf pupils themselves. The comment of a severely deaf young person characterises this view:

Kathy	22 years	'I never got any stick. I never got called names. I think with some of the others that may be because they wouldn't go in with the hearing. They kept themselves out of it, you know and a lot of them were more introverted and I think that's why a lot of them got some stick. They go for you if they think you're stuck up.'

Kathy, along with one or two others, believed that some deaf pupils kept themselves to themselves too much as an exclusive social group and that this antagonised other pupils. Had hearing-impaired pupils made more effort to enter the world of the normally hearing, they would, according to this argument, have been more acceptable to the normally hearing group and less obvious targets for ridicule.

An interesting point of view expressed by one severely deaf girl was that some deaf pupils might, on occasions, *imagine* they are being made fun of when in reality they are not. Her view, referring to a former profoundly deaf classmate, who claimed on occasions to be victimised by others, suggests that deafness by its very nature can facilitate feelings of 'paranoia':

Julie   20 years   'I can't remember anybody tormenting
                                  Paul. He used to have hearing friends. He
                                  could have imagined it. He's deafer than
                                  me and sometimes I feel that somebody's
                                  having a conversation behind me and they
                                  don't want me to listen and I feel they're
                                  talking about me. Paul could have thought
                                  that.'

Given the number of reports of teasing, however, it clearly cannot be
the case that being made fun of was 'all in the mind' of the hearing-
impaired pupil. None the less, the notion that certain over-sensitive
hearing-impaired pupils might exaggerate the extent to which they were
being teased has a certain common-sense appeal and accords with the
evidence presented in Chapter 6, based on the views of normally hearing
pupils. Pupils who are self-conscious about their handicap and who, furthermore, may not be completely 'tuned in' to what is going on around
them might well, like the physically handicapped children studied by
Anderson and Clarke (1982), believe themselves to be more victimised
than they actually are.

However, that some hearing-impaired pupils believed they were
unreasonably tormented is a matter which warrants some attention on
the part of educators. The evidence suggests that whilst the majority of
hearing-impaired pupils were able to withstand pupil ridicule in the ordinary school with more or less equanimity, there were some who suffered considerable emotional upset because they believed they were special
targets for unkind behaviour and mocking attitudes. The following ad-
mission of a severely deaf girl referring to her early years at secondary
school illustrates this point quite poignantly:

Joanne   17 years   'I came home from school and I cried every
                                  single night.'

Such beliefs and feelings are not conducive to integration in any sense
of the word; they merely contribute towards deaf pupils' sense of aliena-
tion. Teachers, therefore, need to be alert to the possibility of a deaf pupil
being anxious or miserable particularly during the early years of secondary education. Educators may be able to help deaf pupils through 'difficult times' by counselling them so that they might become better able
to cope with teasing with good humour. Perhaps even more important
for the well-being of the hearing impaired is the duty of teachers to inform

and educate normally hearing pupils about the very serious problems that are consequential upon deafness. In addition to encouraging more pupils to offer friendly and helpful accommodations to hearing-impaired peers, insights into the problems of deafness might appeal to the finer feelings of those prone to mocking and teasing and discourage them from the victimisation of those already disadvantaged.

Having described and discussed some aspects of hearing-impaired pupils' and young peoples' perceptions of their social experiences in ordinary schools, aspects of their integration into the wider society will now be considered.

Hearing-impaired Young People: Their Place in Society

The follow-up investigation in 1983/4 included interviews with young people who had attended an ordinary school but who had since left. The interviews and discussions provided an invaluable opportunity to explore some key aspects of integration with them: their perceptions of themselves in relation to other people; their sense of being 'normal', 'normalised' or 'different' from other people; their feelings about their hearing impairment; their sense of belonging to or being apart from the hearing-speaking world; their ideas about what constituted obstacles to full participation in normally hearing society; their views about the 'deaf community', 'deaf subculture' and 'deaf language'. I wanted to discover how these hearing-impaired young adults, all of whom had received all or part of their education in an ordinary school, felt on entering the wider society. Did they believe they were 'pale imitations of hearing persons' (McCay Vernon 1981), or did they believe they were fully assimilated individuals, as much a part of normal society as anyone else? Thus, drawing from the interviews with hearing-impaired young people who had left school, a consideration of their concepts and conceptions of integration will be offered.

Perhaps one of the more important findings is that among the hearing-impaired young people a variety of perceptions were held concerning themselves in relation to the wider society. These perceptions were not explicable in terms of any single variable such as hearing loss, educational background, speech intelligibility, or ideology. Clearly, individual, institutional and ideological factors combine in a complex ongoing way to produce a range and diversity of opinions among hearing-impaired young people. Broadly speaking, however, there were three major categories of viewpoint discernible among the hearing-impaired young people concerning their relationship with the wider society. First, there were those who identified with normally hearing people, participated as much as possible in hearing-speaking society and who felt no need for contact with other hearing-impaired people. Second, there were those who spent most of their lives in association with normally hearing people, identified to a large extent with the normally hearing but felt some need of contact with others who were hearing impaired. As a consequence, though they spent most of their time with normally hearing people, they formed part of a more or less loose network of deaf people. Finally, there was a small minority of hearing-impaired young people who were part of the 'normal' world in the sense that they had to cope with everyday life in hearing-speaking society but who formed their closest and most significant relationships within the deaf group.

To consider first those who identified primarily with the normally hearing: these comprised about half my sample. As might be expected some who came into this category did not have profound hearing losses and were thus more able to think of themselves as 'not really deaf'. The following statements by moderately/severely deaf young people characterise this stance:

Richard	16 years	'I hate being surrounded by deaf people. I don't think of myself as deaf. I can understand anything. I don't see the point of being with deaf people.'
Paul	17 years	'Most of my mates don't know that I'm deaf, so they treat me like a normal person. I tried it out with some of the kids — I told them that I was deaf and what have you and they started treating me special, so I don't bother telling them now.'
Lorraine	17 years	'I hate being surrounded by deaf people. I don't think of myself as deaf. I can understand anything. I don't see the point of being with deaf people.'

Several hearing-impaired young people with views similar to those quoted above had attended a unit within an ordinary school and, therefore, had experience of having the status of 'special' pupil. They appear, however, to have shaken off the label 'deaf' or 'partially-deaf' and, as far as can be judged, have become assimilated into normally hearing socie-ty. These young people did not feel deaf or different enough, it would appear, to want or need to associate with other deaf individuals. Clearly, they felt they had more in common with the normally hearing than with deaf people. The rejection of the deaf as friends or associates was in the case of some interviewees forcibly expressed. Comments such as the following illustrate this viewpoint: 'I want nothing to do with them', 'No way do I want deaf friends', 'I just think of myself as normal so I don't need to go around with the deaf.' These hearing-impaired young peo-ple's protestations could signify some underlying awareness of their marginality on the deaf/hearing spectrum. Association with deaf people might, in their eyes, stigmatise them and undermine their ability to sus-tain their view of themselves as 'normal'.

Not all the hearing-impaired young people who wished to be iden-tified with the normally hearing rather than with the deaf had relatively less severe hearing losses. There were three profoundly deaf young peo-ple who were fully aware of their deaf status and fully conscious of the many problems associated with deafness, but who had none the less com-mitted themselves to be part of normally hearing society and had deter-minedly dissociated themselves from social contact with other deaf peo-ple. They chose the hearing world as their reference-group for ideological reasons, not because they felt 'normal'. (For a discussion of reference-group theory see Merton (1968), pp. 335–440.) Citations from two of these three exemplify this point of view:

| Paul | 18 years | 'I only have hearing friends. I don't want to be with deaf people. Hearing people bet-ter. I don't go to Deaf Club; no signing; just normal people.' |
| Kathy | 21 years | 'I don't have deaf friends now. I don't like Deaf Clubs and being with deaf people. All my friends are hearing . . . I go to the pub and I'm in the Ladies Darts Team. I'm not lonely at all.' |

Interviews with the three profoundly deaf young people from this first category indicated that they had serious communication problems: their speech was often intelligible; their voice quality was abnormal and ques-tions frequently had to be repeated and rephrased to make them under-stand what they were required to speak about. Given their communica-tion and other difficulties it might have been expected that these deaf young people would have felt some need for deaf friends to communicate with in a more relaxed way than could ever be possible when talking with the normally hearing. However, these young deaf people did not express such a need and were doing what they were doing because they had elected to do so. They were aware that there was a Deaf Club and other deaf people in their area with whom they could associate if they wished. They had opted to integrate into the wider society of the normally hearing, albeit as a member with a 'different' status.

The second category of hearing-impaired young people, again comprising almost half of the sample, were those who had normally hearing friends and acquaintances but believed that they needed some contact with other people who were deaf like themselves. (A subgroup within this category were those young deaf people who had been individually integrated into their local school and who felt a need for companionship with someone with a similar problem to themselves but who, to their regret, had no such friend or acquaintance. This point of view has been referred to earlier in the chapter so will not be amplified again here.) Some of these young people felt a strong need for deaf friends; others a lesser need; but none in this category wished to be cut off completely from the deaf. A sample of statements made by hearing-impaired young people characterises these views:

Susan	17 years	'I think I got on with hearing better. I don't want to be stuck with just deaf. But I wouldn't want to be completely cut off from the deaf.'
Maria	18 years	'I think it's important really. I don't know why but I think I feel a little bit more at home (with the deaf). We can communicate better. We can talk about our problems, say someone's annoying us and we can understand it as well, being deaf.'
Kathy	22 years	'I do think it's very important to have deaf friends, because like with a hearing person, you can't really talk over your problems with them because they're not deaf themselves, whereas that's something, one thing you have in common with the deaf, you know we've all got the same problems.'
Heidi	22 years	'I need both . . . it is very important to have deaf friends and hearing friends. I like

> going to the Deaf Club, and I have a lot of other friends.'

The opinions cited above demonstrate a need for deaf friends for mutual support and understanding; for the opportunity to be with people with whom they can communicate easily and for the chance to be able to relax with those who, because sharing similar problems, do not make the kinds of difficult demands on them that are typically made by hearing-speaking people.

Some of the deaf young adults had deaf friends but were not sure whether this was because of a need for relationships with others who were deaf or simply because of many years of close contact at school. Here are some examples of their views:

Sally-Anne	17 years	'We've been friends for so long, it's unnatural to split up . . . it's not just they're deaf, they're just friends.'
Susan	17 years	'I like my deaf friends, but then I've known them all these years.'
Maxine	18 years	'I'm close to deaf people, but that's because I know them for a long time. I think I'll always want deaf friends because I find it difficult really surrounded with hearing people, but I'll have to see how I am.'

Regardless of the reasons for maintaining contact with deaf people, and regardless of the amount of contact they had with deaf people, or regardless of whether they attended a Deaf Club or formed part of a large informal network of hearing-impaired people, all of these 'both worlds' young people took for granted that they had to live their lives for most of the time in a normally-hearing society. Generally, they accepted the conventions of the hearing-speaking world. They did not present themselves to the wider hearing-speaking society as a minority group of deaf people with a special identity, culture and language of their own which demanded due respect from those who could hear, nor did they express any desire to do so. They did not question a necessity to conform to the accepted means of communication used in the normally hearing world.

This acceptance of the necessity to conform to the norms of hearing-speaking society was to an extent also true of those young deaf people in the final category. There were only two of these individuals and whilst they spent most of their time with normally hearing people, for example at work or at home, they none the less claimed to be only 'really at ease' among their deaf friends and/or relatives. It is this *strong* social orientation towards the deaf which distinguishes these two individuals from those in the previous group. Statements from them give an indication of their feelings:

Janet (moderately deaf)	22 years	'I'm friends with them at work but not outside. I get on better with deaf than with hearing people. I don't know why. I could have hearing friends but I just get annoyed with them.'
Julia (severely deaf)	21 years	'Most of my friends are partially deaf or deaf. I don't think I like if my friends were hearing. The deaf are more easy to talk to and to understand. The hearing a bit difficult . . . I be very lonely. I can talk but I can't say all the words. Never lonely so long as with deaf.'

Both Janet and Julia had reasonably intelligible speech, particularly Janet, and a reasonable grasp of the English language. They were, thus, less 'handicapped' than many hearing-impaired young people interviewed who in spite of communication difficulties maintained more social contact with hearing people. A brief examination of their biographies may explain their pronounced preference for social contact with deaf people:

Janet has deaf parents, deaf siblings and other deaf relatives and, therefore, it is not unreasonable that she should feel more as ease in the company of deaf people. Julia, until the age of 13 years, attended a school for the deaf where all her companions were deaf. On transferring to a unit which was part of a secondary comprehensive school, she claimed she found the work difficult and communication with normally hearing pupils a perpetual struggle. She, therefore, kept herself very much with the deaf group at the ordinary school as indeed did Janet.[1] These factors, coupled with the fact that Julia is naturally rather

---

1. This 'exclusive' behaviour on the part of these two interviewees was noted earlier in the chapter in the section on social integration in schools.

quiet and shy, may at least in part explain why, as an adult, she chose her close friends from among the deaf rather than from among the hearing group.

Neither of these two young people were completely encapsulated in a tight-knit deaf community. Both lived and worked in the 'real' world and both saw the necessity to observe the conventions of that world: for both of them talking was the main form of communication.

In general, then, whilst there was a diversity of opinions among the young hearing-impaired people, none could be said to form part of a close-knit community of deaf people, nor did there seem to be any desire on their part to belong to such a group. Variations in perceptions about themselves in relation to others were largely in terms of the degree of assimilation into hearing-speaking society. Some of the hearing-impaired young people aspired to become part of, or felt themselves to be part of, the normally hearing world. They had no apparent need for association with other deaf people. Those who believed that they were full members of normally hearing society felt themselves to be 'normal'. Others felt more or less assimilated into the hearing-speaking world and more or less 'normalised' but had maintained contact with other deaf people largely for mutual support and understanding. They did not, however, form part of a socially exclusive deaf group, nor did they confine their friendships and close acquaintances to the deaf: they all had some friends who were normally hearing. Just two young people elected, whenever possible, to spend their social life in the company of other deaf people. Neither felt completely at home in the normally hearing world, and, therefore, cannot be said to be fully assimilated into that world. They both, however, accepted the need to adapt and accommodate to the behavioural norms of the hearing-speaking world when interacting with normally hearing people. They thus accepted an important feature of the principle of 'normalisation': the belief that they had to behave normally and talk normally when interacting with normally hearing people.

This is not to suggest that all the deaf young people interviewed were all personally well adjusted, emotionally trouble-free, never lonely and socially competent at all times. Nor is it claimed that they were unaware of the limitations in their lives imposed by a hearing impairment which meant that at times life was a struggle. It is simply to say that no deaf person interviewed was isolated from others or alienated from the society in which they lived. No one was without friends or regular social contact with other people, most of whom were normally hearing. There was no evidence from my research, therefore, to support the views of writers such as Ladd (1981) that the deaf are merely 'trying to catch on to the coat-tails' of normally hearing society.

An examination of the social relationships and social orientation of the hearing-impaired young people who had left school has indicated that they attached considerable importance to the principle of normalisation and being part of the hearing-speaking world. All of them, regardless of need for occasional or frequent contact with other deaf people, believed that in order to participate in the normally hearing world they had to abide by its rules. They wanted, above all, to be able to talk intelligibly and to be able to understand the speech of others. This does not mean, however, that these young people felt 'normal' or were unaware of themselves as deaf persons with a sense of 'special identity'. It is this sense of 'special identity' which will be examined next.

Hearing-impaired Young People: Their Sense of Special Identity

The majority of young hearing-impaired individuals interviewed *were* aware of being deaf. They acknowledged their special status and attendant problems. The minority who were reluctant to make any such acknowledgement consisted of a few young people with less severe hearing losses and their views of themselves are typified by the comment of a moderately deaf teenager:

Dale   16 years   'I don't think of myself as deaf. I can do anything anyone with hearing can do.'

Most of the young people were, however, often acutely aware that their hearing loss caused some areas of their life to be very difficult to cope with. Thus, whilst most of the deaf interviewees embraced the notion of 'normalisation' in the sense of wanting as much preparation as possible for participation in a normally hearing society, this does not mean that they felt entirely normal. Attitudes towards deafness varied from taking deafness for granted to calm or reluctant resignation to a certain amount of sadness, regret or bitterness. The following comments illustrate the spectrum of attitudes:

Julie   15 years   'I wish I weren't a deaf person because then I could walk about and talk like a normal

		person. Life is very difficult for a deaf person.'
Mark	16 years	'I accept it as I am.'
Peter	16 years	'I've just had to face up to it that I'm deaf an' there's nothing that anyone can do about it.'
Andrew	16 years	'I don't mind being deaf. I'm not ashamed of it. I don't see myself as different from anybody else.'
Mandy	17 years	'I forget I'm deaf most of the time.'
Joanne	17 years	'I'm always aware I'm deaf but on my "off" days I feel it more acutely and I worry about the future. I see people in their 50s and they've always been deaf and it frightens me so much when I look at them that that could be me in 30 years time, *still deaf*; to know that you have a life sentence is quite something . . . I don't think I'll ever be happy so long as I'm deaf.'
Paul	18 years	'When I think about being deaf — I get very upset.'
Gwen	20 years	'I can't imagine being hearing just now. I'm sort of used to it, as it is.'
Julie	20 years	'I don't feel different . . . not at all.'
Kathy	21 years	'I don't like it, but nobody can give me my hearing.'
Heidi	22 years	'I don't think about being deaf not really. You get used to it.'
Kathy	22 years	'I just take it for granted.'

Several citations from the deaf young people have been presented to demonstrate that there was no single, simple response to being deaf among those who had a sense of 'deaf awareness'. The comments of Heidi and Andrew, for example, indicate that it is possible to acknowledge deafness without necessarily believing that this confers on one deviant or different status. The comments of, for example, Julie and Joanne on the other hand indicate a high level of 'deaf awareness' — a sense of 'difference' from others and serious regrets about their handicapping condition. That some individuals feel unhappy, angry and embittered that they are deaf is a sad finding — but not an altogether surprising one. A severe hearing impairment represents a lifelong ineradicable handicap. That not every deaf young person felt upset or bitter about their hearing impairment presumably reflects normal human diversity of qualities such as personality, temperament, character and sensitivity.

Regardless of overall attitudes to deafness the majority of deaf young people acknowledged specific problems associated with their hearing loss and they were well able to exemplify these in some detail. There were enough everyday occurrences which caused problems to these deaf young people to serve as regular reminders that they had a hearing impairment and this in itself helped fuel and maintain the notion in their minds that they had a special deaf identity. Difficulties alluded to ranged from the broad idea that 'life is a struggle when you're deaf' to the more specific one of 'not being able to understand/decipher the public address announcements at railway stations' (who can!). Most commonly cited problems were: not being able to hear or talk on the telephone; hear the doorbell, their dog barking, TV and radio programmes, records and cassettes; not being able to sustain a conversion in a noisy environment, participate in a three- or four-party conversation; not being able to talk, listen and drive a car all at the same time; embarrassment at not being understood in shops or in other public places.

Given that most of these deaf young people were aware of the day-in day-out problems caused by their hearing loss it was surprising to discover that so few knew about the various aids and welfare services available to them. Some of these aids and services could have helped alleviate some of their difficulties. Several interviewees, for example, who could not hear their doorbell or someone speaking over the phone did not know that they could obtain a flashing door bell or an amplifier for their telephone receiver. Even where there was some knowledge of these facilities they seemed uncertain as to how they could find out about obtaining them. There was considerable ignorance concerning local authority welfare services, national information services such as that available at the RNID and the special benefits to which they might, as of right, be entitled. If the overall purpose of deaf education is to help the deaf individual overcome his handicap to the maximum extent possible, then it would seem reasonable to advise a deaf pupil at school about the range of advice, aids and services available to him which may help him to cope with daily living more easily. Educators in their enthusiasm to normalise a deaf pupil should not lose sight of the undeniable fact that a deaf pupil is to become an adult who has to cope with a serious handicap for the rest of his life.

For most deaf children and adults the most important aid available for alleviating the handicap is a hearing aid. A hearing aid can be critical to the deaf person's ability to understand the speech of others and hence 'integrate' into hearing-speaking society. If a person with a substantial hearing loss does not have positive attitudes towards hearing aids, is not willing to wear them, maintain them properly and set them at appropriate volume levels, he greatly reduces his opportunities for social interaction with normally hearing people.

As seen in Part 1 of this chapter some hearing-impaired pupils observed in ordinary classes during the earlier phase of the research adopted the tactic of hiding their aids in order to remove from sight what they believed to be a stigmatising symbol of their handicap. If the practice of not wearing hearing aids continues into adulthood this will have consequences for the deaf person's participation in the wider society. Attitudes towards hearing aids of the young deaf people featuring in the follow-up investigation will thus be examined next.

Hearing-impaired Young People: Attitudes to Hearing Aids

The follow-up interviews with the young deaf adults indicated that the majority wore their hearing aids, and took good care of them. These individuals claimed that they would be 'lost without them'. Some of their comments serve to illustrate their positive attitudes towards hearing aids:

Susan	18 years	'I'm very dependent on my hearing aids. The other day I thought I'd lost both of them — I still can't find one. It might have slipped down under the sofa. But, I wasn't going to go to work that day if I hadn't found my spare hearing aid.'
Lorraine	18 years	'I can't tell I'm deaf when I got my hearing aid in.'
Julie	20 years	'If I didn't have this (post-aural aid) I might as well give up. It's my life-saver.'
Julia	21 years	'I couldn't manage without aids. No, it'd be nice not to wear them, but I must.'
Kathy	21 years	'Without 'em I'm finished.'

This acknowledgement of the value of hearing aids in alleviating the handicap of deafness is likely to be welcomed by those responsible for educating the deaf. So also is the readiness on the part of many hearing-impaired young people to make their aids visible, as this indicates that the deaf person has, in an important sense, come to terms with the handicap. Several hearing-impaired young people were either unembarrassed about their aids showing or even took steps to make the aid visible in order to advertise that they had a hearing loss. The following remarks by deaf young people typify this position:

Mark	16 years	'When I say meet someone for the first time I don't really like telling them you know, that I'm deaf. I wait till they say "oooh, you've got a hearing aid", you know what I mean. I like everybody to know so that they think I'm not being rude, you see.'
Mandy	17 years	'If they can't see your aid they gabble on and don't look at you and they lose you,'
Sally-Anne	17 years	'I like people to see my aid, because I don't want them to think I'm deceiving anyone, you know, like when you go for a job.'
Gwen	20 years	'I've got my hair cut away from the ears now and it's an advantage to let people know because I don't look as though I'm deaf and I don't act as though I'm deaf. People sometimes say to me "You're not deaf", so I say "Oh no — I just wear this little machine in my ear for the sheer fun of it!"'
Julia	21 years	'It's better if they can see my aid really, 'cos then they might speak a bit slow and loud.'

The comments of the deaf young individuals cited above exemplify an interesting viewpoint, namely, that because they look normal and have normal sounding speech, they are frequently judged to be 'normal'. It can be a disadvantage for the hearing-impaired person if people are not aware of his hearing loss because they will not then see a need to take account of his special difficulties in understanding speech and make special accommodations. Making the hearing aid obvious saves deaf individuals from the possibly embarrassing experience of having to explain themselves during the early part of an encounter. Thus whilst the 'normalisation' of a deaf child's spoken language is a central aim in deaf education, it can be problematic for the deaf individual if he is seen as *too* normal and appears to be capable of meeting social expectations which realistically he sometimes cannot do.

Not all the hearing-impaired young people wanted to display their hearing aid in order to signify they were deaf. A small minority chose to use their apparent normality to 'pass for normal'. These young people were aware that they needed to wear hearing aids but preferred to conceal both the aids and their deafness. This stance is typified by the words of a teenage severely deaf girl:

Alison   16 years   'I hate it if people know I'm deaf. If I didn't
                                  tell them they don't know and they treat me
                                  as a normal person.'

That this view was only a minority one is likely to be welcomed by educators since it is indicative of a certain amount of shame and embarrassment about 'being deaf' which is unnecessary and inappropriate. If young people such as Alison meet with condescension or pity from others, or come to be seen by them as 'deviant', then it is perhaps understandable that they should try to conceal their deafness. That most deaf young people claimed that they did not believe they were, generally speaking, treated in a patronising manner by those with normal hearing, suggests that there is no general need for the deaf to pretend to be normally hearing. An absence of shame and embarrassment about 'being deaf' is an attitude which educators might not only welcome but where possible, encourage.

A small proportion of those who had left school, six of the 32, did not wear hearing aids at all. All of these young people had been made to wear their hearing aids at school. Different reasons were given by them for abandoning their aids. Two profoundly deaf young people with average hearing losses in the better ear of 108 dB and 101 dB decided that hearing aids did nothing to help them understand the spoken word. All that the aids did, according to these two, was to make a 'horrible noise'. The other four young people who no longer wore hearing aids had moderate hearing losses and believed that they had sufficient hearing to cope without them. They all agreed that hearing aids were beneficial to some deaf people but were not suitable for themselves. They all believed that because hearing aids amplified unwanted sounds, as well as those they wanted to hear, the disadvantages of hearing aids outweighed the advantages. This viewpoint is exemplified by the statement of one moderately deaf young man:

Michael   18 years   'I didn't like it. I don't think they helped
                                   me. I got a lot of noise and more often than

not they whistled all the time. Like if you're
really deaf like my little brother he needs
them — they're like his best friend — as
they was my enemy.'

None of the four moderately deaf young people had, according to their
statements, stopped wearing hearing aids for cosmetic reasons or because
they did not want others to know they had a hearing loss. They simply
believed aids to be of no benefit to them when talking and listening to
other people. Whether this was a realistic position is arguable. However,
the firm impression gained was that none of these young people had given
up their aids lightly. They all had thought carefully their reasons for not
wearing hearing aids.

In sum then, the interviews revealed that the majority of hearing-
impaired young people wore their hearing aids and acknowledged the
benefits that they derived from them. Most of these deaf young people
were not embarrassed about wearing a hearing aid and did not mind that
other people could see their aids. That their attitudes towards hearing
aids were favourable seems slightly at odds with the evidence drawn from
the earlier period of the investigation when it was demonstrated that at
least some hearing-impaired pupils did not like wearing their hearing aids,
particularly their radio aids, in ordinary classes and adopted strategies
to avoid wearing them. That there appears to have been a change of attitude towards wearing hearing aids among the hearing-impaired young
people since they left school might be for any one or more of several
reasons. In the earlier investigation the hearing aids most disliked were
radio aids which were large, heavy and cumbersome and, because they
were early models of this type of aid, it is also possible that they suffered technical 'teething' problems. More recently new models of radio
aid are being used by hearing-impaired pupils. These aids are a lot less
cumbersome and heavy, more attractive looking and perform better than
earlier models. Since, however, radio aids in this country are generally
available only to pre-school children and school pupils the deaf young
people interviewed were no longer in possession of this type of aid and
hence not in a position to find them troublesome. Furthermore, it may
be that with greater maturity the hearing-impaired young people in the
follow-up investigation had developed more sensible and rational ideas
about their hearing aids and indeed their handicap generally. Moreover,
it is my general impression that over the last few years attitudes towards
hearing aids, for whatever reason, have improved among the hearing-
impaired population and that nowadays hearing aids are perceived more

as necessary props for active participation in a hearing-speaking world than as stigmatising symbols. This too might be a contributory factor to more favourable attitudes towards hearing aids on the part of the interviewees. (These explanations are speculative, but have a certain common-sense appeal. There is scope for further investigation to delineate the factors which help produce positive attitudes to hearing aids. Generally, it would seem to be sensible for hearing aid manufacturers to do some market research on the visual as well as the technical design features of the aid.)

A hearing aid is essential for the deaf person who wishes to adapt to the demands of normally hearing society. Favourable attitudes towards hearing aids might be seen, therefore, as an indication of a wish to assimilate into the hearing-speaking world.

Another indication of a deaf person's view of himself in relation to others in society — his sense of special identity or of being 'assimilated' into society as a 'normalised' member — might be demonstrated by his attitude to sign language and it is on this topic that this chapter concludes.

Hearing-impaired Young People: Their Attitude to Sign Language

As seen in Chapter 3, one of the major criticisms of integration policies by the 'anti-integrationists' was that these policies encourage the deaf individual to discard his special identity as a deaf person and deprive the deaf pupil of the opportunity to develop his 'natural' language — sign language. Educators are condemned, as indicated on pp. 65–8, for trying to make the deaf individual be what he cannot be, namely, a normally hearing person. The argument is that if the deaf child is allowed to acquire sign language rather than forced at all costs to be 'normalised' then he can take pride in his 'special identity' rather than accept his 'spoiled identity' when participating in the normally hearing world. In the context of my own research, therefore, I was interested to discover whether deaf young people who had been educated in ordinary schools felt any sense of deprivation because they were not given much opportunity to learn to sign or whether they willingly and happily accepted the goals of 'normalisation' which their educators in the main had set for them.

The results of the interviews with hearing-impaired young people were straightforward. The majority, 29 of the 40 deaf pupils and young people, did not use nor appeared to wish to learn sign language, so closely did they identify with those who have normal hearing. (For the purpose of the discussion of the views of hearing-impaired individuals on sign language, I have drawn on the interviews with all those featuring in the later investigation 1983/4, that is, school pupils as well as those who had left school.) The other eleven used sign language to a greater or lesser extent when communicating with some of their deaf friends or acquaintances, but none of them considered sign language to be their first language. This is an important finding in view of the current controversy surrounding the issue of whether or not the deaf should develop their own distinct deaf culture.

There were differing views among those who could sign about whether deaf children should be taught to sign in school. All of them believed, in common with their teachers, that schools should be concerned with helping deaf pupils acquire oral and not sign language. A few (seven), however, believed that whilst deaf children should be taught first and foremost to talk, they should be taught to sign in order that they be given the opportunity to communicate more easily among themselves. Several examples of the views of the young people interviewed will be cited to illustrate fully the nature of their feelings and range of opinions on what is considered by many people to be a crucially important issue:

Alison	13 years	'I don't like sign language. I don't like it. I like to talk with lip-reading and not to use my hands. I don't like it.'
Cheryl	13 years	'I don't like to use sign language. I like to talk like other people.'
Christine	14 years	'I sign a bit when I talk to some deaf people, but I prefer to talk.'
Julie	15 years	'I don't want to use sign language because I want to talk to my family at home. People won't talk to me if I use sign language, won't be friends with me.'
Peter	16 years	'I'd never join a Deaf Club. They would do sign language which I want nothing to do with because I can talk normally.'
Mandy	17 years	'I don't like it. I wouldn't want to do sign language. I'd start laughing.'
Susan	17 years	'I pick up some signs but I always talk. I see signing like a game really.'
Deborah	17 years	'No. I don't want that. Everybody looking at you.'

Paul	17 years	'I don't want to go to a Deaf Club and do signing. I don't know what they're on about.'
Maria	18 years	'I think however deaf someone is they should be taught to talk just for the case of needing it.'
Julia	21 years	'I prefer to talk. I'm only deaf person in family. I always talk to them. They can't sign. At Deaf Club I usually sign. Deaf people who can't talk should sign, but it's better to talk than sign.'
Janet	21 years	'I think deaf people should be taught to sign, but they should talk. It's not fair if people learn to sign and never talk.'
Kathy	22 years	'Signing is so useful. I'm grateful I can. Some deaf people I sign to them. Others I don't need to.'
Heidi	22 years	'Deaf children should learn to talk. It's all right if they can sign but they must learn to talk. As soon as they go out there are talking people. They can't sign to them because they won't know what they're talking about. You need to talk.'

Contained within the range of views presented we can see a certain vehemence of feeling against manual communication on the grounds that it is both unnecessary and stigmatising. Some, on the other hand, enjoyed signing or were willing to use signs on those occasions when they felt it to be necessary, for example, when communicating with deaf people whose oral skills were poor. Among this group, however, there was unanimity on the need to acquire the ability to talk and understand the talk of others. Thus, my investigations revealed that the views of deaf young people on signing are consistent with their views of their overall place in society. These deaf young people did not, on the whole, see their hearing impairment as an insurmountable barrier to their participation in normally hearing society. They therefore did not believe that the acquisition of sign language should be a priority in their education.

8 SUMMARY AND CONCLUSIONS

What we have seen in this book is that the policy of making some special educational provision in ordinary schools for pupils with a hearing loss is long established in Britain. Also that more recent trends have been towards integrating into ordinary schools even pupils with more substantial hearing losses. A situation has developed in which the majority of deaf pupils in this country receive their education in an ordinary rather than a special school. The aim of the research reported here was to gain some insight into the way this 'new' situation was working out in practice.

My investigation into aspects of integration in deaf education has, hopefully, provided insights of value not only to those responsible for the education of deaf children, but also to educators in other areas of special education where progress towards integration has up until now been less marked. The knowledge and wisdom revealed through an examination of the experience of educating one category of severely handicapped child, namely, the deaf pupil in the ordinary school has, I believe, relevance and application to the education of other categories of handicapped pupils in ordinary schools. With the implementation of the 1981 Education Act the integration of handicapped children into ordinary schools is likely to accelerate in the near future and therefore, the need for insights into the practice of integration becomes even more important.

Through an examination of my own data, and the research evidence of others, this book has attempted to shed new light on both the practice and the concept of integration. By looking at integration from the perceptions and perspectives of ordinary class teachers, normally hearing pupils, and, perhaps most important of all, the hearing-impaired pupils themselves, the objective has been to illuminate general features of educational integration such as acceptance, adaptation, assimilation, normalisation and mutual accommodation as both educational goals and as social processes. The clarification of these features is of crucial importance to anyone involved with the integrated education of handicapped children.

The examination of the integrated education of deaf pupils in the classroom has attempted to discover whether or not normalisation and assimilation were perceived by teachers, normally hearing pupils and deaf pupils as desirable and realistic goals and whether or not there was in practice mutual accommodation in the ordinary school between those who were deaf and those with normal hearing. The clarification of these matters is of special significance and relevance in deaf education in the context of the current opposition to integration expressed by influential organisations such as the British Deaf Association and the National Union of the Deaf.

Those holding the 'anti-integrationist' view allege that the placement and education of deaf pupils in ordinary schools is not integration but 'pseudo-assimilation'. According to this view the ordinary school, far from presenting an environment which encourages mutual toleration and acceptance between deaf pupils and normally hearing people, relegates the deaf pupil to second-class citizenship as an inferior hearing person. The ordinary school, it is argued, does not normalise the deaf pupil but pervasively destroys his dignity and feelings of self-worth so that he becomes increasingly alienated and isolated from others.

In seeking the views of those young deaf adults who had recently experienced an integrated education I have been concerned specifically to clarify the currently disputed, controversial issue of whether or not the increased integration of severely and profoundly deaf pupils into ordinary schools constitutes a mark of progress in the education of the deaf, or represents a retrograde step leading not to 'integration' but to the 'disintegration' of the deaf and their subcultural institutions in society (Montgomery 1981).

The review of recent research into the educational, social and emotional attainments of hearing-impaired pupils in different educational settings reveals evidence of some support for the notion that normal schools 'normalise' but the evidence is not unequivocal. Whilst formal surveys of the academic, linguistic and speech attainments of hearing-impaired pupils indicate that no matter what the degree of hearing loss, achievements are superior in ordinary rather than in segregated school settings, the evidence also clearly indicates that deaf pupils do not achieve comparable results to those of normally hearing pupils of equivalent intelligence. It would seem that it is degree of hearing loss rather than school setting which is the major determinant of educational attainment. Furthermore, research studies indicate that the deaf pupils, whatever type of school they attend, do not attain normal standards of social and emotional adjustment. The more recent research evidence into the education of deaf pupils in ordinary schools does not, therefore, refute or challenge the long-standing views based on earlier research that a severe and profound hearing loss represents a serious barrier to the educational development and normalisation of a deaf pupil and is hence a barrier to his ultimate full assimilation into normally hearing society. Thus, it can certainly be said on the basis of the research evidence examined that an education in an ordinary school cannot of itself eradicate all the consequences of the handicap of deafness. Those educators in favour of integrated educational policies for deaf children might argue, however, that whether deaf pupils achieve 'normal' or 'abnormal' educational standards in an ordinary school is of lesser importance than that they are accepted by the normally hearing pupils and teachers surrounding and involved with them.

The research literature which focuses on the way hearing-impaired pupils are accepted in ordinary schools indicates that deaf pupils are favourably regarded and well received by others in the ordinary school, *provided certain conditions are met*. So, for example, ordinary class teachers are found to be more accepting of any pupil with special needs if they are teaching in what they believe to be good conditions, such as having a small or an 'easy' class. Class teachers, so the research suggests, need to feel sufficiently knowledgeable about deafness and the special needs and problems of hearing-impaired pupils, and experienced in dealing with deaf pupils in general, in order to feel confident about being able to contribute to a specific deaf pupil's educational progress. Normally hearing pupils are generally accepting of hearing-impaired peers, and become more so the more opportunities they have for interacting and co-operating with such pupils. Relationships between hearing-impaired and normally hearing pupils in ordinary schools are, for the most part, reported by researchers to be 'satisfactory'.

Generally, then, the research evidence reviewed in the early part of this book indicates that whilst an education in an ordinary school goes some way towards 'normalising' the deaf pupil, individuals with substantial hearing losses do not, overall, achieve the academic, linguistic and speech standards attained by those with normal hearing; nor are they as socially and emotionally well adjusted as their normally hearing peers. An integrated education, as the critics of integration policies are quick to point out, does not miraculously convert a deaf person into a hearing one (Merrill 1979). Given, however, that one of the aims of educating a hearing-impaired pupil in an ordinary school is to allow the deaf and the normally hearing to become accustomed to one another from an early age, and to learn to accept each other despite differences, then integration policies can be judged to have had some success. The evidence from research on the social integration of hearing-impaired pupils in ordinary schools, and on their acceptance by teachers and pupils, does not lend support to the view, shared by many of those people opposed to integration policies in deaf education, that deaf pupils in ordinary schools because 'unhearing' are relegated to a low status position by the dominant 'hearing' group (McGrath 1981).

That part of my own research concerned with the reactions, attitudes and behaviour of class teachers and normally hearing pupils towards deaf pupils/classmates in ordinary schools both confirms the picture presented by previous research workers and enlarges upon it. The ordinary class teachers and normally hearing pupils who featured in my investigation were, generally speaking, accepting of the hearing impaired and prepared to make accommodations to their special needs.

The investigation has revealed that some class teachers were more enthusiastic than others about having a deaf pupil in their class. Reasons underlying favourable teacher attitudes, we saw, related to personal characteristics and ideas of the teachers themselves, features of the situation in which they were working, and qualities of the hearing-impaired pupils. 'Enthusiastic' teachers typically felt a sympathy for pupils handicapped by deafness and/or found them appealing in some special way. Deaf pupils were often perceived to be 'well-behaved' and this contributed to their acceptability. Those teachers who had previous experience of a deaf child, knew a deaf person, or who had a deaf relative, were found to be generally favourable towards receiving a deaf pupil into the class, as were teachers who held the firm conviction that handicapped children *ought* to be integrated into ordinary schools and not segregated in a special school.

In addition to exploring the attitudes of class teachers towards receiving a hearing-impaired pupil into their class the behaviour of teachers towards pupils with a hearing handicap was also investigated. It was found that a class teacher might be happy to receive a hearing-impaired pupil into her class but this does not mean that she is necessarily prepared to cater for his special educational needs or offer him appropriate educational attention. Observations in classrooms revealed differentiation in class teachers' responses in terms of the nature and amount of special accommodations that they were prepared to make to a deaf pupil.

Most class teachers made some accommodations to their hearing-impaired pupil and offered some extra help, but generally speaking the majority of teachers made only minor modifications to their teaching practices to accommodate the needs of a pupil with a hearing impairment. Teachers who offered most help to a deaf pupil and who made the most sensitive accommodations were those who were most aware of the severity and complexity of the problems confronting a pupil with a hearing loss *and* who felt that they had the time to devote to such a pupil. Thus the less class teachers were conscious of the 'abnormality' of their 'normal looking' deaf pupil, the less likely were they to offer such a pupil special or extra attention. Also, teachers working in what they believed to be 'difficult' conditions, such as having a large mixed ability class, or a 'tough' class, were found to be less likely than others to offer positive discrimination to a deaf pupil. Thus, it was possible for a teacher to receive a deaf pupil willingly into her class yet not offer him more than minimal special or extra help. This finding demonstrates that a favourable attitude towards a handicapped pupil on the part of the class teacher will not of itself guarantee such a pupil an effective education in the ordinary class. Teachers who treat their deaf pupils 'as normal' may in the long run, paradoxically, be contributing towards the abnormality of these pupils by failing to offer an education which enables the hearing-impaired pupil to reach normal or near-normal standards of attainment. It emerges from my findings, then, that it is important for those with overall responsibility for the education of hearing-impaired pupils in ordinary schools to become aware of the different responses and practices of class teachers who receive hearing-impaired pupils into their class because these responses and practices will influence both the nature of the advice that needs to be given to teachers and also the amount of support for the hearing-impaired pupil that needs to be provided by the specialist services.

Given that hearing-impaired pupils, and indeed other handicapped children, are tending to spend more time in ordinary classes there is a case for encouraging class teachers to make special adjustments to their teaching and for encouraging them to offer extra help and special attention to suit the needs to these pupils, but this will require positive action on the part of educational policy-makers. Only a quarter or so of the class teachers who featured in the investigation made more than minor accommodations to suit the needs of a pupil with a hearing handicap. If more positive discrimination from more class teachers is required, then teachers are going to need not only more guidance but more resources of time, knowledge and possibly ancillary help.

An awareness on the part of class teachers of the special status of a hearing-impaired pupil has been shown to have implications for the education of such pupils in ordinary classes. My research findings also suggest that an awareness on the part of normally hearing pupils of the special features of a pupil with a hearing loss has significance for the integration of the deaf pupil. The consequences of the normally hearing pupil perceiving that a deaf classmate was 'different' could be seen, in the main, to be beneficial. An awareness of the special problems confronting the deaf pupil in the ordinary school led many normally hearing pupils to offer sympathetic understanding and helpful accommodations which played an important part in facilitating the hearing-impaired pupil to adapt to life in ordinary classes. Examples of the kind of support offered the deaf pupil in the ordinary class by pupils with normal hearing included 'cueing-in' to when the teacher was talking, repeating or reformulating information and instructions from teachers, pointing to the right page, offering notes for copying, etc. These kinds of accommodations were acknowledged by the hearing-impaired pupils to be extremely useful in helping them to follow lessons. What should be encouraging to those concerned about the quality of education received by hearing-impaired pupils in ordinary schools is that the more normally hearing pupils become accustomed to being in classrooms alongside deaf pupils the more they take their differences for granted, and the more they routinise their help for their hearing-impaired classmate. Thus, normally hearing pupils could be seen to be offering special help, and making special accommodations to deaf classmates, apparently without needing to pay too much deliberate attention to, or having to reflect upon, what they were doing.

What might also give grounds for optimism to those educators keen to promote integration policies for broad social reasons is that although the normally hearing pupils were conscious that their deaf friends and classmates were in some ways different from themselves this did not appear to lead to imputations that the deaf were inferior. That is to say, deafness was not, in the minds of normally hearing pupils, associated with intellectual weakness. Generally speaking, an awareness that classmates were deaf did not give rise to the notion that deaf pupils were somehow not quite 'proper' pupils or that they were second-class citizens in the ordinary school.

Deaf pupils were, for the most part, liked and disliked according to 'normal' criteria — for qualities such as friendliness, attractiveness, generosity, liveliness, aggressiveness, aloofness, etc. Whilst there were a few examples of over-protective behaviour on the part of some younger normally hearing children, deaf pupils were not, in the main, found to be befriended because they were 'unfortunate' and deserving of pity, patronage or condescension.

That deafness conferred a special status on a pupil in the eyes of normally hearing pupils did, however, have its negative side. The mark of deafness, symbolised, for example, by difficulties of communication, attendance at a special class, etc., according to reports from both normally hearing pupils and teachers, led some pupils on some occasions to make fun of or name-call a hearing-impaired pupil. Neither teachers nor normally hearing pupils, however, believed that the phenomenon of teasing deaf pupils was widespread or serious or that there was any malice underlying the mild 'mickey-taking' which occurred. What did seem to evoke a certain amount of negative feeling in normally hearing pupils was not that a fellow pupil was deaf *per se*, but that such a pupil, because deaf, received more than his fair share of attention from teachers.

Most normally hearing pupils believed that deaf pupils, because of their handicap, merited some special consideration. However, there seemed to be a fine line drawn in the minds of some normally hearing pupils between teachers offering a reasonable amount of extra help to deaf pupils and giving them undue attention and unjustifiable privileges. Normally hearing pupils did not, for the most part, think hearing-impaired classmates should take up too much teacher time and they were particularly resentful if they thought teachers were allowing behaviour from hearing-impaired pupils which would not have been tolerated in themselves. Such 'allowances' appeared to many normally hearing pupils as unacceptable favouritism. Thus, an unintended but possible consequence of teachers offering positive discrimination to a deaf pupil in an ordinary class may be that such a pupil is resented or even ostracised by other pupils because he is believed to be the 'teacher's pet'. That pupils have such a keen sense of justice and are quick to notice what they believe to be the operation by teachers of dual standards of treatment, one for normally hearing pupils and another for the deaf, emphasises a requirement for teachers to offer positive discrimination to special needs pupils in the classroom with some sensitive discretion.

The evidence from my research revealed that pupils with a hearing handicap were generally accepted into the social milieux of normally hearing pupils and were treated in a friendly manner and indeed in many instances were 'made friends with'. In nearly all main school classes there were normally hearing pupils prepared to offer helpful accommodation and constructive support to a deaf classmate in order to facilitate his understanding of lessons and this is, I believe, significant. It is important for educators, concerned to ensure 'an optimum education' for the hearing-impaired pupil in the ordinary class, not only to be aware of this fund of special support from normally hearing pupils but also to take steps to develop and enlarge it. It might well be the case that if normally hearing pupils are given say, talks about deafness, the simulated experience of different types of hearing loss, demonstrations of the way hearing aids work, etc., then they might be even further encouraged to offer sensitive support to their hearing-impaired peers.

If the acceptance of deaf pupils by those with normal hearing, despite acknowledged differences, is considered to be an important objective of educating hearing-impaired pupils in ordinary schools, then my research findings are reassuring. The real test, however, of whether or not deaf pupils are socially integrated into the ordinary school is in terms of how the deaf themselves view their experiences of ordinary school life and whether they have a sense of belonging, or not belonging, to the social world of the normally hearing.

Investigation into the perceptions of and perspectives on an integrated education of hearing-impaired pupils and young people who were attending, or who had attended, ordinary schools, was, as we have seen, a central concern and feature of my research. Interviews with deaf pupils and deaf young adults revealed a mixture of views concerning themselves in relation to the normally hearing and to others who were deaf. Their views reflected both a desire to be as 'normal' as possible, that is, to talk normally, and to be part of the normally hearing group, and to a greater or lesser degree a sense of special identity as a deaf person. At one end of the spectrum of perspectives were hearing-impaired pupils and young people who had a weak sense of their deaf status and who felt to all intents and purposes 'normal'. These interviewees believed themselves to be assimilated into normally hearing society. At the other end of the spectrum were hearing-impaired individuals who had a strong sense of the difference between themselves and those with normal hearing and who, whilst participating on several levels in the hearing-speaking world, generally preferred the company of other deaf people. In many of the hearing-impaired pupils and young people a simultaneous sense of being both 'normal' *and* 'deaf' could be detected.

All the hearing-impaired pupils and young people subscribed to the principle of normalisation in that they all believed the major goal in deaf education should be teaching deaf children to talk. They believed that the ordinary school, in providing a normal spoken language environment, offered them as deaf pupils the best available means of acquiring the ability to talk normally. This view was held by deaf pupils and young people who used sign language together with those who eschewed any form of manual communication. Thus, virtually all the hearing-impaired pupils and young people who had views on the matter stated a preference for an education in an ordinary rather than in a special school. This does not, however, necessarily mean that they found life easy or always pleasant in the ordinary school.

Many hearing-impaired pupils and former pupils acknowledged that there were sometimes problems and even painful experiences in the ordinary school, such as difficulties in following ordinary class lessons, inconvenient and sometimes distressing noise, occasional experiences of being made fun of or victimised by certain of their normally hearing peers. None the less, despite day-to-day problems in and out of the classroom there was considerable agreement that the ordinary school provided the best 'preparation for life' in the adult hearing-speaking world. There seemed to be a universal desire among the deaf interviewees to acquire the behavioural norms of their normally hearing peers in order for them to be able to adapt to, and be accepted in, a hearing-speaking society. None questioned that they would need to conform to the expectations of the normally hearing if they were to cope with life as adults in a hearing-speaking world. The views of the hearing-impaired pupils and young people I interviewed are quite likely to be typical of deaf young people in the country as a whole as they were not specially selected, but I cannot with complete confidence make such a claim. In order to ascertain whether or not the opinions cited are representative of British deaf children and young people generally, it would be necessary to interview a much larger sample of deaf pupils and young people and one which included a proportion who were attending, or who had attended, special schools for all or most of their school lives.

That the research findings indicate a desire on the part of hearing-impaired pupils and young people to talk normally and become socialised into the ways of the normally hearing will undoubtedly be much welcomed by those teachers of the deaf who believe their chief responsibility is to teach deaf children to talk. However, there was evidence that some hearing-impaired pupils displayed on some occasions what might be seen as too strong a desire 'to be normal', or at least too strong a desire *to be perceived* 'as normal'. This was made apparent when deaf pupils tried to conceal their handicap and disattend to or deny the existence of the many problems associated with the handicap of deafness. Attitudes and behaviours reflecting a 'denial of handicap' were most apparent in relation to receiving special attention from teachers in the ordinary classroom.

Negative attitudes towards special attention from class teachers reflect the kind of feelings which perhaps any pupil might have in not wanting to be 'in the limelight', or to be seen by others as the 'teacher's pet'. Special attention was also unwelcome in the opinion of some deaf pupils and young people, though not all of them, because they felt it exposed their handicap and made them feel unacceptably different from other pupils. Some hearing-impaired interviewees admitted that they would 'pretend to understand' rather than admit that they were having difficulties in follow-ing lessons or rather than ask for help from teachers.

Oversubscribing to the idea of being 'normal' or affecting appearing to be 'normal' rather than acknowledging 'abnormality' is likely to be counter-productive for the deaf pupil. The long-term effect of strategies designed to deceive the teacher into believing that they were coping ade-quately and following the lessons, when the converse is true, might well be to increase the gap between hearing-impaired pupils' educational at-tainments and those achieved by normally hearing pupils.

An inspection of the public examination attainments at 16 years of age of the hearing-impaired young people who featured in the study did in-deed reveal that the deaf pupils' attainments were below national norms of attainment for all pupils. This finding reinforces the well established belief that if deaf pupils are to have equal opportunity to develop their educational potential then they require positive discrimination. On the other hand my research has demonstrated that offering positive discrimina-tion to deaf pupils in ordinary classes can be a problem. It may be a problem for class teachers in relation to the scarcity of resources such as time and expertise; it may be a problem for normally hearing pupils in that they are likely to feel resentment if deaf classmates are given what they see to be unfair 'favouritism'; and, very importantly, it may be a problem for hearing-impaired pupils who might not want attention drawn to their special problems and special status. [1]

In addition to ensuring that class teachers have adequate resources to enable them to offer special help to the deaf pupil, and in addition to ensuring that normally hearing pupils are made aware of the special pro-blems caused by a hearing handicap and the consequent special educa-tional attention that deaf pupils so often need, it is also likely to be necessary to counsel hearing-impaired pupils themselves to come to terms with special attention. This is so that they do not feel ashamed or embar-rassed about their handicap, and are not afraid to ask for help when ex-periencing difficulties in following lessons. Deaf pupils should be en-couraged not to feel humiliated if a teacher offers extra help or checks

---

1. The increasingly popular practice of providing support teachers, usually teachers of the deaf, to assist hearing-impaired pupils in ordinary classes relieves class teachers of the extra work such pupils are likely to entail. But, support teachers cannot be in ordinary classes all the time and class teachers have, therefore, to take some responsibility for the education of the deaf pupil despite the demands which doing so might entail. Furthermore, though the presence of a special teacher in the classroom might benefit the class teacher, it is potentially very stigmatising for the deaf pupil receiving the assistance.

their understanding. Indeed, some hearing-impaired pupils in ordinary schools may need to be firmly advised that pretending that their problems in main school classes do not exist might offer short-term relief but is likely in the long run to exacerbate rather than lessen the effects of their handicap.

Consideration might also be given to other additional forms of compensatory education for the hearing impaired. One compensation might be simply to inform the hearing-impaired pupil and his parents that greater than average efforts are required at home and in school in order to enlarge his educational opportunity and help to overcome the effects of a hearing handicap. The deaf child, if possible with the help of his parents, might be encouraged to do extra school work, or extra reading and language work at home. Another form of positive discrimination would be to extend the period of compulsory education for severely and profoundly deaf pupils.

Generally, then, my research findings indicate that however much a deaf pupil appreciates and values the 'normalising' environment of the ordinary school and however much parents and educators support the goal of normalisation in the education of the deaf, normalisation will not just 'happen' simply by placing a hearing-impaired pupil in an ordinary school. Appropriate positive discrimination is clearly necessary if deaf pupils are to fulfil their expressed desire to talk normally and be capable of adapting to the demands and expectations of hearing-speaking society. When a consideration is being made concerning the kinds of special help and extra support that might be offered to deaf pupils in ordinary schools it is crucially important that such help and support is given in a way that is made acceptable to the consumer of the service, namely, the deaf pupil himself.

The major reason why deaf interviewees wanted to talk normally was so that they might mix with, and make friends with, people who have normal hearing and who communicate by oral/aural means. Nearly all the hearing-impaired pupils and young people who featured in my research wanted to interact socially with the normally hearing, though not all wanted to mix exclusively with normally hearing-speaking people. The majority certainly wanted more than just minimal interaction with those who could hear and speak.

Three broad categories of social attitudes and behaviour were discernible among deaf interviewees with reference to the hearing-speaking world. First, there were those who wanted what might be termed 'all-out assimilation' into hearing-speaking society. These hearing-impaired pupils and young people, who constituted almost half the total, wanted as far as possible to shake off their 'deaf' or 'unit' identity tag and to reduce to a minimum their contact with those who were deaf. They wanted to mix as much as possible with those who had normal hearing. Some who were in this 'all-out assimilation' category had only moderate hearing losses and thus felt themselves to be 'not deaf'. Others, whilst having a more severe hearing handicap, none the less chose, and oriented to, the normally hearing as their reference-group.

In the next category were those hearing-impaired pupils and young people who identified to a significant extent with the normally hearing but who felt some need or wish to have contact with others who had a hearing impairment. Approximately half came into this 'dual identity' category. Those still at school had both deaf and normally hearing friends. Those who had left school participated for the most part in the everyday life of the normally hearing but, in addition, formed part of a more or less loose network of deaf people. Some maintained their place 'in the deaf world' by attending Deaf Clubs; others had more casual and informal association with other deaf people, characteristically people who were ex-school friends. Though the deaf young people in this category spent most of their lives in the company of those who had normal hearing they liked to associate, more or less regularly, with friends and acquaintances with a similar handicap in order to talk over shared problems and to experience that sense of commonality which derives from being with people who had in common with themselves the significant feature of deafness.

The third category, comprising very much a minority, participated in the day-to-day hearing-speaking world but were strongly oriented towards others who were deaf: they felt most affinity for deaf people and formed their close social relationships from among the deaf group. Those in this category (there were only two) had a firm sense of their special identity as deaf people.

That the hearing impaired featuring in the research held different viewpoints, and adopted different stances in respect of their relationships with others in society, suggests that they were not subject to a single source of influence. Their attitude and behaviour were almost certainly affected by parents and teachers of the deaf. But there was no evidence that I could detect to suggest that those who chose to identify primarily with the normally hearing had been 'indoctrinated' to espouse 'normality', or compelled to cast off their deaf identity. Likewise, there were no grounds for believing that those who chose to attend Deaf Clubs and use sign language had been told that they must preserve their special identity and participate in deaf culture. Whether or not those deaf pupils and young people, particularly those with profound hearing losses, who strove to be part of the normally hearing world, and who disliked the idea of communicating through sign language had 'false consciousness', or whether, indeed, they were acting in their own best interest is a matter of value judgement. The responses of the hearing-impaired people, no matter what their attitude towards coping with their handicap, did not, however, support the allegation that the ordinary school forced:

> the deaf individual into a situation in which he must try to deny his deafness, imitate a hearing person and pretend he enjoys it. (Merrill 1979)

No hearing-impaired pupil or young person observed or interviewed found it impossible to interact at some level with those who had normal hearing and the majority had regular and frequent social contact with others who were not deaf. Variations among them in their perceptions about themselves in relation to others and variations in their social orientation were manifest mainly in terms of the *degree* of assimilation into handicapped society. Those who believed that they were full members of normally hearing society felt themselves to be 'normal'. Others, who oriented to hearing-speaking society but had maintained contact with other deaf people mainly for mutual support and understanding felt more or less 'normalised'. Even the minority who formed their closest associations from among the deaf group were not part of a close-knit deaf community and no one expressed a wish to belong to any such group.

Some knew sign language and frequently or occasionally used visual/manual communication when interacting with other deaf people. A few deaf young people believed it would be beneficial if deaf children were taught sign language as part of their school education. Such a belief did not, however, detract from the conviction of all the hearing impaired that the acquisition of spoken English was and should be the major goal of their education and of their personal aspiration.

Many of the deaf people interviewed not only felt that they had no need to know sign language but rejected the idea of using sign, mainly on the grounds that to do so would tend to make them too closely identified with what they saw as a rather exclusive and separate deaf world. The hearing-impaired pupils and young people who could not sign did not feel a sense of deprivation at not being able to use their so-called 'biologically preferred mode' of communication.

Generally, though, the findings of this aspect of my investigation suggest that whilst most deaf pupils and young people do not want to be part of a distinctive and exclusive deaf subculture, with its own special language, nearly half felt a need for association and friendship with others who were similarly handicapped. It is significant, I believe, that most of the hearing-impaired pupils and young people who had been individually integrated into their local school, and who did not have the opportunity at school to meet other deaf pupils, expressed some regret at not knowing someone of similar age with a similar handicap. Thus whilst placing a deaf pupil individually in his local school might be considered to be serving his best interests in terms of, say, extending opportunities for increasing his academic or linguistic attainments, such placement can mean a restriction of opportunity in terms of being able to have companionship with other deaf people. Being able to talk about problems shared in common with other deaf people can be very important to the deaf individual's sense of well-being. Enthusiasm for assimilation and normalisation should not blind educators from acknowledging that a severe sensorineural hearing loss represents a permanent and serious handicap for a deaf individual. Education cannot cure deafness; it can only alleviate its worst effects. Thus it may well be necessary for educators to take special measures to enable individually integrated deaf pupils to form contacts with others who are deaf, if they so wish. Education, most people would agree, is concerned with extending opportunities and enlarging choices for individuals and not restricting them. Furthermore, my research indicates that educators, who, we may assume, want to help the deaf individual gain independence and overcome his handicap to the maximum extent possible, might devote more attention to advising deaf pupils of the many special services available for deaf people to make use of because many of the deaf participating in my research were unaware of the range of facilities, services and aids designed to make life easier for someone with a hearing handicap.

Finally, I would propose that in order to help deaf pupils eventually to become more self-sufficient, independent adults, such pupils should be consulted about their education more often than is currently the case. My research findings indicate that an education in an ordinary school is popular with hearing-impaired pupils and young people. This does not mean, as we have seen, that there are no problems associated with an integrated education for the hearing impaired, nor that matters could not be improved so that deaf pupils receive a more effective education in an ordinary school. It would, I suggest, be wrong to assume that teachers of the deaf in this country, who almost invariably have normal hearing, always know what is best for the deaf pupil. Consulting and counselling deaf pupils about the education they are receiving in ordinary schools may not only lead to improvements in their education but also give deaf pupils the experience of having some say in, and influence over, their own destiny. This is particularly important in relation to the current criticisms voiced by 'anti-integrationists' such as Merrill (1979) and McCay Vernon (1981) that too little account is taken of the 'voice of the deaf' when planning educational provision for the hearing impaired.

APPENDIX I

Different Patterns of Integrated Provision for Hearing-impaired Pupils in Ordinary Schools

A variety of patterns of educational provision are plainly discernible in the integrated education of the hearing impaired. One can in the first place distinguish two broad forms of provision: unit provision and individual integration.

What all units have in common is that severely hearing-impaired pupils are educated in one school. The school is, generally speaking, not the pupil's local one, and there is at least one teacher of the deaf based at the school. There are, however, many different ways in which unit provision can be organised and it would probably be true to say that no two units in Britain are alike in their organisation. None the less three major types of unit arrangements for educating hearing-impaired pupils can be distinguished: full or almost full-time education in a special class in the ordinary school; part-time education in a special class/part-time in an ordinary class; full-time, or almost full-time, attendance in ordinary classes with occasional withdrawal to the special class.

Individual integration on the other hand is distinguished from unit provision in that, generally, the hearing-impaired pupil is placed full time in his local school where he is likely to be the only deaf pupil in that school. He can receive specialist educational support either from a peripatetic teacher of the deaf or alternatively, for at least part of the school day, he is assisted by a specially appointed support teacher who works with him in the classroom whilst normal lessons take place. (It is of course possible, and indeed sometimes the pratice where there is unit provision, for a teacher of the deaf to act as a support teacher in the ordinary class.)

Within the two broad forms of provision, unit and individual integration, there are, thus, five broad types of integrated education for hearing-impaired pupils, each with inherent strengths and weaknesses. In order to evaluate the different types of integrated education it is useful, first, to examine the advantages and disadvantages of unit provision in contrast to individual integration before considering more specifically the pros and cons of the different types of integration within those two broad forms.

Unit Provision

Advantages

1. The hearing-impaired pupil has access to someone specially trained to teach the deaf who can offer several different kinds of educational and moral support and extra help.
2. The deaf pupil is given the opportunity to form close relationships with others who are similarly handicapped.
3. Specialised facilities can easily be centralised in a unit so that a hearing-impaired pupil has access to, for example, an acoustically treated room, a speech trainer, hearing aid spare parts, battery recharger, language master, etc.
4. In theory, and often in practice, units can offer a flexibility of arrangements so that a hearing-impaired pupil can receive just the degree and level of specialist support he requires.
5. Teachers in the main school can, over the years, become increasingly knowledgeable about the educational implications of deafness and are, therefore, more able to cater for the special educational needs of hearing-impaired pupils. Thus, there tends to be in a school with a unit, an accumulation of 'specialist' expertise among ordinary class teachers.
6. It is relatively easy and 'cost-effective' to inform and advise both ordinary teachers and pupils in a school with a unit about the special problems resulting from deafness and to demonstrate how they can offer valuable and sensitive support.

Disadvantages

1. Travelling to and from the unit is both tiring for the pupil and expensive for the Local Education Authority. Travel commitments may also preclude deaf children from joining in after-school activities.
2. The distance between home and school may be such that friendships made at school are difficult to sustain out of school.
3. The deaf pupil in a unit, because part of an identifiable group, is more likely to be labelled 'deaf' by other pupils and be subject to teasing and name-calling.
4. The presence of other deaf pupils in the school may reduce the incentive for the hearing-impaired child to make friends and associate with normally hearing pupils.
5. The hearing-impaired pupil may become emotionally and academically over-dependent on the unit teacher of the deaf.

6. The hearing-impaired pupil in a unit receives greater than average surveillance by teachers, particularly by the teacher(s) of the deaf. Whereas this can in some ways be to his advantage it can increase his discomfort and reduce his freedom of action.

7. It might be difficult for the unit teacher of the deaf to fulfil conflicting roles, for example, teacher, academic judge, confidante, etc. Yet the deaf pupil, because of his special difficulties, needs help with his personal problems as well as with his academic work.

Individual Integration

Advantages

1. The individually integrated hearing-impaired pupil does not have to travel to a school outside his neighbourhood so school friendships can be reinforced in the neighbourhood and neighbourhood friendships can be maintained at school.

2. The individually integrated hearing-impaired pupil is obliged to make friends with normally hearing pupils and is more likely to identify with the normally hearing group.

3. Full-time attendance at an ordinary school is challenging and demanding and can stimulate the hearing-impaired pupil to make his best effort both academically and socially.

4. The deaf pupil has to come to terms with his handicap in a *normal* setting.

5. The individually integrated hearing-impaired pupil is not as likely to be labelled and stigmatised as he would be if he were a member of an easily identifiable group of exclusively deaf pupils.

6. Research evidence (for example, Jensema and Trybus 1979; Dale 1984) suggests that, other factors being equal, the individually integrated pupil is academically more successful than his counterpart in a special class.

7. Fully integrated deaf pupils may suffer more of the 'knocks of everyday life' in a hearing society than they would in a more protected environment but they are more likely to develop a healthy resilience which will serve them well on leaving school.

Disadvantages

1. The special educational needs of the fully integrated deaf pupil may be overlooked and he may not understand a lot of what is going on in lessons.

2. The individually integrated deaf pupil may feel isolated and unhappy because he has no one at hand with whom he can talk over or share his special problems. He may daily feel more frustrated by a sense of his own inadequacy in relation to other pupils.

3. The deaf pupil in the ordinary school is deprived of the companionship of other deaf pupils and may not find it easy for logistic reasons to become part of a deaf subgroup or informal social network, should he wish to do so.

4. Ordinary class teachers are possibly less likely to make special accommodations to deaf pupils because they generally are less aware than teachers working in schools with units of the educational implications of a hearing loss.

5. Normally hearing pupils, through lack of awareness of the implications of deafness, are less likely to offer helpful, and sometimes much needed, accommodations to a hearing-impaired classmate.

6. The individually integrated deaf pupil is almost certain to be educated in classrooms which are not acoustically treated and where there is, characteristically, a lot of noise. The hearing-impaired pupil may well feel discomforted and may not get maximum benefit from his hearing aids.

7. The integrated deaf pupil in classrooms with poor acoustic conditions and large numbers of pupils may receive insufficient language input to develop his linguistic potential. It may be a particular problem for the young deaf child to acquire language in the ordinary class because he is not likely to get much individual time and attention from his class teacher. Other children will undoubtedly communicate with him but it is generally recognised that young children do not provide good language models for each other.

So far I have considered some of the benefits and shortcomings of the two broad forms of provision, unit and individual integration. In order to throw more light on the many different practices of the integrated education of hearing-impaired pupils, I want next to itemise the advantages and disdvantages of the major types of provision for deaf pupils in ordinary schools which fall within these two broad categories.

Separate Special Class Provision Within the Ordinary School

Advantages

1. The hearing-impaired child who receives all or almost all his education in a special class within the ordinary school is taught by someone

specially trained to teach the deaf.

2. The listening conditions in the special classroom are likely to be good and the pupils can get maximum benefit from hearing aids.
3. Intensive tuition on any topic of education is possible.
4. The young deaf child with minimal linguistic competence can benefit from considerable language input in optimum acoustic conditions from a skilled adult talker.
5. The deaf pupil is afforded maximum opportunity to form close relationships with others similarly handicapped.
6. Deaf children who are *very* handicapped, that is with poor communication skills, or who have other handicaps in addition to their deafness can none the less be educated within an ordinary school and participate, where appropriate, in some ordinary school activities. These children can live at home rather than be sent away to residential school and, therefore, get some experience of the 'normal' world before leaving school. Parents are generally happier with this arrangement rather than have their children sent to segregated special schools.

Disadvantages

1. The heterogeneity of special classes in terms of age, hearing loss and ability can make it difficult if not impossible for one teacher to teach effectively. Hence, the individualisation of educational programmes, which is in principle possible, in practice tends to be unworkable. Deaf pupils do not get the one-to-one tuition that they might be thought to need.
2. There is the possibility that a deaf pupil is taught by one teacher for several years. This is likely to mean a restriction of educational experience. The unsatisfactory situation is further exacerbated if there is a personality clash between teacher and pupil.
3. There can all too easily be an over-protective, even claustrophobic, atmosphere in a separate special class. Norms of behaviour may develop within the class which are inappropriate and unacceptable within the main school.
4. It is almost certainly impossible within the confines of one, often small, classroom to offer the full range of curricular activities and options available in the main school.
5. Teachers of the deaf in segregated units are likely to become isolated from their colleagues in the main school and out of touch with current educational practice. They may well, because of lack of experience of 'normal' pupils, lower their academic expectations of

their deaf pupils.

6. Deaf pupils are for the most part isolated from their hearing peers and friendships between deaf and normally hearing pupils are likely to be more difficult to make and sustain.

Unit Tutorial or Resource Room Provision

Advantages

1. The hearing-impaired pupil who uses the resources of the unit but who spends nearly all his school day in ordinary classes receives most of the benefits of full-time integration: that is, a 'normal' curriculum, the full facilities of the school, generally higher academic expectations and the opportunity to associate and form friendships with normally hearing classmates.
2. The deaf pupil is not deprived of the opportunity to associate with hearing-impaired pupils should he wish to do so.
3. The hearing-impaired pupil in a school with a teacher of the deaf 'on-site' is secure in the knowledge that he has someone to go to if he has any special educational or other problems. He can, of course, make use of any technical and specialist educational resource facilities of the unit.
4. The almost fully integrated deaf pupil benefits from being educated by several teachers, not just by one teacher of the deaf.

Disadvantages

1. Given the limited amount of time the fully integrated unit pupil spends in the resource room it is difficult to decide what is best to do in that time. The hearing-impaired pupil is likely to have many needs such as: tutorial assistance for main school lessons; general counselling, advice and moral support; help with reading and writing skills, etc. The unit teacher cannot cater for *all* these needs. Thus, some of the hearing-impaired pupil's educational needs must go unmet.
2. The unit deaf pupil who spends nearly all his school day in ordinary classes does not receive much specialist attention yet has the probable disadvantages of having to travel a long distance to school and of being separated from his neighbourhood friends.

Part-time Special Class/Part-time Ordinary Class Provision

Advantages

1. Part-time integration is often thought to be an acceptable compromise between segregation and full integration. With partial integration the deaf pupil experiences the benefits that derive from ordinary class attendance yet has the advantage of being taught for a significant amount of time by a teacher qualified to deal with his special needs.

Disadvantages

1. It may in practice be difficult to decide which subjects can be best pursued in the main school and which in the special class. Decisions can often be based on questionable criteria: for example, a pupil may receive his geography lessons in the unit because the teacher of the deaf is a geography specialist; a pupil may be sent to main school drama lessons because the drama teacher is known to be 'kind' to deaf pupils.
2. The teacher of the deaf has the problem of deciding the balance of activities to be pursued in the special class; of choosing between several options all of which seem crucial to the educational development of the hearing-impaired pupil. Some very desirable and necessary educational topics are likely to have to be rejected because of lack of time.
3. The partially integrated deaf pupil may find it difficult to become attuned to ordinary classroom routines and the ways in which normally hearing pupils behave and think. He may be regarded as a 'marginal' member of the class by other pupils.
4. The main school teacher may not regard her part-time hearing-impaired pupil as her own and may feel absolved from taking responsibility for his educational development.

The Provision of Individual Integration with Peripatetic Support

Advantages

1. The deaf pupil has regular access to a teacher who understands his special educational needs and difficulties.
2. Given a generously staffed peripatetic service, some of the problems associated with full-time integration can be overcome, for example, young deaf children can be given frequent and intensive periods of language tuition; class teachers can be informed about deafness and

advised how to accommodate to the special needs of the hearing-impaired pupil; pupils in the ordinary class can be given a talk about deafness, how hearing aids work, etc. and be shown how to offer helpful support to a deaf classmate.

3. The hearing-impaired pupil with problems, especially as he gets older, is more likely to confide in an 'outside' person than a member of staff in the school.

Disadvantages

1. The deaf child may resent being withdrawn from his class for special attention.
2. The visiting teacher of the deaf cannot help a hearing-impaired pupil with specific day-to-day problems as they occur.
3. The peripatetic teacher has the difficult problem of deciding how to make best use of the short time available at any particular school. This problem is particularly acute when peripatetic teachers have heavy case loads and, therefore, cannot devote much time to any one pupil or his teachers.

The Provision of Individual Supported Integration

Advantages

1. When the teacher is located in the classroom of the fully integrated hearing-impaired pupil she can offer assistance directly relevant to the classwork immediately it is needed.
2. It may be possible at appropriate times for the support teacher to offer tuition to the deaf pupil in speech and language.
3. Individually supported integration allows pupils with more serious handicaps to remain in the ordinary class.
4. The support teacher can on occasions, and where appropriate, offer help to other pupils in the class.
5. The presence of a support teacher in the classroom can have the effect of sensitising class teachers and other pupils to the special needs of deaf pupils.

Disadvantages

1. There is a danger that the deaf pupil becomes too dependent on the support teacher and does not try hard enough to sort out problems for himself.

2. The deaf pupil might feel unduly singled out and stigmatised by having a teacher close by him scrutinising his work and surveying his every move.
3. The deaf pupil might resent the special attention which serves as a constant reminder of his handicap and his difference from others.
4. Whilst some teachers might readily welcome another pair of skilled teaching hands in the class not all teachers would welcome the presence of another teacher in the classroom.

Once a particular educational option is decided upon, it is useful to be mindful of the inherent disadvantages of that provision and to try to compensate for those disadvantages. For example, if a young deaf child needs to be in a special class for the sake of his language development the problem of social isolation arising from this type of provision might be overcome by a policy of inviting into the unit, periodically, a few children from the ordinary class.

It should be stressed that it is because there are no easy solutions to the difficulties of educating a hearing-impaired pupil that careful thought should be given to the disadvantages, and ways of overcoming them, as well as to the advantages of the type of integration offered in the ordinary school.

Case Studies of Four Hearing-impaired Pupils Integrated Into Ordinary Schools

In order to make comparisons between the four pupils easier the description and discussion is confined to the secondary experiences of each pupil.

Mark

Mark has an average hearing loss in the better ear of 70 dB and wears a post-aural aid. He attended a special school for the hearing impaired as a young child (aged four to six years) and was then transferred to his local primary school: there he was visited regularly once a week by a peripatetic teacher of the deaf. Mark was believed to have coped well at his junior school and achieved just above average attainments. A move in residence on the part of his family meant that he changed LEAs when transferred to secondary school.

Mark's speech sounds normal, apart from his very rapid rate of utterance. He claims to understand the speech of others but none the less finds the effort a strain in some situations. For example, throughout his school life he reports that he always made every attempt to follow lessons but that this effort often resulted in his having a headache by the end of the day.

For the first term at secondary school Mark was visited by a peripatetic teacher of the deaf. She visited Mark every fortnight for about 20–30 minutes during which time she listened to him read. After the first term Mark received no further visits from a teacher of the deaf until his final year at school. Subsequently a newly appointed peripatetic teacher visited Mark regularly, though not frequently (once every three or four weeks). She devoted her time to advising him about further education and employment.

For most of his time at secondary school Mark felt he was treated as any other pupil by teachers. No teacher, according to him, made any special concessions to his handicap; he states that no one ever checked whether he had understood the lesson, obtained the information he needed, etc. He says he would have liked more concern to have been shown about his special problems.

Mark took six CSEs and achieved one Grade 1 and five at Grades 2

263

or 3. He now attends an FE College where he is taking some GCE 'O' levels.

Mark is sociable and amiable and has many friends, none of whom has a hearing impairment.

Alison

Alison has an average hearing loss of 65 dB in the better ear: she wears one post-aural aid. Alison received both her primary and secondary education in a phu. Her speech is intelligible and apart from a few minor defects such as a sloppy 's' and a slightly nasal voice, she sounds reasonably normal. Her understanding of speech is nearly normal. Alison tends to look intently at the face of a speaker and occasionally asks for repetitions of what was previously said.

On entering secondary school Alison was believed to have 'about average' intelligence though her educational attainments were slightly 'below average'. She was regarded by teachers as being a sensible, friendly girl with a stable personality. She had no difficulty in forming relationships with others be they hearing impaired or normally hearing.

For the first two years at secondary school Alison spent 40–50 per cent of her time in the phu: there she was taught Maths, English and some History and Geography in a small group of similarly aged hearing-impaired pupils. At this stage of education she attended main school classes for non-academic subjects such as needlework and PE and those subjects such as science, for example, which could not easily be taught in the special classroom. As was general for phu pupils in this school, the time spent in ordinary classes increased as Alison became older. By the age of 16 years she spent 80 per cent of her time in the main school, returning to the unit for language work and for back-up support for some of her ordinary class lessons.

Throughout her secondary school years Alison mixed with both hearing-impaired and normally hearing pupils. At age 16 her 'best' friend was one with normal hearing. Alison passed two CSEs with average grades and left school to take a Secretarial Course at a local FE college.

Paul

Paul is profoundly deaf with an average hearing loss of 108 dB in the better ear. He wore a hearing aid at school because recommended to do so by teachers, but subsequently has ceased to wear an aid as he believes: 'They no good to me. I'm too deaf.' Paul's speech has always been unintelligible to most people: his voice is deep and monotonous; his rhythm is deviant; his articulation of consonants is poor and there is virtually no differentiation between his vowels. His spoken language shows many syntactical errors though he has a reasonably sophisticated vocabulary. Paul's comprehension of speech is limited: he understands little of normal conversations unless utterances are simplified and directed specifically towards him.

Paul attended a special school for the deaf until he was twelve, at which age, along with many other deaf children in his LEA, he was transferred to a newly opened secondary phu. Paul was judged to be much above average in intelligence. His reading age at twelve was, however, only 8.5 years: this was more a reflection of his weak sense of language structure than of poor vocabulary.

For all his years at the secondary phu Paul attended ordinary classes for about 90 per cent of the time. He returned to the unit for about four periods a week, mainly for help with material he had not understood in main school lessons. Paul claimed to understand very little of what teachers said when addressing the class as a whole. Most class teachers were, however, sensitive to the severity of Paul's handicap and would generally go over points with him during the latter part of the lesson. Given this extra help, Paul claimed to be able to 'catch on' to the content of lessons reasonably easily and this is borne out by his fairly good examination performance at 16 years of age. Paul obtained two GCE 'O' levels and two CSEs at Grade 1 with three further CSEs at other grades.

Paul did not make any close friends at school either with the hearing-impaired or normally hearing pupils. He had great difficulty in understanding his classmates and they experienced problems in understanding him. Consequently, according to the reports of several teachers, many of Paul's normally hearing peers tended to avoid contact with him in order to escape embarrassment.

On leaving school, Paul obtained a BEC qualification in Computer Studies and is now working in the Medical Records Department of a local hospital.

Gwen

Gwen is severely deaf with an average hearing loss in the better ear of 75 dB: she wears one high-powered post-aural aid. For the whole of her school life Gwen was placed full time in the ordinary school.

By the age of eleven years Gwen had achieved above average attainments in reading, writing and maths and was considered by her teachers to be a 'bright' girl. She was also regarded as very likeable, lively and full of fun. Her speech is 'near normal': her voice has a slightly deep 'laryngeal' quality and she occasionally leaves off word endings.

Otherwise she sounds normal, so much so that she makes a special point of making her hearing aid visible so that others know that she has a hearing problem. Gwen's understanding of the speech of others varies according to circumstances and she acknowledges that she has great difficulty in following conversations among groups of people. Because of her personal and intellectual qualities full-time individual placement in an ordinary school seemed the most suitable option for Gwen at the secondary stage of education. She was placed in a relatively small girls' school which had a reputation for its academic standards and also for being a 'caring' school. It was believed that Gwen had sufficient intelligence to cope with the academic work and would benefit, as a handicapped pupil, from the small size of the school and the sympathetic attitudes of the staff.

Gwen claimed to be very happy throughout her secondary school years. She refers to her 'comfortable compact little life' at secondary school. She was generally popular with both pupils and staff and had two very close friends from her class.

Gwen was visited about once a fortnight by a peripatetic teacher of the deaf who acted mainly as a counsellor to her and as an adviser to the teaching staff at the school. On the whole both staff and pupils in the school were sensitive to Gwen's special needs and many teachers adapted their teaching styles in order to help her understand the content of lessons. Gwen was extremely dependent on her friends for support during lessons and she admitted that in some classes she had 'nil idea of what was going on'. Her friends would frequently relay to Gwen what the teacher had said and offer their notes and sometimes homework for Gwen to copy. Gwen did not welcome 'a lot of fuss' from teachers and preferred not to be singled out for too much special attention.

In spite of being happy at secondary school, Gwen did not, for some reason, take academic work seriously and at age 16 years failed all six of the GCE 'O' levels she took. Gwen passed at low grades in two CSE subjects, the only ones offered by the school.

Discrepancies in Provision: A Brief Discussion

It is not my intention here to make judgements about the appropriateness of provision for each of these 'integrated' hearing-impaired pupils. My intention is simply to demonstrate that there were disparities in the amount and type of special support offered to these pupils which cannot be accounted for in terms of individual features such as hearing loss, intellectual ability, or linguistic attainments. Interesting yet puzzling questions emerge from these case studies. Why for instance was Alison, the least deaf of all, placed in the most protected educational environment? Why did Mark receive such minimal special support during most of his secondary school years compared to the other three pupils? Why did Mark's first peripatetic teacher think it important to check his reading ability whereas Gwen's peripatetic teacher of the deaf preferred to talk about problems in general? Why did Paul, given the severity of his hearing loss and level of linguistic attainments, both spoken and written, receive virtually no specialist tuition in speech and language? The list of questions such as these could be extended.

Explanations for some of the differences in the educational treatment received by each pupil can be given in terms of the heritage of educational institutions for the deaf in each respective LEA and in terms of their financial resources. It should be remembered, however, that the amount of money LEAs are prepared to devote to services for hearing-impaired children, and the degree to which they are prepared to retain or change existing structures of educational provision, is very much a political and ideological matter. Even the brief outline I have given of the experiences of four hearing-impaired pupils living in four different LEAs demonstrates that integration as a practice is interpreted in different ways by different people. There are different notions of, say, 'individual special needs', 'optimum provision' and 'most appropriate environment'. In all LEAs there was a consensus of view that deaf children should develop competence in oral language and, as far as possible become assimilated into normally hearing society. In these four cases, therefore, variations in provision almost certainly relate not so much to divergences of opinion on broad aims but to differences in thinking on the best way to achieve those aims. Similar ends are sought but different routes have been selected in order to arrive at those ends.

Informal Interviews with Hearing-impaired Pupils and Young People 1983–4: Main Areas of Enquiry

The interviews, in keeping with my epistemological approach, were informal and for the most part loosely structured so as to capture the rich incarnate character of opinions and views of interviewees on integration, but this does not imply that 'just anything' was asked or discussed or that no interviewer control was exercised. After exploring the literature on integration and undertaking a wide range of sensitising discussions and observations with both teachers and pupils the following schedule of relevant 'obligatory' topic areas was compiled and used as an *aide-mémoire*, or guide, in interviewing.

1. General attitudes to ordinary school placement.
2. Reasons for liking/disliking, preferring/not preferring an education in an ordinary rather than a special school.
3. Features of an ordinary school education which were believed to be significant, for example, a normal social and academic environment; opportunities for mixing with normally hearing pupils; preparation for life and work in a hearing-speaking society.
4. Ideas and beliefs about what constitutes proper goals in the education of deaf pupils.
5. Difficulties and day-to-day problems experienced in ordinary classrooms, for example, noise; understanding the spoken and written lesson material, class discussions, dictation, teacher lectures, video and soundtapes, radio and TV.
6. Strategies for overcoming problems in ordinary classes, for example, seeking help from a neighbouring pupil; copying from another pupil; seeking help from class teacher; seeking help from teacher of the deaf; seeking help from parents; day-dreaming; pretending to understand; acting naughty; concentrating harder; doing extra work at home; reading as much as possible.
7. Attitudes to extra or special help from class teachers; feelings about special attention from teachers.
8. Views concerning experiences in ordinary and special classes; ideas about full-time and part-time integration and the advantages and

disadvantages of being in a unit or full time in a local school.

9. Satisfaction or otherwise with their academic attainments; perceptions of academic achievements when compared with those of normally hearing pupils.
10. General attitudes towards normally hearing pupils in ordinary school.
11. Need or wish for interaction and friendship with normally hearing pupils.
12. Nature and quality of social relationships with normally hearing pupils — close and intimate or distant and remote.
13. Difficulties experienced in interacting with normally hearing parents.
14. Preferences for normally hearing and hearing-impaired friends.
15. Attitudes to victimisation, teasing and name-calling; awareness of the phenomenon; perception of the foregoing as a 'problem'; strategies for coping with being made fun of, or called names.
16. Attitudes to wearing hearing aids both in and outside school.
17. Views of the hearing-impaired young people who had left school about how well the ordinary school had prepared them for life in a normally hearing society; their place in a normally hearing world; the nature and amount of participation in ordinary society; the need and wish to associate with other people with impaired hearing; feelings about being deaf; their views on using sign language as a means of communication.

GLOSSARY OF TERMS AND ABBREVIATIONS

BATOD   British Association of Teachers of the Deaf
BDA   British Deaf Association
BSAG   Bristol Social Adjustment Guide
CSE   Certificate of Secondary Education
DES   Department of Education and Science
DHSS   Department of Health and Social Security
FE   Further Education
GCE   General Certificate of Education
LEA   Local Education Authority
NDCS   National Deaf Children's Society
NUD   National Union of the Deaf
phu   partially-hearing unit

Definitions Relating to Levels of Hearing Loss in Children (BATOD 1981)

Slightly hearing-impaired	Children whose average hearing loss does not exceed 40 dB.
Moderately hearing-impaired	Children whose average hearing loss is from 41 dB to 70 dB.
Severely hearing-impaired	Children whose average hearing loss is from 71 dB to 95 dB.
Profoundly hearing-impaired	Children who were born with, or who acquired before the age of 18 months, an average hearing loss of 96 dB or greater.

The terms 'deaf' and 'hearing-impaired' are used throughout the book to refer to pupils or young people with significant hearing losses; they do not imply a specific degree of hearing loss.

REFERENCES

Alexander, C. and Strain, P (1978) 'A Review of Educators' Attitudes Toward Handicapped Children and the Concept of Mainstreaming', *Journal of Psychology in Schools*, 15 (3), 390–6

Allsop, J. (1980) 'Mainstreaming Physically Handicapped Students', *Journal of Research and Development in Education*, 13 (4), 37–44

Anderson, E.M. (1973) *The Disabled Schoolchild*, London: Methuen

—— and Clarke, L. (1982) *Disability in Adolescence*, London: Methuen

Antia, S.D. (1982) 'Mainstreaming of Hearing-Impaired Children Though Affected by the Law is not a Recent Phenomenon in the History of the Education of the Hearing Impaired', *American Annals of the Deaf*, 127, 18–25

Baker, J.L. and Gottlieb, J. (1980) 'Attitudes of Teachers Toward Mainstreaming Retarded Children' in Gottlieb, J. (ed.), *Educating Mentally Retarded Persons in the Mainstream*, Baltimore: University Park Press

Barnard, H.C. (1961) *A History of English Education*, London: University of London Press

BATOD National Executive Committee (1981) 'Audiological Definitions and Forms for Recording Audiometric Information', *Journal of British Association of Teachers of the Deaf*, 5 (3), 83–7

BATOD (1984) '1983 Survey on Staffing, Salaries, Numbers of Hearing-Impaired Children and Use of Manual Communication', *Journal of British Association of Teachers of the Deaf*, 8 (1), 11–15 (Association Magazine)

Baum, B.R. and Frazita, R.F. (1979) 'Educating the Exceptional Child in the Regular Classroom', *Journal of Teacher Education*, 30 (6), 21–1

Bender, R. (1960) *The Conquest of Deafness*, Cleveland, Ohio: the Press of Western Reserve University

Bishop, M.E. (1977) 'Integration: Some Critical Issues to be Faced' Keynote address delivered to the European Federation of Teachers of the Deaf, September 1977, NTID Rochester, NY

Bitter, G. and Johnston, K.A. (1973) *Project NEED for Facilitating the Integration of Hearing-Impaired Children into Regular Public School Classes*, Final Report, Salt Lake City: University of Utah

Blumberg, C. (1973) 'A School for the Deaf Facilitates Integration' in Northcott, W.H. (ed.), *The Hearing Impaired Child in a Regular Classroom*, Washington: Alexander Graham Bell Association

Bookbinder, G. (1983) 'A New Deal or Dashed Hopes', *Special Education: Forward Trends*, 10 (1), 6–7

Booth, T. (1983) 'Integrating Special Education' in Booth, T. and Potts, P. (eds), *Integrating Special Education*, Oxford: Blackwell

Bowlby, J. (1965) *Child Care and the Growth of Love*, London: Penguin

Braybrook, D. (1980) '1980 — One Hundred Years After Milan', Triennial Congress, Scarborough 1980, British Deaf Association, Carlisle

British Deaf Association (1982) *The BDA 1982 Annual Report*, Carlisle

Bunting, C. (1981) *Public Attitudes to Deafness*, A survey carried out for the DHSS. Office of Population Censuses and Surveys Social Survey Division, London: HMSO

Byford, E.M. (1979) 'Mainstreaming: The Effect of Regular Teacher Training Programmes', *Journal of Teacher Education*, 30 (6), 23–4

Cameron, M. (1979) The Social and Emotional Adjustment of Hearing-Impaired Children in Ordinary Schools, MEd Thesis, University of Manchester

Cattell, R.B. (1952) *Factor Analysis: An Introduction and Manual for Psychologist and*

Social Scientist, New York: Harper

Cave, C and Madison, P. (1978) *A Survey of Recent Research in Special Education*, Windsor: NFER

Chazan, M. (1970) 'Maladjusted Children' in Mittler, P. (ed.), *The Psychological Assessment of Mental and Physical Handicaps*, London: Methuen

Cicourel, A.V. (1966) *Method and Measurement in Sociology*, New York: Free Press

Clark, M. (1978) 'Preparation of Deaf Children for Hearing Society', *Journal of British Association of Teachers of the Deaf*, 2 (5), 146–54

Conrad, R. (1979) *The Deaf Schoolchild*, London: Harper and Row

Cope, C. and Anderson, E.M. (1977) *Special Units in Ordinary Schools*, Studies in Education 6, London: University of London, Institute of Education

Cosper, C.H. (1976) 'Mainstreaming of the Junior High and Senior High Student' in Nix, G. (ed.), *Mainstream Education for Hearing-Impaired Children and Youth*, New York: Grune and Stratton

Craig, H.B. (1965) 'A Sociometric Investigation of the Self-Concept of the Deaf Child', *American Annals of the Deaf*, 110, 456–78

Curtis, S. (1968) *History of Education in Great Britain*, London: London University Tutorial Press

Dale, D.M.C. (1966) 'Units for Deaf Children', *Volta Review*, 68 (7), 496–9

——(1978) 'Educating Deaf and Partially Hearing Children Individually in Ordinary Schools', *the Lancet*, 8095 (11), 884–7

——(1984) *Individualised Integration*, London: Hodder and Stoughton

——and Hemmings, I. (1971) *Report on Integration Research*, London: Ewing Foundation

Delamont, S. and Hamilton, D. (1976) 'Classroom Research: A Critique and a New Approach' in Stubbs, M. and Delamont, S. (eds), *Explorations in Classroom Observation*, Chichester: John Wiley

Denmark, J. (1981) 'A Psychiatric View of the Importance of the Early Use of Sign Language' in Woll, B., Kyle, J. and Deuchar, M. (eds), *Perspectives on British Sign Language*, London: Croom Helm

Deno, E. (1970) 'Special Education as Developmental Capital', *Exceptional Children*, 37 (3), 229–37

DES (1967) *Children and Their Primary Schools* (The Plowden Report), London: HMSO

—— (1967) *Units for Partially Hearing Children*, Education Survey 1, London: HMSO

—— (1968) *The Education of Deaf Children: The Possible Place of Finger Spelling and Signing*, London: HMSO

—— (1969) *Peripatetic Teachers of the Deaf*, Education Survey 6, London: HMSO

—— (1970–84) *Statistics of Education, Schools*, London: HMSO

—— (1972) *Aspects of Special Education*, Education Survey 17, London: HMSO

—— (1973) *Special Education - A Fresh Look*, London: HMSO

—— (1974) *Integrating Handicapped Children*, London: HMSO

—— (1978) *Primary Education in England*, London: HMSO

—— (1978) *Special Educational Needs* (The Warnock Report), London: HMSO

—— (1979) *Aspects of Secondary Education in England*, London: HMSO

—— (1980) *Special Needs in Education*, London: HMSO

—— (1984) *Statistical Bulletin*, 11/84, London: HMSO

Douglas, J.D. (1971) *Understanding Everyday Life*, London: Routledge and Kegan Paul

Education of All Handicapped Children Act, 1975: Public Law 94–142. *US Code Congressional and Administrative News*, 94th Congress, First Session, 2

Elsner, R. (1959) 'The Social Position of Hearing-Impaired Children in Regular Grades', *Exceptional Children*, 25 (7), 305–9

Esposito, B. and Peach, N.J. (1983) 'Changing Attitudes of Pre-School Children Toward Handicapped persons', *Exceptional Children*, 49 (4), 361–3

Eyre, W. and Hall, D.E. (1983) 'Deaf Children in an Ordinary School', *Forum*, 25 (2), 43–5

Farrugia, D. and Austin, G. (1980) 'A Study of Socio-emotional Adjustment Patterns of

Hearing-Impaired Students in Different Educational Settings', *American Annals of the Deaf, 125,* 535–41

Filstead, W.J. (1971) *Qualitative Methodology,* Chicago: Markham Publishing Co.

Fisher, B. (1965) The Social and Emotional Adjustment of Children with Impaired Hearing in Ordinary Classes, MEd. Thesis, University of Manchester

Force, D. (1956) 'Social Status of Physically Handicapped Children', *Exceptional Children, 23 (3),* 104–7

Foster, K.W. (1965) 'Physically Handicapped Children in an Ordinary Primary School — a New Dimension' in Loring, J. and Burn, G. (eds), *Integration of Handicapped Children in Society,* London: Routledge and Kegan Paul

Garrison, W. and Tesch, S. (1978) 'Self-concept and Deafness: A Review of Research Literature', *Volta Review, 80 (7),* 457–66

Gesell, A.L. (1970) *The Child from Five to Ten,* London: Hamish Hamilton

Glaser, B.G. and Strauss, A.L. (1971) 'Discovering of Substantive Theory: A Basic Strategy Underlying Qualitative Research' in Filstead, W.J. (ed.), *Qualitative Methodology,* Chicago: Markham Publishing Co.

Goffman, E. (1968) *Stigma,* London: Penguin

Gottlieb, J. (1980) 'Improving Attitudes Towards Retarded Children by Using Group Discussion', *Exceptional Children, 47 (2),* 106–10

Gregory, S. and Bishop, J. (1981) 'Language at Home and School of Young Hearing-Impaired Children', *Proceedings of Conference for Heads of Schools and Services for Hearing-Impaired Children,* Department of Audiology and Education of the Deaf, University of Manchester

Gresham, F.M. (1982) 'Misguided Mainstreaming: the Case for Social Skills Training with Handicapped Children', *Exceptional Children, 48 (5),* 422–33

Hadfield, J.A. (1962) *Childhood and Adolescence,* London: Penguin

Hamilton, D.F. and Delamont, S. (1974) 'Classroom Research: A Cautionary Tale', *Research in Education,* 11 May

Hamilton, P. and Owrid, H.L. (1974) 'Comparisons of Hearing Impaired and Sociocultural Disadvantage in Relation to Verbal Retardation', *British Journal of Audiology, 8 (1),* 27–32

Handlers, A and Austin, K. (1980) 'Improving Attitudes of High School Students Towards their Handicapped Peers', *Exceptional Children,* 47 (3), 228–9

Hargreaves, D.H. (1967) *Social Relations in a Secondary School,* London: Routledge and Kegan Paul

Haring, N.G., Stern, G. and Cruickshank, W. (1958) 'Attitudes of Educators Towards Exceptional Children', *Syracuse University Special Education and Rehabilitation Monograph,* Series 3, Syracuse: Syracuse University Press

Hay, J. (1981) 'Quiet Flows the Mainstream' in Montgomery, G. (ed.), *The Integration and Disintegration of the Deaf in Society,* Edinburgh: Scottish Workshop Publications

Hegarty, S., Pocklington, K. with Lucas, D. (1981) *Educating Pupils with Special Needs in the Ordinary School,* Windsor: NFER-Nelson

—— (1982) *Integration in Action: Case Studies in the Integration of Pupils with Special Needs,* Windsor: NFER-Nelson

Hemmings, I. (1972) 'A Survey of Units for Hearing-Impaired Children in Schools for Normally Hearing Children', *Teacher of the Deaf, 70,* 445–66

Hine, W.D. (1970) 'The Abilities of Partially Hearing Children', *British Journal of Educational Psychology, 40 (2),* 171–8

Hoben, M. (1980) 'Toward Integration in the Mainstream', *Exceptional Children,* 47 (2), 100–5

Hodgson, A., Clunies-Ross, L. and Hegarty, S. (1984) *Learning Together,* Windsor: NFER-Nelson

Hodgson, K. (1953) *The Deaf and their Problems,* London: Watts and Co.

Horne, M.D. (1979) 'Attitudes and Mainstreaming: A Literature Review for School Psychologists', *Psychology in the Schools, 16 (1),* 61–5

Hunt, P. (ed.) (1966) *Stigma: the Experience of Disability,* London: Chapman

Ives, L.A. (1973) 'Deaf and Partially Hearing Children' in Varma, V. (ed.), *Stresses in Children*, London: University of London Press

Jensema, C.J. (1975) *The Relationship between Academic Achievement and the Demographic Characteristics of Hearing-Impaired Children and Youth*, Office of Demographic Studies, Gallaudet College, Series R, No. 2

Jensema, C.J., Karchmer, M.A. and Trybus, B.J. (1978) *The Rated Speech Intelligibility of Hearing Impaired Children: Basic Relationships and a Detailed Analysis*, Office of Demographic Studies, Gallaudet College, Series R, No. 6

Jensema, C.J. and Trybus, R.J. (1979) *Communication Patterns and Educational Achievement of Hearing Impaired Students*, Office of Demographic Studies, Gallaudet College, Series T, No. 2

Johnson, A.B. and Cartwright, C.A. (1979) 'The Roles of Information and Experience in Improving Teachers' Knowledge and Attitudes about Mainstreaming', *Journal of Special Education*, 13 (4), 453-62

Johnson, D. and Johnson, R. (1980) 'Integrating Handicapped Students into the Mainstream', *Exceptional Children*, 47 (2), 90-8

Johnson, J.C. (1962) *Educating Hearing-Impaired Children in Ordinary Schools*, Manchester: Manchester University Press

Johnson, M. (1963) A Report on a Survey of Deaf Children who have been Transferred from Special Schools or Units to Ordinary Schools (DES Pamphlet), London: HMSO

Jordan, K. (1981) 'Integration and Total Communication in the Education of Deaf Children' in Montgomery, G. (ed.), *The Integration and Disintegration of the Deaf in Society*, Edinburgh: Scottish Workshop Publications

Katz, L., Mathis, S.L. and Merrill, E.C. (1974) *The Deaf Child in the Public Schools*, Illinois: Interstate

Kennedy, P. and Bruininks, R.H. (1974) 'Social Status of Hearing-Impaired Children in Regular Classrooms', *Exceptional Children*, 40 (5), 336-42

Kindred, E. (1976) 'Integration at the Secondary School Level', *Volta Review*, 78 (1), 35-43

Ladd, P. (1981) 'The Erosion of Self-Identity by the Mainstream: A Personal Experience' in Montgomery, G. (ed.), *The Integration and Disintegration of the Deaf in Society*, Edinburgh: Scottish Workshop Publications

Larrivee, B. (1981) 'Effect of Inservice Training Intensity on Teachers' Attitudes Towards Mainstreaming', *Exceptional Children*, 48 (1), 34-9

Larrivee, B. and Cook, L. (1979) 'Mainstreaming: A Study of the Variables Affecting Teacher Attitude', *Journal of Special Education*, 13 (3), 315-24

Levine, E.S. (1960) *The Psychology of Deafness*, New York: Columbia University Press

Löwe, A. (1977) 'Mainstream Education for Hearing-Impaired Children', *Journal of the British Association of Teachers of the Deaf*, 1 (3), 101-7

Loxham, E. (1982) 'A Survey of Mainstream Teachers' Attitudes in Three Schools Containing Units for the Hearing Impaired', *Journal of British Association of Teachers of the Deaf*, 6 (6), 161-71

Lynas, W. (1984) 'The Education of Hearing-Impaired Pupils in Ordinary Schools: Integration or Pseudo-Assimilation?', *Journal of British Association of Teachers of the Deaf*, 8 (5), 129-36

MacDonald, P.J. (1980) 'What does the English Picture Vocabulary Scale Measure with the Hearing Impaired?', *Journal of British Association of Teachers of the Deaf*, 4 (6), 178-84

MacDougall, J.C. (1971) 'The Education of the Deaf in Canada', *Canadian Psychologist*, 12, 534-40

Madebrink, R. (1972) 'Integration of the Deaf — a Must?', *Scandinavian Audiology*, 2, 13

Markham, R. (1972) 'Psychological Aspects of Deafness', *The Deaf American*, 1972, July/August, pp. 11-12

McCauley, R., Bruininks, R.H. and Kennedy, P. (1976) 'Behavioural Interactions of Hearing-Impaired Children in Regular Classrooms', *Journal of Special Education*, 10, 277-84

McCay Vernon (1981) 'Public Law and Private Distress' in Montgomery, G. (ed.), *The Integration and Disintegration of the Deaf in Society*, Edinburgh: Scottish Workshop Publications

McGrath, G. (1981) 'Language Competency in the Evaluation of Integration: A View from Australia' in Montgomery, G. (ed.), *The Integration and Disintegration of the Deaf in Society*, Edinburgh: Scottish Workshop Publications

Meadow, K.P. (1969) 'Self-Image, Family Climate and Deafness', *Social Forces*, *47*, 428–38
—— (1980) *Deafness and Child Development*, London: Edward Arnold

Merrill, E.C. (1979) 'A Deaf Presence in Education', Supplement to *British Deaf News*, August, 1979, Carlisle

Merton, R.K. (1968) *Social Theory and Social Structure*, New York: The Free Press

Ministry of Education (1963) *A Report on a Survey of Deaf Children who have been Transferred from Special Schools or Units to Ordinary Schools*, London: HMSO

Montgomery, G. (1968) 'A Factorial Study of Communication and Ability in Deaf School Leavers', *British Journal of Educational Psychology*, *38 (1)*, 27–37
—— (1981) 'The Ideal of a Workshop with the Deaf' in Montgomery, G. (ed.), *The Integration and Disintegration of the Deaf in Society*, Edinburgh: Scottish Workshop Publications

Moores, D. (1971) 'Psycholinguistics and Deafness' in Jones, R.L., *Problems and Issues in the Education of Exceptional Children*, Boston, Houghton Miflin

Murphy, A., Dickstein, J. and Dripps, E. (1960) 'Acceptance, Rejection and the Hearing Handicapped', *Volta Review*, *62*, 208–11

Mykelbust, H.R. (1960) *The Psychology of Deafness*, New York: Grune and Stratton

Naor, M. and Milgram, R.M. (1980) 'Two Pre-service Strategies for Preparing Regular Class Teachers for Mainstreaming', *Exceptional Children*, *47 (2)*, 126–9

National Deaf Children's Society, *Yearbooks*, 1971–84

Needleman, H. (1977) 'Effects of Hearing Loss from Early Recurrent Otitis Media on Speech and Language Development', in Jaffe, B. (ed.), *Hearing Loss in Children: A Comprehensive Text*, Baltimore: University Park Press

Nix, G. (1977) *Mainstream Education for Hearing Impaired Children and Youth*, New York: Grune and Stratton

Opie, I. and Opie, P. (1969) *Children's Games in Street and Playground*, Oxford: Clarendon Press
—— (1972) *The Lore and Language of Schoolchildren*, Oxford: Clarendon Press

Oxford Polytechnic (1980) *1980 — One Hundred Years After Milan*, Videotape, Lady Spencer Churchill College, Oxford Polytechnic

Paul, R.L. and Young, B. (1975) 'The Child with a Mild Sensori-neural Hearing Loss; the Failure Syndrome', Paper delivered at the International Congress, Education of the Deaf, Tokyo

Payne, R. and Murray, C. (1974) 'Principals' Attitudes Towards Integration of the Handicapped', *Exceptional Children*, *41 (2)*, 123–5

Peatey, B.C. (1984) 'The National Plan', *Proceedings of Conference of Heads of Schools and Services for Hearing-Impaired Children*, Department of Audiology and Education of the Deaf, University of Manchester

Peckham, C.S., Sheridan, M. and Butler, N.R. (1972) 'School Attainment of Seven-Year Old Children with Hearing Difficulties', *Developmental Medicine and Child Neurology*, *14*, 592–602

Porter, G. (1975) 'The Missing Dimension in Successful Integration', *Volta Review*, *77 (7)*, 416–22

Pritchard, D.G. (1963) *Education and the Handicapped*, London: Routledge and Kegan Paul

Quigley, S.P. and Kretschmer, R. (1982) *The Education of Deaf Children: Issues, Theory and Practice*, Baltimore: University Park Press

Rauth, M. (1981) 'What Can Be Expected of the Regular Education Teacher? Ideals and Realities', *Exceptional Education Quarterly*, *2 (2)*, 27–36

Reeves, K. (1983) 'The Education Act, 1981', *Journal of British Association of Teachers of the Deaf*, 7 (6), 170–6

Reich, C., Hambleton, D. and Houldin, B.K. (1977) 'The Integration of Hearing Impaired Children in Regular Classrooms', *American Annals of the Deaf*, 122, 534–43

Ringlaben, R.P. and Price, J.R. (1981) 'Regular Classroom Teachers' Perceptions of Mainstreaming Effects', *Exceptional Children*, 47 (4), 302–4

Rister, A. (1975) 'Deaf Children in Mainstream Education', *Volta Review*, 77 (5), 279–90

Rodda, M. (1970) *The Hearing-Impaired School Leaver*, London: University of London Press

Ross, M. with Brackett, D. and Maxon, A. (1982) *Hard of Hearing Children in Regular Schools*, New Jersey: Prentice Hall

Sacks, H., Schegloff, E.A. and Jefferson, G. (1974) A Simplest Systematics for the Organization of Turn Taking in Conversation. Unpublished paper available from the Department of Sociology University of Manchester

Schultz, L.R. (1982) 'Educating the Special Needs Student in the Regular Classroom', *Exceptional Children*, 48 (4), 366–8

Snowdon Report (1976) *Integrating the Disabled*, Horsham, Surrey: National Fund for Research into Crippling Diseases

Spredley, T.S. (1980) 'Deaf Like Me', Book Review in *British Deaf News*, 12 (8), 261

Stephens, T. and Braun, B. (1980) 'Measures of Regular Classroom Teachers' Attitudes Toward Handicapped Children', *Exceptional Children*, 46 (4), 292–4

Stott, D.H. (1958) Manual to, Bristol Social Adjustment Guide, London: University of London Press

—— (1963) *The Social Adjustment of Children: Manual to Bristol Social Adjustment Guide*, 2nd edn, London: University of London Press

—— and Marston, N.C. (1974) *The Child in the School — Boy*, Bristol Social Adjustment Guide, London: University of London Press

—— (1975) *The Child in the School — Girl*, Bristol Social Adjustment Guide, London: University of London Press

Sussman, A.E. (1973) An Investigation into the Relationship between Self-Concepts of Deaf Adults and Their Perceived Attitudes Towards Deafness, Unpublished Phd Thesis, New York University

Taylor, I.G. (1981) 'Medicine and Education', *Journal of British Association of Teachers of the Deaf*, 5 (5), 134–43

Tomlinson, S. (1982) *A Sociology of Special Education*, London: Routledge and Kegan Paul

Tough, J. (1973) *Focus on Meaning*, London: Allen and Unwin

Townsend, P. (1962) *The Last Refuge*, London: Routledge and Kegan Paul

Turfus, S. (1982) 'Integration or Pseudo-assimilation?', Letter to *WHERE* (July/August) 180, 10

Van den Horst, A.P. (1971) 'Defective Hearing, School Achievements and School Choice', *Teacher of the Deaf*, 69, 398–414

Van Uden, A. (1977) *A World of Language for Deaf Children*, Amsterdam: Swets and Zeitlinger

Washington, D. (1981) 'What Have You Done to Us?' in Montgomery, G. (ed.), *The Integration and Disintegration of the Deaf in Society*, Edinburgh: Scottish Workshop Publications

Watson, T.J. (1967) *The Education of Hearing-Handicapped Children*, London: University of London Press

Webster, A. and Ellwood, J. (1985) *The Hearing-Impaired Child in the Ordinary School* London: Croom Helm

Wild, B.M. (1976) The Formulation of Opinion: Some Aspects of the Organisation of Talk. Unpublished Phd Thesis, University of Manchester

Yater, V.V. (1977) *The Mainstreaming of Children with a Hearing Loss*, Illinois: Charles C. Thomas

Zinkus, P.W. and Gottlieb, M.I. (1980) 'Patterns of Perceptual and Academic Deficits Related to Early Chronic Otitis Media', *Pediatrics*, 66, 246–53

INDEX